TEACHING IN A PLURALISTIC SOCIETY
Concepts, Models, Strategies

Second Edition

RICARDO L. GARCIA
Kansas State University

HarperCollins*Publishers*

To my wife, Sharon, and the twins,
Shane and Maria, for their patience.

Senior Editor: Christopher Jennison
Project Editor: Diane Rowell
Design Supervisor: Pete Noa
Cover Designer: Merlin Communications, Inc.
Production Administrator: Beth Maglione
Compositor: American–Stratford Graphic Services, Inc.
Printer and Binder: R. R. Donnelley & Sons Company
Cover Printer: Lynn Art Offset Corporation

Teaching in a Pluralistic Society: Concepts, Models, Strategies, Second Edition

Library of Congress Cataloging-in-Publication Data

Garcia, Ricardo L.
    Teaching in a pluralistic society : concepts, models, strategies /
Ricardo L. Garcia.—2nd ed.
        p.   cm.
    Includes bibliographical references and index.
    ISBN 0-06-042237-8
    1. Intercultural education—United States.   2. Minorities
—Education—United States.   3. Teaching.   I. Title.
LC1099.3.G37   1991
371.1′02—dc20   90-48835
                                                   CIP

91 92 93 94   9 8 7 6 5 4 3 2 1

Contents

Preface

We live in a pluralistic society. Before you finish your teaching career, you will more than likely teach all kinds of students—African-American, Spanish-speaking, Native American, Asian, Appalachian, and White ethnic—to name a few. They may represent most social classes, religious affiliations, regions of the country, and the world. The challenge will be to make a difference in their lives: to teach them all that they are capable, unique individuals, who have a right to be respected by others and a responsibility to respect others.

Our society is undergoing rapid changes as it moves toward the twenty-first century. There are no panaceas for teaching in a pluralistic society. The text's first edition focused on the role of ethnicity in teaching and learning; this second edition takes a broader focus by examining the role of gender, handicapping conditions, religion, social class, race, and ethnicity in teaching and learning. The text offers theoretical and practical premises—drawn from the social and behavioral sciences—to understand teaching in a pluralistic society.

The text is divided into two parts. Part One provides the theoretical concepts necessary for understanding teaching and learning in a pluralistic society. Part One highlights the philosophic posture of cultural relativism, explaining what the posture means and how it applies to pluralistic teaching and learning. A description of communal life in the United States provides the societal context and ideologies embedded in pluralistic teaching. School and community relationships are then examined, along with the impact of ethnocentrisms on schooling. Gender, handicap, religious, social class, race, and ethnic issues are confronted head-on. Part One also provides an overview of fundamental sociocultural concepts as theoretical constructs as well as teaching and learning realities.

Part Two describes instructional models and strategies appropriate for teaching and learning in a pluralistic society. Two instructional models are examined, cultural education and language education; then two instructional strategies are described, intergroup relations and human rights. Specific demonstration lessons are provided for the cultural education and language education models as well as the intergroup relations strategy; specific human rights guidelines for managing the day-to-day affairs of the classroom are also provided with the human rights strategy. The lessons and guidelines are intended to assist teachers with the application of the models and strategies described in Part Two.

The text can be used for these purposes: (1) pre-service teacher education in courses such as "Educational Foundations," "Sociology of Education," "Introduction to Education," and "Multicultural Education"; (2) in-service multicultural education; (3) pre- or in-service education that attempts to comply with the NCATE multicultural education standard; (4) human relations, equal opportunity, or desegregation workshops and institutes. The text could also be used as supplemental reading in courses that focus on the nature of teaching and learning, such as courses in "Human Growth and Development" or "Educational Psychology" whose texts traditionally do not include pluralistic perspectives.

The text is introductory, and it encourages a thoughtful approach to pluralistic teaching and learning. It should help teachers make reasoned judgments about the many difficult issues that arise, but it provides no pat answers for specific situations. Teaching is a changing, ongoing process for which recipes are inappropriate. What makes good teaching difficult is that there are few consistent answers. To raise questions and consider answers, each chapter is organized thus: each lists key terms central to the chapter's thesis; after a brief introduction, each chapter is divided into subtopics that are summarized at the chapter's end. Then discussion questions and exercises are provided. The questions and exercises can be used to review the chapter's contents as well as to provide depth and clarity to the chapter's topics.

Good teachers should develop sophistication in cross-cultural teaching. If they teach in suburban schools, I believe they should teach their students about the diversity of American society, even though their schools may appear monolithic. If they teach in the ghetto, the barrio, or on a Native American reservation, I believe they should build upon the cultural differences of their students rather than treat differences as deficiencies to be ignored or purged.

Good teachers should develop sophistication in dealing with human differences. Students not only differ in terms of culture but they also differ in terms of cognitive and physical abilities, ethnic, gender, religious, and social class orientations. Ultimately, teachers are challenged to empower students to think for themselves, to rise above whatever sociocultural constraints they have acquired so that they can improve their own lives as well as the lives of others.

ACKNOWLEDGMENTS

Special thanks go to Bob Bullough and Carlos Diaz, and other colleagues who chose to remain anonymous, for comments pertinent to this second edition.

Ricardo L. Garcia

PART
One

CONCEPTS

Chapter
1

The Cultural Factor

Key Terms:

Copernican perspective
cultural relativism
ethical transcendence
global interdependence

knowledge escalation
Ptolemaic perspective
socialization

Imagine that you are a good literature teacher. Your ninth-grade class has just finished reading a series of short stories on liberation themes. As the group leader, you have led the class through the labyrinth of personal, human struggles for liberation from hunger, poverty, racism, sexism, and political and religious suppression. As a final project the class members want to organize into small groups and, using magazine and newspaper clippings and pictures, construct a collage that summarizes the human struggle for liberation. "Why not?" you think. "That's a creative way to have the students show they understand the themes." Okay, you'll permit it. The next day, students bring their material. You provide scissors and glue, help organize the groups, and set a deadline. Halfway through the project, one male student hollers, "Aw, hell! This stinks! Cutting paper dolls is girl's stuff! I won't do it!" He takes the collage from his group, tears it up, and throws it on the floor.

So what's the problem? Forty years ago you could beat the youngster for his deviant behavior. Ten years ago you could paddle him, and now you could beat or paddle the youngster. Now, of course, you'd have to face a lawsuit. But if you really are a good teacher, you will approach the whole situation differently. You will treat each classroom experience, planned or unplanned, as a learning experience for students and a teaching experience for you.

In this case, what is being taught and learned by the young man's protest? Have you somehow created a climate in your classroom that discourages or encourages dissent? Is this good? Bad? Is the student's self-concept threatened? Has he learned from his cultural background that there are distinct role behaviors for men and women? Is cutting pictures for a project synonymous with cutting paper dolls to him? Or did you, in your zeal to teach about the liberation of the poor, the religious, and women, unintentionally teach that the oppressor in American society is the White male? Did the youngster, an American White male, find no positive White males in the liberation literature and thereby infer that his kind was responsible for all of the oppression in American society? Did you mean to teach the inference? If so, is the inference that White males are responsible for all religious, social, and racial oppression valid, given a rigorous study of American social history? If the inference is valid, how does it relate to the angry young man in your class? What rights does he have? Does he have the right to dissent? The right to gender-role stereotype? Do you have a responsibility to change the student's attitudes or values, especially if the student has a cultural reason why the project threatens his self-concept? What about the rights of other students? Do they have to listen to foul language? Do they have property rights in the torn collage?

And then, you ask, just what are you teaching? Literature? Liberation? Democratic living? The answer is that you are teaching all three, because you are a good teacher who knows that you have a responsibility to transmit more than data about literature—to provide your students with basic literary skills and to socialize them to live and work in a democratic, pluralistic society. So, as a good teacher, what do you do about the angry young man whose self-concept is threatened by your assignment, and who, in turn, violates some of the rights of his peers? You can ignore the problem, hoping that in some vague way someone will teach your students their rights and responsibilities within the human community. After all, what difference does your teaching make? Do teachers really make a difference in the lives of students? No doubt some great leaders once had teachers who influenced them. Yet, most of the prisoners in American jails, including corrupt political leaders, had a few teachers in their lives. Did teachers perversely influence the latter just as they positively influenced great leaders and good citizens?

The question defies an answer. I believe that teachers can make a difference, and while they do not deliberately lead students to lives of crime or political corruption, they may forget to take the active role in the socialization of students that could circumvent criminal tendencies.

Teachers should be a liberating force in the lives of students. Their classrooms should be guided by justice so students will be free to learn, thereby liberating themselves from ignorance: the social ignorance caused by happenstance of birth—we are all born provincials—and the academic ignorance caused by the illiteracy of youth. Age is, after all, a fundamental impediment to the education of the young. Since World War II we have witnessed an escalation of knowledge and an awareness of global interdependence. Now we have more access to knowledge than ever before. With computer technology and telecommunications we are able to access data instantaneously on a global scale. How to understand it? How to evaluate it? How to use it? These are central questions teachers must answer with their students if academic ignorance is to be confronted.

We also have more access to other humans. What happens in a small toolshed in Japan is felt by workers in Paris, Texas and Paris, France. The fates of others in faraway nations are intertwined with our fates. We need to know about each other. Why do certain groups live in peace in a contentious world? Why do some nations resent our well-intentioned generosity? What can we learn from some cultures about quality and efficiency? These questions mirror the need to know other cultures and their languages.

Realize that teaching is a scholarly pursuit. Public school teachers are mandated under law to teach the basic skills and knowledge of traditional subjects. This is correct; teachers should be scholars. They must teach the basic skills and academic knowledge of traditional subjects if academic ignorance is to be confronted. Teachers should also teach skills and knowledge to live in a pluralistic society. Teaching traditional academic knowledge and cultural awareness are not mutually exclusive; they can be taught concurrently.

Teaching is a challenging profession, a difficult task, and a poorly rewarded one. What you must keep in mind is that teaching in the public schools is an exceedingly complicated task that is worth doing. Everything about teaching is always changing. Each group of students is new. Facilities, social conditions, and curriculum goals change. Parents, school boards, administrators, professional education organizations, teacher educators, and civic groups inundate the teacher with their views on the nature of students, learning, teaching, and the good life. Usually, the views conflict. Teaching complexities are not new, but they are real. There is nothing simple about teaching. Even on a daily basis, students and teachers are influenced by factors such as the day of the week, the time of day, the weather, and the seasons. There are constant, general factors central to the teaching-learning situation. The quality of classroom management and instructional strategies and the student's and the teacher's self-concepts are important in good teaching practices. For teaching in a pluralistic society such as the United States, consideration of *cultural* differences is fundamental to good teaching (see Figure 1.1).

The cultural factor is not just another teaching-learning complication. Cultural differences have always existed in classrooms. At one time, the function of a good teacher was to melt away ethnic differences. To Americanize and homogenize students of immigrant families, teachers discouraged any indications of ethnic heritage and ancestral ties. English-only laws were enacted, prohibiting the use of any language other than English in the public classroom. Students could be and were punished for speaking a non-English language. Teachers could lose their certification, go to jail, and be fined. Later, it was fashionable to ignore cultural differences, to claim that, "I treat all my students *as though* they are alike." Ignoring differences by pretending they didn't exist served to submerge rather than purge cultural differences in the classroom and ignored the students' fundamental humanity.

All classroom activities and factors—classroom management techniques, instructional strategies, and, of course, self-concepts—operate on assumptions which are embedded in cultural values, attitudes, and beliefs. There is no such thing as a culturally neutral or culturally free teaching activity. The search for culturally free techniques, curriculum materials, or tests is in vain. Teaching activities spring from unconscious assumptions one makes: they are based on one's cultural perspectives. Likewise, students' learning and behaving are in-

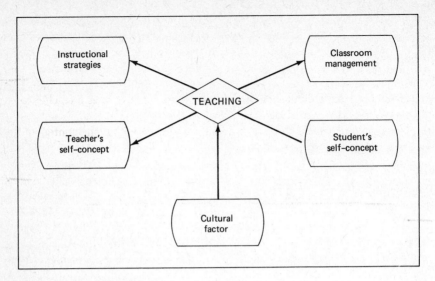

Figure 1.1 The cultural factor

fluenced by their cultural perspectives. What students learn and what teachers teach are ultimately filtered and strained through their cultural sieves. Understanding the cultural factor creates the consciousness necessary to perceive that transmitting culture and socializing students are inherent in classroom teaching and learning.

It's easy to forget, once you begin analyzing and evaluating the complexities of teaching and learning in a pluralistic society, who or why anyone would teach. Keep in mind that we live in a global society. Nations, cultures, and peoples throughout the world are interdependent even though at times certain cultures and nations consider themselves aloof from the global society. The fact is that we inhabit one planet, breathe the same air, and depend on the same sun. We are challenged with a new image, the image of global citizens within a pluralistic world. Remember that all cultures, nations, and peoples have in common the enemies of ignorance, disease, famine, and poverty. Even in our affluent society, there are undernourished, hungry, sick, and illiterate people. If you as a teacher determine to liberate your students—even only one student—from one of these common enemies, you will achieve the respect given only to excellent teachers. I am not referring to pie-in-the-sky liberalism or missionary zeal. Rather, I mean that a good teacher must be committed to making a difference in the lives of students.

Students, for the most part, are captive audiences with little real say in who will teach them or what they will be taught. Essentially, students in the classroom are sentenced (compulsory education) to attend and their teachers are mandated (equal educational opportunity) to teach any and all students. This being the case, teachers must accept the reality of their students and the cultural milieu from which the students emerge. One teacher who did this was

Sylvia Ashton-Warner, who made a difference in the lives of her students by committing herself to eliciting excellence. In her book, *Teacher*,[1] she tells of her experiences teaching English among New Zealand Maori infants. Rather than pouring the English language into her students, Ashton-Warner activated students to generate language and content from their individual cultural perspectives. To make a difference in the lives of students, you as a teacher must liberate yourself from provincial and narrow conceptions about people, teaching, learning, and yourself and try to elicit excellence within the context of the students' own cultural perspectives.

CULTURAL RELATIVISM AND TEACHING

To teach in a pluralistic society, in my view, one must take the position that all cultures should be examined relatively, that is, looked at from the vantage point of the group under consideration. Rather than viewing the value of a certain culture from the perspective of one's own culture, a teacher in a pluralistic society should develop the ability to see how other cultural groups perceive their social reality. Not an easy task! Most of us have been taught to think that our cultural ways are better than others—ethnocentrism—and the idea that other groups may differ does not always seem to convince us that our way may be good only for our group. Nevertheless, we are faced with cultural differences in a pluralistic society.

Cultural relativism was developed by anthropologists as a conceptual approach toward understanding other cultures without judging them from an ethnocentric, normative perspective. During the late nineteenth and early twentieth centuries, anthropologists compared other cultures to those of the United States or nations of Western Europe. Compared to the United States and Western European cultures, the other cultures were judged to be "primitive," "barbaric," or "underdeveloped." The normative approach judged other cultures to be superior or inferior to the cultures of the anthropologists, but the normative approach did not help anthropologists understand other cultural groups. Consequently, an approach that studied other cultures from the viewpoint of the members of the group was instituted and has taken on several labels, observation-participation, ethnographic studies, qualitative research, which require a researcher to take a relative posture toward the group under study. The researcher's intent is to get an insider's view of the culture by actually being a part of the group. Once becoming involved with the group, the researcher can better understand why group members behave or believe as they do because the researcher will have experienced group membership. Subjective understanding rather than objective examination is the purpose. Cultural relativism requires researchers to study other peoples and their cultures by becoming actively involved in the everyday affairs of the group under study. The researcher is an active participant in the culture of the group being studied. Teachers, because they are actively involved in their classrooms, are in an ideal position to qualitatively research the culture of their classrooms.

CULTURAL RELATIVISM AND ETHICAL TRANSCENDENCE

Difficult ethical problems exist with cultural relativism. Some might argue that violence is a basic value in their culture, and thus they have a right to inflict violence on others. (In fact, few known cultures condone violence for the sake of violence. Because violence begets violence, it is, in the final analysis, self-destructive and contrary to group survival.) Violence *qua* violence in the classroom would not only disrupt learning activities but would violate the students' right to personal safety. Further, some teachers might argue that their culture supports racist attitudes toward racial minority students, and because of cultural relativism, racist teachers have a right to promote their brand of racism; or, some teachers might believe in traditional gender roles. While these teachers are free to believe what they wish, they must not use cultural relativism to justify racial discrimination or gender-role stereotyping in their classes. While we live in a democratic society that allows academic and individual freedom of opinion, cultural relativism should be used by teachers as a conceptual tool to understand other cultures or groups rather than as a rationalization to place limits on the students' life options and opportunities.

Teacher attitudes are not the only complicating factors with the use of cultural relativism; there may be aspects of the students' cultures that are inimical to learning, and if maintained in the name of cultural relativism, these parts of the cultures will hinder the students' chances for learning. Yes, I am saying that there may be parts of a student's culture that the teacher may have to change. For example, if a student's cultural group views reading as a middle-class activity, and if the student views middle-class people as the enemy, then the student may refuse to learn to read. (This example is not farfetched; see Chapter 4 for a discussion of the "reading and talking middle class" phenomenon.) By refusing to read, the student shuts the door to the universe of knowledge, thereby impeding his or her chances for knowledge empowerment.

Subsumed in the preceding arguments is the attitude that ethical anarchy or ethical neutrality prevails in a cultural relativist classroom. Clearly, the attitude is unacceptable. Teachers are legally and morally bound to manage a classroom that protects the fundamental right of all students to equal educational opportunity. As such, teachers are mandated to assert equitable leadership in the classroom. Ethical anarchy and neutrality can be destructive of human survival. In other words, there are times when teachers have to judge and prohibit certain behavior as inimical to the rights of students. This is predicated on the faith that teachers can assume ethical leadership in the classroom. My hope is that teachers will use cultural relativism to enhance the teaching-learning process and to better understand the many cultural differences that exist within the United States. And, teachers must practice ethical transcendence, that is, develop an ethical system of classroom management that transcends all cultural differences and operates on norms that are fair to all students (see Chapter 10 for ethical classroom management).

There is a parallel between what I am proposing and what the astronomer

Copernicus proposed many centuries ago. Until the time of Copernicus, European scholars accepted the Ptolemaic view of the physical universe which placed the earth at the center. This was a simple, cozy, and stable viewpoint. Elaborate but easily comprehensible theological systems of beliefs were based on the view. Still, it limited human knowledge of the earth itself and of an even greater universe filled with immense constellations and galaxies. Copernicus proposed that the earth was not the center of the universe and that, in fact, the earth revolved around the sun. Although religious leaders proclaimed Copernicus's view as heretical because it challenged established religious beliefs about the order of nature and God, time and history have verified the truth of the Copernican view.

In the cultural universe of teaching and learning in U.S. public schools there still persists a Ptolemaic view. In the Ptolemaic view of the teaching and learning universe, the values, attitudes, and beliefs of middle-class Americans have prevailed, seeming to reflect the nature of all students and presuming to provide standards of that culture as the final criteria of right and wrong. In this synoptic view, middle-class culture sits at the hub of the teaching-learning universe; other cultures are far removed or nonexistent. The presumption is that only one model citizen exists,[2] and variations from this middle-class model are perceived as deviancies requiring remediation. This is not meant to demean middle-class culture, but rather to place it in perspective within the myriad other American cultures. The Ptolemaic, geocentric view of teaching and learning is simple, stable, and cozy; it is also dysfunctional. It limits our view of the cultural universe available for our classrooms. We fail to benefit from the cultural diversity of American society.

Time and history will verify the validity of a Copernican view of teaching and learning. Once freed from the Ptolemaic view, we can see the teaching universe from a Copernican perspective. The astronomer Copernicus transcended the myopic vision of the Ptolemaic view and opened our vision to a universe of innumerable galaxies and infinite space. The Copernican view broadened our horizons and revealed an endless array of planets, stars, and possibly other worlds. A Copernican view of teaching—the view that the universe of teaching and learning consists of vast galaxies of cultures and human groups—abandons the fiction that the hub and center of the teaching universe is the middle-class American culture. The Copernican view calls for a radically different perspective based on the cultural diversity of American society. It calls for viewing all cultures as coexistent, abandoning paradigms that speak of cultures as "underdeveloped," "overdeveloped," and "primitive." It discards educational labels that describe nonwhite, non-middle-class students as "culturally deprived," "disadvantaged," or "culturally deficient." Bilingualism becomes an asset rather than a liability and Black English becomes another dialect of American English rather than substandard English. Embracing a Copernican reorientation to the universe of teaching and learning can serve to liberate teachers and assist them in transcending the narrow confines of their cultures.

Once committed to a Copernican view of the cultural universe of teaching and learning, consider the idea that there exist in the teaching-learning universe many progressive cultures, each rich, complex, and worthy of knowing. A caveat is necessary here. The words "progress" and "progressive" connote positive developments in White, middle-class culture. They imply growth and development, but they also create confusion because what is viewed as progress or progressive in one culture may be perceived as decadence in another. Rather than getting caught in the semantics of what is progressive cultural develop- ment, it would be better to free cultures from the notion of industrial progress, keeping in mind that all cultures, if they are to grow and develop continuously, must adapt and change according to present exigencies while yet conserving aspects of their past. All cultures, if they are to remain viable, must constantly strive toward self-improvement by balancing forces of change and conservation. Within any cultural group, there will be people of change and conservation. Within any cultural group, there will be people who advocate change as a means to improve and adapt the culture to meet current and future situations. Within the same cultural group there will be people who oppose or resist change, arguing that conservation of present and past practices or customs will serve to meet current and future situations. Too much conservation of the past can lead to decadence and ultimately to cultural decay. Yet too much change can lead to instability and ultimately to cultural chaos. "Progressive" cultural development requires an equilibrium between the forces of change and con- servation. Any cultural group that maintains an equilibrium between these forces, changing by degrees and conserving by degrees, will constantly improve within its own context as a cultural group.

Cultural development should not be viewed in an industrial format, with cultures evolving from the primitive, to the medieval, and then to the "mod- ern" stages of industrial development. The industrial progression theory—the notion that cultures progress in a linear thrust and can be compared according to their degree of progress toward industrialization—pervades European and American thinking.[3] This progress theory posits that cultures progress from so-called primitive food gathering or hunting stages to more advanced agricul- tural and economic stages. Industrialized cultures, such as the United States, are somehow the most advanced and modern. But what practices are more advanced? Examine the customs dealing with the elderly in Eskimo and middle- class American cultures. In the Eskimo culture—a "primitive" hunting culture according to the progress theory—when elders are too old to help with fishing, hunting, or housekeeping, they are given a position of social eminence within the family and are then sought for advice and guidance. Eventually, when they no longer feel of use to the younger family members, they leave the household to freeze to death on the Alaskan ice plains. In middle-class culture—a "mod- ern" industrial culture according to the progress theory—elders are often placed in an "old folks' home" when they are no longer useful to the family. Many times, they do not choose to go to the homes but are compelled to confinement because they are perceived as a burden to the family. In the rest home, the elders are further demeaned by inane, time-killing activities. Their knowledge and experience are for naught. Like broken-down machines, the elders are discarded to finish their lives among other discards. They cannot choose when, where, or with whom to die, and so must die slowly among other dying strangers. Which culture is more advanced? More modern? Which preserves human dignity and conserves the wisdom that comes with age and experience? According to the progress theory, the "modern" industrialized culture is more complicated and therefore "progressive"; the "primitive" hunting culture is ostensibly less complicated and therefore "less progressive" than the industrialized culture. Which culture is more advanced in its treatment of the elderly? The answer is apparent.

As a person who may have been influenced by the progress theory, can you view cultures as different without making judgments about the differences? Can you reconcile the differences of other cultures with your cultural orientations and be comfortable? Obviously, you need to understand yourself as a member of some cultural or social group. As you read this book, ask the questions: From my group's perspective, how do I feel about the particular values and issues that are raised? Why do I feel this way? From his perspective (the author's), how does he feel about these values and issues? Why does he feel that way? To start the task of understanding you and your cultural group, try to develop an in-group/out-group perspective about yourself. In other words, how do you appear to someone outside your group?

CULTURAL RELATIVISM AND TEACHING MYTHS

There are some myths, if not outright misconceptions, about teaching and teachers that need to be dispelled. *Roll over Copernicus and tell Ptolemy the news.* Teachers need not be charismatic. Among the folklore about teachers is the myth that good teachers have charisma, all too often perceived as personal attraction and magnitude. I think a charismatic person will not necessarily make a good teacher. So-called charismatic teachers are led to believe that students respond to those whom they sense are committed to liberation of the mind. Now if charisma involves having an insatiable curiosity—that is, an inquiring mind, and a burning desire to share the inquiry—and if charisma involves the desire and ability to help others develop an inquiring mind, then it is essential to teaching that liberates. But if charisma merely means being a "nice guy," then charismatic teachers are expendable.

One can have an inquiring mind about many things. The football coach and the elementary math teacher who are self-impelled searchers for new patterns and combinations and who can share this quality with students so they too can develop such compulsions are on the path to releasing students' curiosities. Releasing students' minds to probe the unconventional and to explore the dimensions of their curiosities is vastly different from holding over students a charismatic power which allows one to deposit data in their minds. Freire calls this the "banking method"[4] of teaching. In regular installments, a teacher places knowledge in the students' data banks. From time to time, students record the installments by taking a test or in some manner demonstrating that they have memorized the data in their banks. Teachers own all the data and make deposits as the occasion permits. Students are used as depositories who are expected to store the data but are not expected to use it in any way. Holding this type of charismatic power over students creates a dependence upon you, the teacher; rather than freeing students from impoverished minds or bodies, the teacher makes them subjects.

Ultimately, you cannot liberate students, per se. Liberation is an act of self-assertion, a leap of faith that students will take when you have created the correct set of conditions and circumstances for them. Consider the mother and father robins who care for and feed their fledglings, creating the correct set of circumstances for them. One day as the fledglings approach the brink of the nest, the mother and father robins encourage the fledglings to take a leap, spread their wings, and fly. And they do.

Roll over Copernicus and tell Ptolemy the news. A teacher need not know everything about all groups in a pluralistic society. Actually, a teacher can't possibly know everything about most groups. Further, to admit ignorance is the first step toward understanding. Rather than seeing teachers as transmitters of knowledge (the banking method), consider them as leaders or facilitators who assist students in their pursuit of cultural understanding. As a teacher-leader, one initiates action, maintains the teaching-learning process, sets individual and group guidelines, assures equalitarian individual and group relations, and evaluates the students' experiences and products. As the teacher-leader, you confront the problem of leading your students to a goal that you desire and value. I am not referring to subtle, covert manipulative maneuvers which program students to pursue your interests. Rather, I am referring to an open, unhidden agenda of values that you clearly explain to students. If you are committed to the goal of preparing students to live in a pluralistic society, it is critical that you explain this to your students and then commence to lead them toward the goal, learning with them about the diversity of U.S. society.

Before you can create correct sets of conditions and circumstances—before you can bring students to the brink of knowledge or encourage them to make a guess, take a position, follow up on a hunch, expand their knowledge, and explore the vast panorama of speculation and creation—you must liberate your mind from a provincial, Ptolemaic view of teaching and learning.

SUMMARY

Teachers can make a difference in the lives of their students by keeping in mind that while teaching is an incredibly complex task the goals of teaching are straightforward. All elementary and secondary education teachers, regardless of their academic specialties or the grades they teach, are charged with two basic goals: (1) to transmit the knowledge, skills, and attendant attitudes about one or more academic subjects, and (2) to socialize students to live in a democratic, pluralistic society that exists within the context of an interdependent world.[5] To achieve both goals, teachers should keep their focus first on transcending problems that are common to all societies, nations, and students—

ignorance, poverty, hunger, disease—and second on the cultural differences manifest in their students' learning orientations and ways of behaving. Even the most monolithic appearing group of students manifest cultural variances, differences that are not readily apparent but are nonetheless real due to the dynamics caused by the interactions between social stratification, religiosity and ethnicity, racial and gender-role stereotyping, and handicapping conditions. A posture of cultural relativism, which views students and cultural groups from their own vantage points, can assist the teacher with the awesome task of dealing with teaching in a pluralistic society.

Cultural relativism takes the attitude that cultures are different but not necessarily inferior or superior. In fact, cultures differ because groups of people develop them to accommodate unique physical, demographic, political, and economic situations. Cultural relativism requires that we perceive cultures and the people who hold them from their own unique perspectives rather than solely from the perspective of the White, middle-class American. Some may argue that cultural relativism is amoral or that "anything goes." For example, do the cultures of groups who advocate violence for the sake of violence have to be respected? Or, do extreme racial theories such as bigotry and biological racism have to be accepted under cultural relativism? These questions defy answers. The purpose of cultural relativism is to foster open attitudes about cultures and groups.

Cultural relativism is a conceptual tool which may be used to create a climate of understanding toward differences; it is a tool teachers can use to understand cultural differences and create a climate in their classrooms that accommodates these differences when appropriate. Still, teachers need to develop ethical principles to manage their classrooms. Otherwise, in a pluralistic classroom, chaos would prevail in the name of cultural relativism and little real learning would occur. While cultural relativism is a useful tool for understanding differences, it must be kept subordinate to ethics which transcend all cultural differences. (Chapter 10 discusses ethical principles for classroom management.) These principles attempt to transcend cultural differences while allowing for appropriate differences to exist. Therefore, cultural relativism should not be perceived as a philosophy of nihilism where "anything goes" but rather as a way of building acceptance of differences. Good teaching is not amoral. Good teaching does not endorse political, economic, or religious philosophies that suppress the dignity of human life. Philosophies, policies, or practices that suppress the dignity of human life are alien to good teaching.

STUDY QUESTIONS

1. How would a teacher who takes a Ptolemaic attitude deal with culturally different students?
2. How would a teacher who takes a Copernican view deal with culturally different students?

3. Define cultural relativism by providing an example taken from your personal experiences or from the experiences of others.

4. What makes cultural relativism an effective teaching tool in a pluralistic society? What makes cultural relativism a dangerous tool in a pluralistic society?

5. What are the two basic goals of all teachers? How are these goals important to the individual student? How are the goals important to the society as a whole?

NOTES

1. Sylvia Ashton-Warner. *Teacher*. New York: Simon & Schuster, 1963; see also, Herbert Kohl. *Thirty-six Children*. New York: New American Library, 1967.
2. Peter McLaren. *Life in Schools: An Introduction to Critical Pedagogy in the Foundation of Education*. New York: Longman, 1989, pp. 186–188; see also, Robert Howsam, et al., *Educating a Profession*. Washington, D.C.: American Association of Colleges for Teacher Education, 1976, pp. 23–24.
3. Kenneth A. Strike and Jonas F. Soltis. *The Ethics of Teaching*. New York: Teachers College Press, 1985, pp. 3–7; see also, Melvin Rader. *Ethics and the Human Community*. New York: Holt, Rinehart and Winston, 1964, p. 231.
4. Paulo Freire. *Pedagogy of the Oppressed*. New York: Seabury Press, 1978, pp. 53–56.
5. Rodman B. Webb and Robert Sherman. "Liberal Education: An Aim for Colleges of Education," *Journal of Teacher Education* (April 1983): 23–26.

Chapter
2

Communal Ideologies in American Culture

Key Terms

American Creed
Anglo Conformity
apartheid
cultural pluralism
desegregation
ethnic pluralism
feminism
ideology

institutionalization
integration
interdependence
melting pot
nationalism
religious pluralism
social class consciousness

It's true. "When you are waist-deep in a swamp filled with alligators, it is easy to forget that your initial goal was to drain the swamp." Concepts like *cultural relativism* and *ethical transcendence* are mind-boggling terms that make the head spin. They, like the alligators mentioned above, cause one to lose sight of one's goals. Before we lose sight of the *why* of teaching, let's examine the nature of the pluralistic society so we do not forget that schools, and educational institutions as a whole, serve the society in which they are housed. This chapter analyzes and describes the core American culture, pervasive communal ideologies, the basic forces of social class conflict, and the desegregation-integration issue as a way of providing a framework or societal mileau, of teaching in a pluralistic society.

How have people in the United States gone about the business of living together? The way people live together in a community is a result of social and historical forces as well as regional and local circumstances. Children growing up in the many different communities in the United States acquire their family's culture as well as the regional culture that pervades their community. Also, because the public schools teach a secular version of the Protestant Work Ethic—allegiance to free enterprise, individualism and self-reliance, the virtues of hard work, punctuality, and competitiveness—as well as a universal culture governed by constitutional doctrines and laws, living in America is a complicated affair. This chapter examines the forces and ideologies endemic to American society within the context of a pervasive American culture as a way of describing how individuals manage the complexities of communal living.

E PLURIBUS UNUM

E Pluribus Unum—one out of many—is the motto of the U.S. government. This Latin phrase summarizes the idea that the United States is a singular society forged from many cultural groups. Cultural groups are subsumed within the context of a broad, societal structure, the American nation-state. (I use the term *American* to denote U.S. citizens and residents even though the term can apply to all nations and peoples of the American continents.) The subordinate cultural groups function as the nation's infrastructure; the nation-state functions as the society's basic structure providing the diverse cultural, ethnic, class, and religious groups unity, cohesion, and a pervasive sense of peoplehood, or nationalism, as exemplified by the opening words of the U.S. Constitution, "*We, the People . . .*"

Nationalism, as a unifying, cohering social force, expands and transforms ethnic and cultural group identity.

> Nationalism—including language loyalty—is made up of the stuff of primordial ethnicity; indeed, it is transformed ethnicity with all the accoutrements for functioning at a larger scale of political, social, and intellectual activity.[1]

What cultural groups do for individuals at a community or regional level, nationalism does countrywide to cohere the variegated cultural groups into a unified whole, thereby providing the country with a national culture. (In Chapter 4, culture is defined as the interaction between mores, folkways, technology, and tools that comprises a total way of life to promote a group's survival and enhance its quality of living.) What follows is a sketch of the American national culture using the anthropologic definition.

American Mores. The central mores of the American culture are individualism and equality. Both are crucial to the culture's testament of faith, what can be called the *American Creed.* At the core of the Creed is the belief that capitalism is inviolably and absolutely good—*the greatest good comes to the greatest number of people when persons pursue their individual economic self-interests.* The virtues of capitalism are entrepreneurship, competitiveness, and ownership of property. The role of government is to make sure capitalism works. Hofstadter described the Creed as the

> sanctity of private property, the right of the individual to dispose of and invest it, the value of opportunity, and the natural evolution of self-interest and self-assertion. . . . The business of politics—so the creed runs—is to protect this competitive world, to foster it on occasion . . . but not to cripple it with a plan for common collective action. American traditions also show a strong bias in favor of equalitarian democracy, but it has been a democracy in cupidity rather than a democracy of fraternity.[2]

The Creed is a faith that all citizens can prosper. Prosperity is possible through work; work is everywhere waiting to be done. One must take the initiative to seek out the work or to create it. The Creed contains a presumption of human equality, a feeling intertwined with general Christian notions which holds that all people are brothers and sisters under the skin, that all peoples are equal in the eyes of the law. Implicit in the Creed is the Protestant work ethic: work is one's salvation, and if one works hard, spends wisely, takes advantage of opportunities, and leads a clean life, salvation will be at hand.[3] Material gain, such as money in the bank, a new house, and two cars, is tangible proof that one is saved. The American Creed basically holds that any person in American society can prosper materially by capitalizing on the opportunities offered in the society. This is sometimes called the "bootstrap theory," from the adage, "if you want to succeed, you must pull yourself up by the bootstraps." The Creed assumes that all persons are equal under the law, and with this general protection, all persons can prosper on their own merit. Those who do not prosper, according to the Creed, fail because they do not capitalize on opportunities provided them. They fail, therefore, because of some character flaw, such as laziness or slovenly living, rather than a flaw or breakdown in the workings of the Creed. Circumstances of birth, such as the social class or racial or ethnic group one inherits, are considered irrelevant.

[handwritten margin note: not successful with other ethnic groups!]

The American creed has been expressed eloquently in the Declaration of Independence, "we hold these truths to be self evident: that all men are created equal; that they are endowed by the Creator with inherent and inalienable rights. . . ." Abraham Lincoln succinctly expressed the Creed when he said in his Gettysburg Address: ". . . our fathers brought forth on this continent a new nation, conceived in liberty, and dedicated to the proposition that all men are created equal. . . ." In our time, Martin Luther King, Jr., reaffirmed the American Creed, calling for all Americans to join him when he delivered his "I Have a Dream" speech at the end of a historic march on Washington, D.C. in August 1963.

American Folkways. American folkways vary because of the nation's religious and cultural pluralism (see discussion later in this chapter). Theoretically, individuals are free to live and work where they wish, and they are free to join any cultural group they desire. But, where one lives and with whom one associates are mediated by communal ideologies and the attitudes held by their adherents. Mobility and freedom of association, then, are basic folkways which may or may not be restricted by communal ideologies.

There are some universal traditions observed by many citizens, such as the Fourth of July, Christmas, and Thanksgiving holidays. Even deeper, there exists a conscious national history with its attendant ideals, heroes, and martyrs. The virtue of honesty is taught in the legend of George Washington and the chopping down of the cherry tree. As a lad, Washington actually did not chop down his father's cherry tree, but the legend has taken on the quality of mythic truth. The virtues of education self-gained are taught with the legend of Abraham Lincoln's climb from poverty to prominence. In our time, two martyrs stand prominent, John F. Kennedy, "Ask not what your country can do for you, but ask what you can do for your country," and Martin Luther King, Jr., "I have a dream—that my . . . children will live in a nation where they will not be judged by the color of their skin . . . ." Both envisioned a greater America whose youth were charged to crusade for freedom and justice.

Common Language. The English language as adapted by Americans over a 200-year separation from the mother culture, England, is the nation's _lingua franca_ serving as the language of business, commerce, education, and government. As the nation's lingua franca, English serves straightforward functions such as providing government and education with a standardized language by which they conduct daily affairs. Neither the administration of government nor education would be possible, in a nation as large as the United States, without a standardized language. As the nation's lingua franca, English serves less straightforward functions, such as conveying national symbols and myths in a language common to all citizens. For example, while there is a standard form of American English there is no government institute or academy that regulates the language, especially its vocabulary. Rather, the American English lexicon reflects a democratic culture as attested by its tendency to incorporate vocabulary items from diverse ethnic groups. Following are common American English words borrowed from various ethnic or national groups:

Native American	French	Dutch	German	Spanish
hickory	pumpkin	cookie	dunk	alfalfa
pecan	bureau	boss	noodle	coyote
skunk	depot	spook	pretzel	cafeteria
chipmunk	gopher	waffle	ouch	corral
moose	chowder	pit or seed	bum	ranch

These terms adapted from five different early American groups are but a few of the many terms incorporated into the development of American English. The terms are not exceptional or esoteric; they are plain words uniquely American, drawn from different subcultural groups and integrated into the English vernacular.

American English also conveys an American oral and literary tradition. For example, the larger-than-life tall tales about Pecos Bill and Paul Bunyan, the plaintive folksongs about John Henry and the Chisholm Trail, and the Negro Spirituals are cast in oral American idioms. The literary tradition, composed by a large number of essayists, novelists, and poets, are also cast in unique American idioms. These opening sentences from American novels, _Call me Ishmael, You don't know about me without you have read a book by the name of_ "The Adventures of Tom Sawyer," _To the red country and part of the gray country of Oklahoma,_ and these lines by American poets, _When lilacs last in the dooryard bloom'd, Something there is that doesn't love a wall, What happens to a_ *dream deferred?* are but a small number that chronicle experiences in the idiom of American English.

In our time, E.D. Hirsch in his text, *Cultural Literacy: What Every American Needs to Know,*[4] described the country's national language and culture and then developed a list of terms that every literate American ought to know. Since publication of the text, he and his colleagues have developed a dictionary that further describes a body of knowledge as basic to the American literary culture. Cultural literacy is focused on the commonality of American culture as reflected in scientific and political terms, literary and religious allusions, place names, dates, and idioms. The position serves to remind us that in our push to recognize the pluralism of American life we have slighted the commonality of the American experience; we have slighted the *one* and emphasized the *many* in *e pluribus unum.* Studying and learning the American national culture helps to balance the "one" with the "many". (Teaching and learning cultural education will be discussed in Chapter 7.)

Norms. Central American norms are codified in the Declaration of Independence and the U.S. Constitution. The Declaration is predicated on a presumption that all humans have rights: life, liberty, and the pursuit of happiness. The Constitution provides the framework, substantive and procedural civil rights, that effectuates the natural rights of the Declaration. Both documents are based on humanistic principles of the social contract, especially as described in John Locke's *Second Treatise on Government.* Each state operates under the auspices of the U.S. Constitution as recorded in its respective state Constitution.

Essentially, the American social contract revolves around the idea that citizens make a compact with each other; they agree to respect the rights of others, and in return, expect that their individual rights will be respected. The courts are the arbitrators that resolve contract disputes. The social contract, like most contracts, requires a quid pro quo; the "something for something" in the contract is the reciprocity expected when citizens respect each other's rights. As such, citizens are interdependent, making a human community possible. The norms of the community are broadly construed state and federal laws, more localized city ordinances, and the unique folkways and mores of local cultural groups. In larger cities, for example, it is common to speak of various "communities," for example, the Baptist community, the Greek community, the blue-color community, each having its distinctive folkways and mores. Sometimes, the community folkways and mores are more powerful than the state and federal laws in terms of controlling people's behavior. Sometimes, the community folkways and norms consciously contradict federal and state laws. For example, there are communities in the American Southwest that tolerate polygamous families even though state laws prohibit polygamy. People in the community, including law officials, are aware of these polygamous families, but so long as they otherwise adhere to state laws, they are allowed to live in relative peace within the community.

No surprise that the United States of America, as a nation-state, meets all the requirements for a culture. Here the intent is not to describe the entire American culture but rather to show that its broadly conceived norms, along with a distinct language, literary heritage, and history, provide the American scene with a pervasive core culture. Because of the culture's broad scope and grand sweep, day-to-day communal affairs, or how people go about the business of living in their communities, are mediated at the local and regional levels under the aegis of distinctively rendered communal ideologies. *Communal ideologies* refer to conceptual frames of reference which allow individuals to understand their social roles within a community. A communal ideology provides ways of thinking and behaving that allow individuals to live and work in a community. Often, the ideology is apotheosized in metaphoric symbolism, such as the *Melting Pot*, giving it the potency of mythic truth.

RELIGIOUS FREEDOM AND PLURALISM

The pre-Revolutionary era of U.S. history was an era of people seeking the right to practice their own religion. Early religious freedom seekers were Puritans in the Massachusetts Bay Colony, Quakers and Amish in Pennsylvania, Roman Catholics in Maryland, Dutch Reformed in New York, and Anglicans in the South. During this era, the Spanish established Roman Catholic missions in Arizona, New Mexico, and California among the Native American tribes. A little later, other religious groups settled in particular parts of the Eastern Seaboard and then moved west. By the time the U.S. Constitution was promulgated, Scandinavian Lutherans, German Catholics, Scotch-Irish Protestants, French Catholics, and Jews had settled villages and farming areas or established neighborhoods in such cities as New York City, Boston, and Philadelphia.

By the time the Constitution was ratified, religious pluralism was a fact of U.S. communal life. When Congress enacted the Bill of Rights, religious pluralism was officially recognized by the First Amendment: "Congress shall make no law respecting an establishment of religion, or prohibiting the free exercise thereof. . . ." The First Amendment provided all citizens freedom of conscience (the free exercise thereof) and freedom from an established church. The amendment was supported by religious and political leaders. The Protestant leaders distrusted the power of clergymen in highly centralized churches; matters of conscience were between the individual and God; theological issues were to be settled at the community church level; a democratic *ethos* emerged of congregational "local control" which applied to most Protestant denominations. Yet, the influence of the local control ethos was eventually felt by centralized churches such as the Presbyterians and Catholics, leading Pope Pius IX in his encyclical *Quanta Cura* (1864) to condemn the "modern" American notion of local control over congregational matters.[5] Protestant churches developed a vigorous sense of local control and a concomitantly vigorous notion that denominational membership was a voluntary act of conscience. One had freedom from religion or freedom to any religion of choice.

The First Amendment separated church and state, resulting in the formation of a secular government. The new nation would be governed by broad-based, humanist morals and ethics—European concepts such as natural rights and social contracts—rather than by specific dogmas and creeds of theocratic-based governments. The source of authority and power to run the secular government would be the will of the people rather than the will of God, thereby effectuating a binary structure for communal life and social control.

Political and economic affairs would be regulated by government; cultural and religious affairs would be mediated by the church working with the individual who would be free to organize communes, religious denominations, and ethnic groups in farming areas, towns, and villages. The new nation would have a "civil" religion,[6] a transcending belief in the American Creed, reverence for democratic institutions, observance of national holidays (*holy* days), and codified ethical precepts in The Declaration of Independence and the Constitution.

Jefferson's goal to erect a wall of separation between church and state was intended to insure freedom of conscience and freedom of thought, both critical in a democracy. Yet, Jefferson saw the need for a unifying ethical structure to guide a democratic nation which had no established religious creed.

> The interests of society require the observation of those moral precepts only in which all religions agree . . .(for all forbid us to murder, steal, plunder, or bear false witness) and that we should not intermeddle with the particular dogmas in which all religions differ.[7]

The state's ethical structure needed to focus on a religious function that, in Jefferson's words, would not meddle ". . . with the particular dogma in which all religions differ." The binary structure for communal life divided the functions of religion between the church and state, the church appropriating the private and the state the public function.

The ethical underpinnings of the Declaration of Independence and the Constitution were based on John Locke's natural rights philosophy. Locke's natural rights philosophy presupposed that pre-political men acted as independent individuals whose natural conditions included life, liberty, and ownership of property. As independent, individual families evolved into clans, tribes, and eventually communities, the pre-political man could no longer operate independently. He was now political. He exchanged independence for interdependence within a community, thereby establishing a social contract with all members of the community. He retained the natural rights of life, liberty, property as did all other community members. The community—now "political men"—formed a government to insure everyone's natural rights. For each individual's right there existed a parallel responsibility to respect the rights of others. Each individual was bound to respect the natural rights of others. To insure mutual interdependence the community members formed a government whose powers were limited so that it would serve the individuals for whom it was established. The social contract idea, further developed by Jean-Jacques Rousseau, and the Natural Rights doctrine were based on a philosophy of humanism that sought the best political organizations and the best social conditions for humans. The humanist philosophy sought to make life bearable as an end in itself rather than a test for life after death, a Renaissance idea couched

in a belief that individuals are entitled to happiness on earth. The individualistic ethic refocused the Christian ethic that individuals should be virtuous to
go to heaven and join God; humanism espoused virtuous behavior as a necessity
for the common good of the community.

The origins of humanism are found in Greek classics rather than Christian
literature. The belief that the Declaration of Independence and the Constitution are "Christian" documents is a misconception probably based on Jefferson's use of the words in the Declaration: ". . . to which the Laws of Nature and
of Nature's God entitle them . . ." As one study of humanism concluded: "The
principles of democracy have their roots in Humanistic ideals."[8] Of course, the
documents' ethical themes are found in most major religions: Christian, Bud-
dhist, Hebrew, Hindu, and Islamic. The ethics of the Declaration of Independence and the Constitution, limited to public functions of religion, are the
central guiding principles of the U.S. pluralistic society. Variously called a
"civil religion, the American Way, the religion of democracy, the common
American faith," the documents' ethics are also central to what I have described
as the American Creed.

We see that church and state both act as institutions that provide important
moral functions. Both need to be on guard to insure that neither intrudes on the
province of the other. Churches must not mandate public laws (they can express ethical and moral opinions about public laws) nor should governments
mandate worldviews (they can provide knowledge about different worldviews).
The relationship between God and the individual is the province of religion; the
relationship between the individual and the society as a whole is the province
of the state. Of course there are overlapping beliefs that deal with the relationship between God and the individual which speak to God's will in human
relationships. For example, the New Testament ethic, "Do unto others as you
would have others do unto you," is conceivably the underpinning of the Constitution's equal protection clause, "No state shall . . . deny to any person . . .
equal protection of the law." The ethic and the clause both deal with the
individual's relationship with society members; the New Testament is expressed as God's will; the Constitution is expressed as the people's will. We also
see in a pluralistic society that church and state have tandem responsibilities to
"promote the general welfare." Yet, neither is to dominate.

U.S. religious pluralism was intended to allow freedom of conscience and
prevent the medieval European condition of coercive church controlled
states. De Tocqueville noted in *Democracy in America* in the early nineteenth century that religious pluralism and the separation of church and state
benefitted the church.[9] Lord James Bryce, writing in *The American
Commonwealth*[10] about religious pluralism at the end of the nineteenth century, noted that the vast array of Christian denominations enhanced free
choice of religious beliefs. Further, he concluded, the separation of church
and state was accepted as axiomatic among church leaders because it fostered
religious freedom.

Beneath the glittering generalizations about religious pluralism all is not
well. Inherent in religious pluralism—as with all forms of pluralism—is conflict

and competition. The relationship between church and state is often strained, especially when religious groups perceive that public institutions are intruding on the province of the church. During the 1920s Christian fundamentalists successfully campaigned for laws prohibiting the teaching of evolution. Oklahoma (1923), Florida (1923), Mississippi (1926), Arkansas (1927) legislatures enacted antievolution laws, which Christian fundamentalists considered incompatible with their literal interpretations of the Book of Genesis in the Old Testament. The infamous 1925 "Scopes Monkey Trial" in Dayton, Tennessee, tested the constitutionality of a state law mandating that " . . . it shall be unlawful for any teacher in . . . public schools . . . to teach any theory that denies the story of the Divine Creation of man as taught in the Bible, and to teach instead that man has descended from a lower form of animal."[11] A biology teacher, John Scopes, was indicted for teaching the theory of evolution contrary to the state law. William Jennings Bryan argued for, and Clarence Darrow argued against, the law. The two famous lawyers drew attention to the case's epic nature: scientific progress and religious orthodoxy in conflict. The two lawyers, each convinced of the truth of his argument, managed to draw attention to the clash between science and religion but did little to resolve the church and state constitutional issue. The Tennessee Supreme Court upheld Scopes' conviction for violating the law and then dismissed the charges because of technical irregularities during the trial. Eventually, the laws were repealed with Arkansas repealing its antievolution law as late as 1966.

In the early 1970s Christian fundamentalists again campaigned against the theory of evolution. Rather than conducting an antiscience campaign, as did the earlier fundamentalists, the Christian fundamentalists conducted a proknowledge campaign, i.e., they proposed that "Creation Science" be given equal time with the theory of evolution in public school science classes. "Creation Science" or "Creationism" is a belief that the earth was created as described in Genesis, the first book of the Old Testament.[12] Creationists argued that scientific evidence exists to support the belief that an omniscient being created all living forms pretty much as they currently exist. The creationist theory contradicts the evolutionist theory which posits that all living forms progressed from simpler forms. The evolutionists claim that any changes in the life forms are a matter of natural selection while the creationists claim that any changes are directed by an omniscient being.

Both belief systems operate from different assumptions about the creation of life. Creationists attribute the entire creation to an act of God; some evolutionists attribute the original conceptualization of life to God but believe that God chose evolution as the method to implement His original idea. In other words, "God created the idea and then let it happen." Other evolutionists attribute life to happenstance. In other words, "life just happened." There are also several different camps among the creationists. Some believe that there were several series of creations. Others believe there was only one, single, instantaneous creation.[13] What is crucial is that the weight of current empirical data leans heavily in favor of the Darwinian notion of evolution. While much has been added to the theory since Darwin's research at the Galapagos Islands, the theory's fundamental premises that life forms evolve from simple to more complex forms, that all known groups of plants and animals emerged from ancestors over periods of time, and that most groups of plants and animals can be traced to the lowest forms of life existent at the dawn of the earth, have been validated through the study of plant and animal fossils.

Advocates of creationism argue that teaching the evolution theory erodes traditional beliefs about human creation, thereby violating their freedom of religion. The state, they argue, has intruded on the province of the church. Creation advocates managed to pass a law in Louisiana in 1982 that provided equal time for creation science to be taught in public schools. The law was tested in the Supreme Court, *Edwards* v. *Agguillard*,[14] and ruled violative of separation of church and state. The Court ruled that creation science was a religious doctrine rather than a scientifically based theory and could not be given equal time to evolution.

Having lost the pro-knowledge creationism campaign, the fundamentalists refocused their campaign on the broader issue that public schools violated the First Amendment because they operated on the purportedly religious doctrine of secular humanism, and thereby violated the Christian students' freedom from religion in public schools. Advocates of secular humanism described their views in the *Secular Humanist Declaration:*

> Secular humanism is not a dogma or a creed. There are wide differences of opinion among secular humanists on many issues. Nevertheless, there is a loose consensus with respect to several propositions.[15]

The *Secular Humanist Declaration* supported the following propositions:

Free inquiry and rational inquiry;

Separation of church and state;

Ideal of freedom;

Ethics based on critical intelligence;

Moral education;

Religious skepticism

Scientific inquiry and evolution;

Education for critical intelligence[16]

The Declaration ended with a brief statement that a more humane world is possible through reason and principles of tolerance, compromise, and the negotiation of differences.

Senator Jesse Helms, a member of the special interest group, the Moral Majority, wrote that ". . . when the U.S. Supreme Court prohibited children from participating in voluntary prayers in public schools . . . it established a national religion in the United States—the religion of secular humanism."[17]

One observer noted that the deeper motives of the fundamentalists, such as Helms, were to restore prayer and Bible reading in schools, replace the free marketplace of ideas (academic inquiry and freedom) with censorship of ideas and books, and, possibly, replace public education with government-funded private education.[18]

CULTURAL PLURALISM

Cultural pluralism is an expansion of religious pluralism with emphasis placed on broader cultural affairs rather than solely religious affairs; as ideologies, however, the two are akin. From its inception, cultural pluralism called for the economic and political integration of White ethnics into U.S. society, but called also for retention of their languages, cultures, and religions. Berkson called this notion the community theory:

> The Community Theory differs from the Americanization and Melting Pot theories in that it refuses to set up as ideal such a fusion as will lead to the obliteration of all ethnic distinction.[19]

For Berkson, ideal cultural pluralism would allow people to select ethnic or cultural communities compatible with their ethnic preferences. These communities would be home base, the source of sustenance, retreat, and renewal. People could voluntarily select their ethnic affiliation and enclave. On this point, Berkson and the recognized originator of cultural pluralism, Horace Kallen, disagreed. Kallen[20] felt that ethnic-group affiliation was involuntary, that people could not change their past heritage and their parents would inevitably socialize them according to their past ethnic heritage. People really had no choice about their ethnic group; they were thoroughly indoctrinated with it before reaching adulthood. In later years, Kallen softened his stance, conceding that adults could possibly select ethnic-group affiliation if accepted by a particular ethnic group.

Because Kallen's writings were the beginning of cultural pluralism, let us examine his three basic themes. The first was that almost everyone had an ethnic group. Considering that Kallen wrote in the early twentieth century, the theme made sense. At that time, most people could identify some ethnic or national group as their own. Also, Kallen thought that most people had no choice but to belong to their ethnic group of birth: that is, most people inherited a family which belonged to some ethnic group, and the family would socialize its youth into that ethnic group. Kallen's second theme was that cultural pluralism was in agreement with the democratic, American way. Because it allowed people to be different and yet be American, the theory allowed people to define themselves freely. Third, Kallen emphasized a unity-within-diversity theme. He argued that it was possible for a society to be diverse as well as unified. Further, he argued that the society could benefit from diversity.

Cultural pluralism devolved into what Herberg called "the triple melting pot."[21] In his study on the sociology of American religions, Herberg found that in the first four decades of this century Americans tended to marry within their religious group—Protestants, Catholics, and Jews. In other words, interreligious marriages occurred in relatively small numbers. The study also revealed that within religious groups, minimal intermarriage occurred between ethnic minorities and Whites: African American and White Protestants rarely married, and Mexican American or Puerto Rican Catholics rarely married White Catholics. Glazer and Moynihan's similar study conducted in New York City, *Beyond the Melting Pot*,[22] reaffirmed Herberg's thesis. The limitation of the triple melting pot concept is that the role of non-Christian religions is not treated. Nevertheless, the triple melting pot thesis does point to the tenacity of religious plurality and ethnic stratification in American society.

Cultural pluralism is often described with the salad bowl analogy. In a salad bowl, each ingredient adds to the overall taste and flavor of the salad, yet each retains its individual identity. A society based on cultural pluralism is like a salad bowl in that each ethnic group retains its identity while contributing to the overall society. The salad would not be complete without the participation of all ingredients; under cultural pluralism, the society would not be complete without the involvement of all ethnic groups. Another analogy is that of the orchestra. In an orchestra, each instrument belongs to a group that retains its identity; each group is interdependent with other instrument groups, and each instrument group contributes to the overall orchestral harmony. In a culturally pluralistic society each group retains its group identity, is interdependent with other groups, and contributes to the overall social harmony.

THE NEW ETHNIC PLURALISM

The new ethnic pluralism is a reaffirmation of religious and cultural pluralism within the context of a mass, industrialized society. The ideology posits that ethnicity remains an ingredient in American communal life; ethnic pluralism does not advocate racial or ethnic separation; rather, it reaffirms the unity-within-diversity notion of cultural pluralism. But, considerable debate revolves around the issue of the degree to which ethnicity remains salient for particular ethnic groups. Novak, in *The Rise of the Unmeltable Ethnics*,[23] developed the thesis that White ethnics have not melted into a homogeneous single group. Instead, White ethnic groups have adapted their ancestral ethnicity to fit contemporary communal requirements while retaining some basic elements of their ancestral customs and traditions.

Allen and Turner, in *We the People, An Atlas of America's Ethnic Diversity*,[24] argued that ethnicity is symbolic for many White ethnic groups. They based their argument on the fact that ethnic groups were dispersed throughout most of the nation. Using 1980 census data from the nation's counties, they developed an atlas which shows the dispersion of ethnic groups in the more than 3,100 of the nation's counties. At least 67 different groups of White and racial minority ethnic groups are shown to be dispersed throughout the country. But the atlas also shows that racial minorities tend to concentrate in certain regions, states, cities, and Indian reservations. Allen and Turner concluded that

> People still think of their ethnic identity as a sense of peoplehood, but this is more typically based on an abstract collective than on a closely interacting group. . . . For people of color [racial minorities] and many of Hispanic origin, ethnic identity usually remains salient because their physical appearances makes them distinguishable from whites.[25]

In 1975–1976, the National Council for the Social Studies appointed a task force to develop an educational rationale focused on the ethnic diversity in the United States. The task force of educators, in conjunction with an advisory board representative of various U.S. ethnic groups, provided an affirmation of ethnic pluralism:

> In the United States, ethnic diversity has remained visible despite the assimilation process that takes place in any society made up of many different ethnic groups. Although ethnic affiliations are weak for many Americans, a large number still demonstrate at least some attachments to their ethnic cultures and to the symbols of their ancestral traditions. The values and behavior of many Americans are heavily influenced by their ethnicity. Ethnic identification may also be increased by many because of their racial characteristics, language, or culture.[26]

ANGLO CONFORMITY

The Anglo Conformity assimilation ideology, developed from the eastern colonial American belief that all immigrants should renounce their former ethnic and national culture and adopt the ways of the English (Anglo) cultural groups living in the Atlantic seaboard colonies. The ideology was conceived for White Europeans; African Americans and Native Americans were not to be melted into the Anglo conformity pot. African Americans were to serve the society as slaves. The institution of slavery clearly defined African Americans' role in colonial society. Native Americans were considered people of different nations. They were to be kept out of the society by treaties that placed them west of the eastern seaboard states. Treatment of Native Americans as separate nations rather than as assimilable human groups clearly defined their role.

The French scholar, Alexis de Tocqueville, noted in his study[27] of the emerging American republic that exclusion of Native Americans and slavery of African Americans threatened the unity and stability of the republic. Since the White groups considered Native Americans unmeltable, de Tocqueville felt that Native Americans had only the options of war with the American republic or withdrawal to the west. If the Native Americans attempted to remain within the republic, de Tocqueville predicted that the Whites would resist, isolate, and eventually expel them. For African Americans, de Tocqueville thought emancipation or expatriation to Africa was inevitable. He also predicted that if African Americans were emancipated, Whites would remain hostile to them for years to come; assimilation of African Americans, according to de Tocqueville, would not inevitably follow emancipation.

Anglo Conformity was an ideology of racial separation, or *apartheid*. America for Whites-only as an ideology is attributed to early colonial attitudes that racial minorities—African Americans and Native Americans during the colonial era—should not be assimilated into American society. The belief was predicated on the presumed genetic inferiority of racial minorities, as well as the presumed excessive prejudice and discrimination racial minorities would experience at the hands of Whites if an attempt were made to assimilate them. Some U.S. Presidents practiced the racial separation ideology to varying degrees.[28] Thomas Jefferson, Andrew Jackson, Abraham Lincoln, and Franklin D. Roosevelt implemented policies and programs to isolate, relocate, or export African Americans, Native Americans, and Japanese Americans.

Thomas Jefferson proposed that all African Americans be educated in a trade or craft. At the age of 18 for females and 21 for males, they would be freed and exported to some other country or to the western United States. He believed that African Americans could not be amalgamated into the Eastern colonies. He felt, too, that White prejudices and discrimination against African Americans would intensify if attempts were made to assimilate them.[29] Andrew Jackson made his reputation as an Indian fighter. Once President, he supported the southern "states righters" who wanted to export all Native Americans from the South to the Oklahoma Indian Territory. When his removal activities were declared unconstitutional by the U.S. Supreme Court, Jackson reportedly said about the Chief Justice of the Supreme Court, "John Marshall has made his decision, now let him enforce it." In violation of the U.S. Constitution, President Jackson exported almost all Native Americans from the South.[30]

President Abraham Lincoln vacillated between colonizing African Americans in other countries and emancipating African Americans within the United States. Between 1862 and 1864, Lincoln experimented with colonization of African Americans on Cow Island, off Haiti. The experiment ended in failure. Lincoln was aware of the American Colonization Society which advocated colonization and exported African Americans from the United States. It was founded in 1817 to establish colonies in Africa for African Americans, sending them to live in Sierra Leone and Liberia. Supporters of this "back to Africa" society were prominent political leaders, including James Monroe, James Madison, John Marshall, and Henry Clay; however, it was not supported by the African American leadership because it was viewed as an expatriation ploy. Before the society's demise after the Civil War, more than 15,000 African Americans had been expatriated to Africa.[31] Lincoln knew that the colonization movement was opposed by the African American leadership and that it failed to attract a significant number of African Americans. He thus supported both African American exportation and emancipation.[32] President Franklin Roosevelt developed a pro-civil rights record while acting as president, but signed the executive order (Executive Order 9066) that dispossessed some 112,000 Japanese Americans of their property. U.S. armed forces then relocated them from the West Coast to internment camps in the interior United States as a means to prevent Japanese sabotage in California.[33]

Before and during World War I, the public's voice was raised to Ameri-

canize all immigrants, "make them 100% American." Americanization rose out
of the fears of older immigrant groups whose roots were in the Atlantic Seaboard colonies. They feared that the so-called Nordic American race would be
diluted, especially by Jewish, Polish, Italian, and other darker-hued immigrants.

Concurrent with the emergence of Americanization, a popular racial theory
emerged which categorized people into two races, the White and the colored.[34]
People were then subdivided into a hierarchy within the two races. In the
hierarchy of the White race, the "Nordic" or "Aryan" strain was the purest
strain, consisting of the older German and English immigrant groups, who
were ostensibly tall, blond, blue-eyed people. The "Alpine" strains were less
pure, consisting of the darker, eastern European immigrants who were the
in-between strains; the lowest White strains were the Mediterranean, consisting
of the dark-haired southern Europeans. The colored race, "people of color,"
was at the bottom. People of color were members of the "yellow" races (Chinese, Japanese, etc.), the "red" races (Native Americans), and the African
American race. All were considered unmeltable into the White race. Paradox-
ically, racial separation existed concurrently with melting pot and pluralistic
ideologies. Gunnar Myrdal, in his classic study *The American Dilemma*,[35] called
the paradox an "antiamalgamation" doctrine. Under the doctrine, racial minorities could not be assimilated into American society without diluting it. Therefore, it was necessary to segregate, relocate, or export racial minorities as a
means of preserving the racial and ethnic purity of White American society.

THE MELTING POT

This ideology envisioned a biological fusion and ethnic synthesis of all Americans regardless of race, national origin, or religion. From this merger would
evolve a new American culture. The ideology emerged from the large-scale
immigration of people from southeastern and central Europe in the years between 1880 and 1914. The ideology was popularized by Israel Zangwill's play,
The Melting Pot. The notion of racial fusion and ethnic synthesis can be traced
to 1756 in an essay by Hector St. John de Crevecoeur[36] who wrote that in the
Eastern colonies individuals were being melted into a new race.

One other melting pot ideology that merits mention is the frontier melting
pot idea of historian Frederick Jackson Turner.[37] Turner's thesis was that frontier exigencies of White pioneers forged a type of cultural synthesis in the
American West. On the frontier, pioneers of all nationalities were compelled to
merge by the austere social and physical environments, according to Turner.
Regardless of past status in Europe or on the Eastern Seaboard, on the frontier
all were equalized by their ability to contribute to human survival. The forced
merger of all national groups in the frontier's crucible fused a new American
nationality, the transnational White Americans, with their unique frontier values and beliefs. Turner's melting pot is essentially the same as Zangwill's with
the important difference that Zangwill described the communal ideal of urban

European immigrants, and Turner described similar desires for rural European immigrant pioneers.

DESEGREGATION AND INTEGRATION

The forces of desegregation and integration countered the racial separation ideology. The forces percolated from the civil rights movement of the 1950s and 1960s and from various U.S. Supreme Court decisions, primarily the *Brown* v. *Topeka Board of Education* decision, which declared that schools segregated on the basis of race were inherently unequal. The decision and subsequent civil rights legislation provided legal authority to dismantle the residue of institutions formed on the basis of the racial separation ideology. Miscegenation (anti-interracial marriage) laws and Jim Crow laws, which allowed official segregation and discrimination against racial minorities, were abrogated.[38]

But the segregation-desegregation-integration thrust did not spring suddenly from the civil rights movement; it underlies the legal changes ethnic and racial minorities have historically struggled to bring about in American society. Aware that U.S. society was legally segregated and that they were legally impeded from full participation in American society, minorities have striven through legal and democratic channels to abolish the segregation laws and thereby desegregate formal institutions such as schools, the armed forces, and federally financed corporations.

Once formal segregation was made illegal, the second phase of the process, desegregation, began, leading to the third phase, integration into American society. The civil rights movement of the 1950s and 1960s sought to abrogate formal and legal societal segregation, which then began the desegregation phase of the process. To a large extent, legal segregation has been ended, and the desegregation phase has been engaged and continues to operate. The third phase, integration, is yet to come. Until the desegregation phase is successfully completed, integration is not possible because it is more than mere elimination of legal segregation and discrimination; it is the condition of full participation for ethnic and racial minorities in all realms of American life. To set the stage for integration, the current desegregation phase must successfully wipe out the racist traditions, folkways, and beliefs, and buttress the political, economic, and social power bases of the ethnic minority groups.

WOMEN'S STRUGGLE FOR EQUALITY

The women's movement did not suddenly spring from the civil rights movement although the two movements are historically intertwined. The women's movement for equal rights (feminism) gained its first impetus from women involved in the abolition movement before the Civil War. During the 1830s, two sisters, Sarah and Angelina Grimké, advocated the abolition of slavery to mixed audiences consisting of men and women. They were criticized, by men and women alike, for daring to speak to mixed groups.[39] The women retorted by asking rhetorically: Do women in America have freedom of expression and opinion only when they talk to other women? The answer was yes! Speaking before audiences filled with men violated a chauvinistic folkway. Sarah Grimké's book, *Letters on the Condition of Women and the Equality of the Sexes* (1838) reaffirmed the ideological basis for the feminist movement which was formulated earlier by Mary Wollstonecraft in her book *Vindication of the Rights of Women* (1792).[40]

During the 1840s female abolitionists, such as Elizabeth Cady Stanton, Lucretia Mott, Maria Child, Maria Weston Chapman, and the Grimké sisters, discovered a dual standard among the male abolitionists; the men valued the women's views on abolition but devalued their views on women's equality. At the World Anti-Slavery Convention which met in London in 1840, female abolitionists were not allowed to sit in the main convention center with men; rather, the women were segregated behind a curtain and bar from where they could observe the convention's proceedings, but the men could not see them.[41]

The London snub was too much. American women, and their British peers, determined that they must launch a movement that would advocate their own rights separate from the slavery issue, which took place July 19–20, 1848 in Seneca Falls, New York. The Seneca Conference is regarded as the birth of the American women's movement. During the time between 1848 and 1919 when Congress enacted the Nineteenth Amendment granting women the right to vote, women launched highly focused campaigns to achieve specific laws or programs of concern to women. Susan B. Anthony and Elizabeth Cady Stanton organized the National Woman Suffrage Association (1869) to launch a campaign to gain the right to vote. Other organizations were formed, such as the International Ladies Garment Workers Union (1900) and the National Women's Trade Union League (1903) to specifically focus on the working conditions and inequities experienced by women in the garment industry.

After a hiatus between 1919–1960, the women's movement experienced a resurgence in the 1960s with three events: (1) Betty Friedan's book *The Feminine Mystique* (1963), which chronicled the ideological basis for feminism in the second half of the twentieth century; (2) the Civil Rights Act of 1964 which prohibited employment discrimination based on a person's race, color, national origins, religion, and sex; the Act's Title IX specifically referred to the rights of women in the workplace, including public and higher education (Title IX is described in Chapter 3); and (3) the formation of the National Organization for Women (NOW), organized in 1966 with the goal of taking action to place women in full participation and equal partnership with men in the American mainstream.

NOW's broadly-based focus is an integration goal, a thrust on the part of women to be integrated into the American mainstream as equals to men. Events of the 1980s, such as Geraldine Ferraro's bid for the Vice Presidency, Sandra Day O'Connor's appointment to the U.S. Supreme Court, and some advances in business and education, indicate that women are experiencing the early phases of desegregation as they undergo the segregation-desegregation-integration process.

INSTITUTIONALIZATION OF THE HANDICAPPED

A much less visible group, the handicapped, has also grappled with segregation and desegregation in a quest for integration. Like minorities and women, the handicapped have experienced formal (legal) segregation as well as informal segregation. Both in England and the United States, mentally retarded and physically disabled individuals were legally isolated from their mainstream societies as epitomized in the word *bedlam*. Bedlam, meaning uproar or confusion was originally The Hospital of St. Mary of Bethlehem, an insane asylum in London. Bethlehem became slurred into Bedlam with its connotation of madness. The treatment in Bedlam consisted mainly of restraints:

> Those who visited Bedlam in London in 1814 could see countless patients clad only in loose shrouds and chained by their arms or legs to the wall. . . . One patient wore rings around his neck and waist and was tethered to a wall for twelve years . . . .[42]

The development of eugenics provided justification for segregating the disabled and mentally retarded. Sir Francis Galton's book, *Hereditary Genius* (1869) evoked eugenics by advocating selective breeding, sterilization, and institutionalization of disabled and mentally retarded individuals. By the early 1900s, compulsory sterilization was legalized in various states. Attitudes toward the mentally retarded were especially vicious:

> The mentally defective were viewed as a menace to civilization, incorrigible at home, burdens to the schools, sexually promiscuous, breeders of feeble-minded offsprings. . . . Consequently, there was a cry for the segregation of the mentally defectives, with the aim of purifying society. . . .[43]

During the 1920s as eugenics was losing its scientific credibility, a more humane attitude toward disabled and mentally retarded individuals was forming. The Vocational Rehabilitation Act (1920), enacted for disabled World War I veterans, included provisions for the handicapped. In 1922, the International Council for the Education of Exceptional Children (today known as the Council for Exceptional Children [CEC]) was founded by Elizabeth Farrell. Yet, until the middle 1950s, there existed an informal public school policy to reject, or refuse admission, handicapped children from matriculating in their local public schools. Rather, handicapped children were to attend special training schools funded by the state. The schools were typically located near isolated communities far from the children's home, parents, and neighborhood.

As school began admitting handicapped students, the students were placed in "special education" rooms or outbuildings segregated from the regular or mainstream classrooms. Special education teachers were charged with educating groups of students who differed in every possible way and to every possible degree, resurrecting the irony of Bedlam—those needing the greatest amount of individualized attention received it the least; treatment consisted primarily of methods to constrain students. Of course, the teachers could not use chains and tethers nor could they possibly be expected to provide their students with an equal opportunity to learn given the immensity of individual differences and the paucity of resources made available to the teachers.

Only until passage of P.L. 94–142: Education for All Handicapped Children Act (1975), were handicapped students legally freed from segregation in public education. The Act mandated the desegregation of all handicapped students as well as their eventual integration into the mainstream of public schools. (For more on the Act, see Chapters 3 and 4.) Currently, handicapped students are experiencing the desegregation phase of the segregation to integration process.

SOCIAL CLASS CONSCIOUSNESS AND CONFLICT

During the nation's early decades citizens envisioned a relatively class-free society. So long as a family could own a farm, the family could be self-sufficient, independent, and equal among other farm families. Frontier land was always there, free for the taking. In the cities and towns, workers formed guilds in which the master or business owner directed the activities of the journeymen and apprentices. The owner and the employees were interdependent and functioned much like a team. The vision of a class-free society dimmed as the frontier closed and the economy shifted from an agricultural to an industrial basis. Working a farm, or working in a small shop in a small town, was quite different from working in a large factory, in a mine, or on a railroad. Theodore Roosevelt described the transition:

> The old familiar relations between employer and employee were passing. . . . There was no such relation between the railroad magnates, who controlled the anthracite industry, and the one hundred fifty thousand men who worked in their mines. The great coal mining companies could easily dispense with the services of any particular miner. The miner could not dispense with the companies. He needed a job. [44]

Industrialization and mass production created a need for large numbers of workers who would work cheaply and efficiently in highly routinized tasks.

A worker's labor was viewed as a commodity, something to be bought. As a commodity, a worker was likened to a machine part. When the machine part decreased in efficiency for any reason, old age, sickness, industrial accident, it could be discarded and replaced with a new part, that is another worker. Carrying the analogy to its logical conclusion, the indispensable work was done by a real machine; the worker's labor was considered ancillary to the primary task. Of course, to the worker, labor was all that he or she had. It was the source of his or her sustenance.

During the industrial transformation, state and federal laws and court de-

cisions favored the development of big business and large industrial enterprises, which fostered a laissez-faire economic policy that protected the
interests of the owners and managers of the large enterprises. "In fact, however, the business community sought . . . a minimum of restrictive legislation
for management and a maximum of beneficent legislation for business
enterprises."[45] The courts readily provided minimum restrictions as reflected
in the tort liability doctrine of "assumed risk." A person entering employment
in dangerous occupations assumed the risk of the occupation. If a coal miner
were injured in a cave-in of the mine's ceiling, his employment would be
terminated, and he would be replaced by another miner. There would be no
workmen's compensation or medical coverage. The injured miner had assumed
the risk of injury by accepting employment in the mine and consequently was
not entitled to any compensation from the mine owner. Never mind that the
mine owner failed to repair the faulty ceiling that caused the accident. The
doctrine protected the property rights of the owner. Without such protection,
the courts and state legislatures reasoned, big business enterprises would be
hampered by the fear of lawsuits. The laws worked to the disadvantage of labor.
As historians Morison and Commager concluded ". . . there developed in certain major industries a species of industrial feudalism in which the laborer
occupied a position in many respects less secure than that of the medieval
serfs."[46]

Workers were easily replaced by the increasing number of immigrants
from southern and eastern Europe, the "new" immigrants. During the decades
between 1890 and 1920, the national origins of immigrants were dominantly
southern and eastern Europe, especially the Balkin countries (Albania, Bul-
garia, Romania, Yugoslavia, Greece, and Turkey).[47] The older immigrants
feared displacement by the newer groups in the labor market. The newer
immigrants were willing to work for lower wages and longer hours in hazardous
working conditions. Grateful to have a job, many were not cognizant of how
they were being used as strikebreakers. The owners often labelled union or-
ganizers as "foreign" or "alien agitators." Most were members of the older
immigrant groups who lobbied for immigration restrictions to protect their
jobs, fanning the flames of xenophobia against the southeastern European
immigrants.[48] Resentment toward the newer immigrants and its consequent
restrictive legislation were a reaction to the practice of employers who hired the
newer immigrants as strikebreakers or wage levelers. Were the seeds of social
class conflict being sown? Would the industrialization of the American economy
fulfill the Marxian prophecy? Would there be the emergence of two antago-
nistic classes, the bourgeois and the proletariat? And would the proletariat,
with a heightened sense of class consciousness, seek to overthrow the bourgeois
masters? These questions were answered by the American labor union movement.

The first major union, the Noble Order of the Knights of Labor (Philadelphia, 1869) was primarily a trade union open to men and women alike. In 1885
it won a major battle in a southwestern railroad strike. Railroad financier Jay
Gould, as a result of a successful strike, was forced to meet on equal terms with

the Knights' executive board; acceding to their demands, Gould symbolically enshrined the union's power to strike.[49] Generally, boycotts, pickets, and strikes were construed as restraints of interstate commerce and were treated by officials as unlawful. Owners called on the state's power of injunction to stop strikes. When enjoined from striking, the workers were compelled to return to work or face replacement by other nonunion workers. Often, the owners would use racial minorities (Chinese, Blacks, Mexican Americans) or the "new" immigrants to break strikes, touching off volatile tensions between the various ethnic groups.

Other unions—the American Federation of Labor (AFL), a craft union led by Samuel Gompers, and the International Workers of the World (IWW) or the Wobblies—used the boycott, picket, and strike to achieve union goals. The IWW proclaimed open warfare on American capitalism. Adopting a Marxist ideology, the preamble to the IWW constitution declared there could be no peace so long as the working people remained poor and the employing people rich:

> Between these two classes a struggle must go on until the workers of the world organize as a class, take possession of the earth and the machinery of production . . . .[50]

The IWW's aggressive anticapitalistic tactics contributed to its demise when it threatened production in munitions plants during World War I. Union leaders were quick to see that anticapitalistic ideologies were self-defeating. The greater bulk of rank-and-file workers placed faith in the American Creed; unions could improve working conditions but this must be accomplished within the system. Gompers deftly drew a line between the union movement and the communist ideology, arguing that the union movement wished to improve the working conditions of workers without intentions of abolishing the capitalistic system, a communist party goal. In the words of a coal miner and union organizer of the 1930s:

> In 1933 the law was passed that allowed us to have a union. We believed we should have a good union, not a company union. Before that time I used to belong to the I.W.W. So we invited a speaker from the I.W.W. He made a very good speech but we didn't believe everything he had to say. He was a communist, you see. He wanted to overthrow the government. That was terrible. So we decided to go with the United Mine Workers of America.[51]

The United Mine Workers of America took hold with coal miners because of the dogged determination of its leader, John L. Lewis, in the 1930s when labor unions won the right to strike and bargain collectively under the National Labor Relations Act (NLRA).

The NLRA of 1935 was the result of Franklin D. Roosevelt's New Deal administration. More deeply, it was the result of the Great Depression which revealed the failures of the laissez-faire economic policy. In its place, the New Deal engaged a policy of governmental intervention, "liberal nationalism," which was rooted in the Progressive Era when strong federal regulations were needed to combat monopolies, trusts, and price fixing. Liberal nationalism pervaded most areas of economic activity, but it had a special impact on labor relations. Estimates for the years 1880–1906 are that 38,000 strikes occurred with another 26,000 strikes during the post-World War I years, 1918–1935, roughly an average of 1,500 strikes per year over 43 years.[52]

The NLRA established a federal mechanism for unions and owners to mediate through collective bargaining. Unions were allowed to strike, and if necessary, the National Labor Relations Board would arbitrate a dispute. Through collective bargaining, unions won concessions with working conditions, wages, medical and retirement benefits. The federal and state governments buttressed the gains by enacting legislation providing social security plans, industrial safety regulations, workmen's compensation, and minimum wage regulations. The hard won union victories benefitted the nonunion workers who were granted similar benefits by their employers, thereby increasing the purchasing power of workers and increasing the overall standard of living. The unions also lobbied for compulsory education, child labor laws, and fair wages for women.

This brief review of the evolution of labor unions reveals that a broad-based working class consciousness (Marx's proletariat/bourgeois conflict) or the impending schism prophesied by the *Communist Manifesto* did not occur. Several social forces prevented the schism. Many immigrants identified strongly with their ethnic groups and were not attracted by proletarian, collectivistic ideologies. Many espoused conformity to the American Creed, that is, loyalty to rugged individualism and free enterprise. The schism was also prevented by the intervention of the policy of liberal nationalism. Without the policy and its parallel social welfare legislation regarding unions, the outcome might have been vastly different. Nonetheless, the bitter, bloody history of the labor union struggle rendered an adversarial relationship between workers and owners. While a binary type of social class consciousness did not evolve, the industrial transformation negated the vision of a class-free society.

ASSIMILATION AS CULTURAL IMPERIALISM

The above discussion of communal ideologies is not all-inclusive. Other theories, such as Warner's class/caste,[53] Myrdal's moral dilemma,[54] and various leftist paradigms,[55] are helpful explanations of some aspects of communal living. Communal ideologies are sometimes referred to as assimilation theories. A common political definition—assimilation means total obliteration of an indigenous culture by a conquering culture—defines assimilation as a weapon for cultural imperialism or the means for a total takeover of one group by another. This was the policy of seventeenth and eighteenth century European colonial powers.

European countries wishing to expand their mineral and food resources conducted "discovery" expeditions to locate land on the American, Asian, and African continents for purposes of exploitation. To exploit the mineral and agricultural resources and transport them to the mother country, indigenous groups were also exploited. The Europeans developed policies and practices which enabled them to control and use the indigenous groups as a labor source. In return, the Europeans gave the indigenous groups the "benefits" of European civilization; that is, Europeans felt they had a responsibility to "civilize" indigenous groups. This ethnocentric attitude of the superiority of European civilization became known as the "white man's burden." Another policy was to send groups of people who would establish a colony and home base for the mother country. The first Europeans on the North American continent—the English, French, and Spanish—combined use of all three practices. Militia, Christian missionaries, and pilgrims were sent to colonize the continent. Later, the U.S. government colonized in the western hemisphere—in Puerto Rico, the Hawaiian Islands, and the Philippines. The colonizing country would send its militia, its Christian missionaries, and sometimes its own citizens. By force and by education (the indigenous groups were taught Christianity and the language of the mother country), the colonizers imposed their cultures on the indigenous groups, subjugating them to a lower class/caste status, and by degrees, encapsulating their cultures. The indigenous groups confronted three dubious options: (1) to be "assimilated" and subordinated by the colonizer, (2) to be expelled from one's home, family, and group, or (3) to be killed for not choosing assimilation or expulsion.

SUMMARY

The U.S. society is a cluster of human and legal communities cohered by a national culture and a pervasive ethos, the *American Creed*. The Creed is a testament of faith that individual free enterprise coupled with equality under the law is the archetypic American communal ideology based as it is on humanistic beliefs and natural rights. To determine a social identity, to answer the basic question "what is my role in society?", one is given broad but vague guidelines by the Creed. One must turn to more specific value and belief systems like those rooted in the home, the school, and the local community. Then one must reconcile the more specific value or belief systems with the broad-based beliefs of the Creed. In American society, U.S. citizens have an American nationality, a more specific group affiliation(s)—ethnic, racial, religious, or social class group—a localized self-concept, and a specific occupational identity.

Given only the broad ideals of the American Creed, people have devised their own belief systems to guide their day-to-day social transactions. Communal ideologies provide a modus operandi by which one's convivial needs can be satisfied. We should not forget that the communal ideologies discussed in this chapter are products of other centuries and other social conditions. The ideologies evolved from the eighteenth and nineteenth centuries when European nations as well as the United States were undergoing a transformation from feudal, agrarian economies to urban, industrial economies. In the feudal, agrarian economies, cultural groups formed around the family, the manor, the village, the church, or the geographic region. Traditions, customs, language—the stuff of ethnicity—were transmitted orally. There was little need for literacy; affairs could be conducted by speaking (not writing or reading) in the vernacular. Customs, language, and myths were maintained by an oral tradition.

As nations industrialized, nation-states replaced ethnic groups as basic forms of social organization. People were concentrated in large, urban areas; they often lived in their own ethnic enclaves where they could maintain a semblance of their former cultures, but the workplace, government, and education all required a standardized language and a common culture to cohere the ethnic and cultural diversity into a united whole. In the United States, the rhetoric of the common school advocates was to establish a common culture using a common language for all citizens. The stuff of ethnicity—customs, traditions, language—was nationalized and standardized with less reliance on oral tradition and more on a literary tradition. American history with its myths and legends and American English with its unique idioms and spellings were written. Literacy replaced the oral tradition, at least within the spheres of government, commerce, the workplace, and education.

Industrialization in the United States, especially through universal public education with its emphasis on a common American history and a standard American English, elevated nationalism and leveled ethnic groups to the private sphere as forms of social organization. Now the nation is in the throes of a postindustrial shift, whirling in the direction of international interdependence so that old-fashioned American nationalism with its tendency toward isolationism is no longer viable. Interdependence is not new; it has existed as long as people have lived in communities; in the American pluralistic society, people are still interdependent at local and regional levels with the added complication that our society is very much interdependent upon the rest of the world. Clearly, new isms and new ideologies are needed to guide us toward global interdependence.

STUDY QUESTIONS

1. Religious beliefs about basic conditions—birth, death, the meaning and purpose of life—influence a person's way of behaving. Analyze how answers to the following questions might influence a teacher's or a student's behavior.

   (a) To what extent do people have control over their ultimate fates? Are their fates predetermined or self-willed? How might a student who believes that one's fate is predetermined behave toward learning difficult subjects?

   (b) Do you consider life to be a trial period in which hard work can earn salvation? Or, should hard work, or anything else that makes life less enjoyable, be avoided so that life can be enjoyed as an end in itself? How would the latter belief (enjoy! enjoy!) affect a student's attitude toward doing homework?

2. How well does the American Creed work? Are all people really able to prosper if they work hard and live a life of thrift? Or, is the American Creed dead, killed by social

class conflict or racial prejudice? In other words, "who you know," or "what you can buy" determines one's prosperity much more than "what you know or do" in the pluralistic society?

3. Currently, how active is the Anglo-Conformity Racial Separation ideology? Before answering, consider the resurgence of racial conflict on American college campuses during the mid-to-late 1980s.

4. Would an ethnic synthesis in American society—the Melting Pot ideology—be desirable? Or, would the ideology suppress religious and cultural freedoms that vitalize society?

5. What are the limits of cultural pluralism? Is it possible for a society to be "too" pluralistic, that is, would too much pluralism fragment American society?

6. Why is separation of Church and State considered important in a democratic society? And, when is it possible to separate the Church and State: in matters of ethics? dogma? observances? What's right (or wrong) with the practice of the U.S. Congress opening each session with a prayer?

7. Read the following passages. Identify which ideology each passage best represents. Then defend your answer by explaining why your answer is correct. The ideologies: Anglo-Conformity, Cultural Pluralism, Melting Pot, Religious Pluralism.

> Female and male, Indian, Negro and White, Irishman, Scotchman and Englishman, German and Spaniard and Frenchman, Italian and Swede and Pole, Hindu and Chinaman, butcher, baker and candlestick maker, workingman and gentleman, rich man and poor man, Jew and Quaker and Unitarian and Congregationalist and Presbyterian and Catholic—they are all different from each other, and different as they are, all equal to each other.[56]

> What . . . is the American, this new man? He is either an European, or the descendant of an European, hence that strange mixture of blood, which you will find in no other country. I could point out to you a family whose grandfather was an Englishman, whose wife was Dutch, whose son married a French woman, and whose present four sons have now four wives of different nations. He is an American, who leaving behind him all his ancient prejudices and manners, receives new ones from the new mode of life he has embraced, the new government he obeys, and the new rank he holds. He becomes an American by being received in the broad lap of our great Alma Mater. Here individuals of all nations are melted into a new race of men, whose labours and posterity will one day cause great changes in the world.[57]

> The [immigrants to America] come to a life of independence, but to a life of labor—and, if they cannot accommodate themselves to the character, moral, political and physical, of this country with all its compensating balances of good and evil, the Atlantic is always open to them to return to the land of their nativity and their fathers. To one thing they must make up their minds, or they will be disappointed in every expectation of happiness as Americans. They must cast off the European skin, never to resume it. They must look forward to their posterity rather than backward to their ancestors; they must be sure that whatever their own feelings may be, those of their children will cling to the prejudices of this country.[58]

> Our progress in degeneracy appears to me to be pretty rapid. As a nation, we began by declaring that "all men are created equal." We now practically read it

"all men are created equal, except negroes." When the Know-Nothings get control, it will read "all men are created equal, except negroes, and foreigners and Catholics." When it comes to this I should prefer emigrating to some country where they make no pretense of loving liberty. . . .[59]

The people of the United States, considered as a whole, are composed of immigrants and their descendants from almost every country. The principal portion of them, however, derived their origin from the British nation, comprehending by this term the English, the Scotch and the Irish. The English language is almost wholly used; the English manners, modified to be sure, predominate, and the spirit of English liberty and enterprise animates the energies of the whole people. English laws and institutions, adapted to the circumstances of the country, have been adopted here. . . .[60]

Under the execrable race of the Stuarts and the struggle between the people and the confederacy of temporal and spiritual tyranny became formidable, violent, and bloody. It was this great struggle that peopled America . . . it was a love of universal liberty, and a hatred, a dread, a horror, of the internal confederacy [of an ecclesiastical hierarchy and despotic rulers] that . . . accomplished the settlement of America. After their arrival here, they . . . formed their plan, both of ecclesiastical and civil government, in direct opposition to the canon and feudal systems.[61]

To our reproach it must be said, that though for a century and a half we have had under our eyes the races of black and of red men, they have never yet been viewed by us as subjects of natural history. I advance it therefore as a suspicion only, that the blacks whether originally a distinct race, or made distinct by time and circumstances, are inferior to the whites in the endowments both of body and mind. It is not against experience to suppose, that different species of the same genus or varieties of the same species, may possess different qualifications. Will not a lover of natural history then, one who views the gradations in all the races of animals with the eye of philosophy, excuse an effort to keep those in the department of man as distinct as nature has formed them? This unfortunate difference of colour, and perhaps of faculty, is a powerful obstacle to the emancipation of these people. Many of their advocates while they wish to vindicate the liberty of human nature are anxious also to preserve its dignity and beauty. Some of these, embarrassed by the question "What further is to be done with them?" join themselves in opposition with those who are actuated by sordid avarice only. Among the Romans emancipation required but one effort. The slave when made free, might mix with, without staining the blood of his master. But with us a second is necessary unknown to history. When freed, he is to be removed beyond the reach of mixture.[62]

These new immigrants were no longer exclusively members of the Nordic race as were the earlier ones who came of their own impulse to improve their social conditions. The transportation lines advertised America as a land flowing with milk and honey and the European governments took the opportunity to unload upon careless, wealthy and hospitable America the sweepings of their jails and asylums. The result was that the new immigration . . . contained a large and increasing number of the weak, the broken and the mentally crippled of all races drawn from the lowest stratum of the Mediterranean basin and the Balkans, together with hordes of the wretched, submerged populations of the Polish Ghettos. Our jails, insane asylums and almshouses are filled with this human flotsam and the whole tone of American life, social, moral and political has been lowered and vulgarized by them.[63]

We live in a diverse society held together by dynamic democratic principles and economic values based on the ethic of individual free enterprise. While some elements of white ethnic groups have blended and melded, and while legal segregation of racial minorities is unconstitutional, we still live in a society in which individuals discriminate against others for religious, economic, and racial preferences. Vestiges of the past percolate into the present.[64]

There is an innumerable multitude of sects in the United States. They are all different in the worship they offer to the Creator, but all agree concerning the duties of men to one another. Each sect worships God in its own fashion, but all preach the same morality in the name of God. . . . Moreover, all the sects in the United States belong to the great unity of Christendom, and Christian morality is everywhere the same.[65]

NOTES

1. Joshua Fishman. *Language in Sociocultural Change*. Palo Alto: Stanford University Press, 1972, p. 182.
2. Richard Hofstadter. *The American Political Tradition*. New York: Vintage Press, 1973, p. xxxvii; see also, Henry B. Parkes. *The American Experience*. New York: Random House, 1955.
3. W. Lloyd Warner. *American Life: Dream and Reality*. Chicago: University of Chicago Press, 1962.
4. E. D. Hirsch, Jr. *Cultural Literacy: What Every American Needs to Know*. New York: Vintage Books, 1988.
5. Sydney E. Ahlstrom, *Religious History of the American People*. New Haven: Yale University Press, 1972, p. 547.
6. Robert Bellah, "Civil Religion in America," in *Religion in America*, eds. W. G. McLoughlin and R. Bellah. Boston: Houghton Mifflin, 1968, pp. 3–23.
7. Thomas Jefferson in Saul K. Padover ed., *Thomas Jefferson on Democracy*. New York: Pelican, 1939, p. 116.
8. Eugene Bewkes, Howard Jefferson, Eugene Adams, and Herman Braatigarn. *Experience, Faith and Reason*. New York: Harper & Brothers, 1940, p. 438.
9. Alexis de Tocqueville. *Democracy in America*, ed. J. P. Mayer and Max Lerner. New York: Harper & Row, 1966, p. 272.
10. James Bryce. *The American Commonwealth*. New York: Macmillan, 1910, II, p. 766.
11. Samuel E. Morison and Henry Steele Commager. *The Growth of the American Republic*. New York: Oxford University Press, 1962, p. 661.
12. John H. Moore. "Why Are There Creationists?" *Journal of Geological Education*, 31, 1983, pp. 95–104.
13. Arthur N. Strahler. "Toward a Broader Perspective in the Evolution-Creationism Debate." *Journal of Geological Education*, 31, 1983, pp. 87–93.
14. *Edwin W. Edwards et al.* v. *Don Aguillard, et al.* 85 U.S. 1513 (1987).
15. "A Secular Humanist Declaration," *Free Inquiry*, 1, 1, Winter 1980.
16. "Secular Declaration," p. 10.

17. From the introduction to Horner Duncan's *Secular Humanism: The Most Dangerous Religion in America.* Lubbock, TX: Missionary Crusade, 1979, p. 4.

18. Edward Jenkinson. *The Schoolbook Protest Movement.* Phi Delta Kappa: Bloomington, Ind., 1983, p. 82.

19. Isaac B. Berkson. *Theories of Americanization.* New York: Arno Press, 1969.

20. Horace Kallen. *Cultural Pluralism and the American Ideal.* Philadelphia: University of Pennsylvania Press, 1956.

21. Will Herberg. *Protestant, Catholic, Jew.* Garden City, N.Y.: Doubleday (Anchor Books), 1960.

22. Nathan Glazer and Patrick Moynihan. *Beyond the Melting Pot.* Cambridge, Mass.: Harvard University Press, 1963.

23. Michael Novak. *The Rise of the Unmeltable Ethnics.* New York: Macmillan, 1971.

24. James A. Allen and Eugene J. Turner. *We The People: An Atlas of America's Ethnic Diversity.* New York: Macmillan, 1986.

25. Allen and Turner, We The People, p. ix.

26. National Council for the Social Studies. *Curriculum Guidelines for Multiethnic Education.* Arlington, Va.: NCSS, 1976, p. 9. Reprinted with permission of the National Council for the Social Studies.

27. Alexis de Tocqueville. *Democracy in America.* New York: Harper & Row, 1966, pp. 291–312.

28. Pierre L. van den Berghe. *Race and Racism, A Comparative Perspective.* New York: Wiley, 1967, pp. 77–79. (van den Berghe argues that almost all U.S. presidents until Kennedy espoused racist positions regarding African Americans and other ethnic minority groups.)

29. Thomas Jefferson. "Notes on the State of Virginia," in Gilbert Osofsky, *The Burden of Race: A Documentary History of Negro-White Relations in America.* New York: Harper & Row, 1967, pp. 49–58.

30. John A. Garraty. *The American Nation.* New York: Harper & Row, 1966, pp. 256–266.

31. Osofsky. *Burden of Race*, p. 74.

32. "Abraham Lincoln's Address on Colonization," in Osofsky, *Burden of Race*, pp. 122–123.

33. Garraty. *American Nation*, p. 768; see also Roger Daniels, *Concentration Camps USA: Japanese Americans and World War II.* New York: Holt, Rinehart and Winston, 1971.

34. Henry Fairchild. *The Melting Pot Mistake.* Boston: Little, Brown, 1962; see also, Elwood Cubberley. *Changing Conceptions of Education.* New York: Riverside Educational Mimeographs, 1909.

35. Gunnar Myrdal. *An American Dilemma.* New York: Harper & Row, 1944.

36. Hector St. John de Crevecoeur. "Letters from an American Farmer," In Oscar Handlin's, *Immigration as a Factor in American History.* Englewood Cliffs, N.J.: Prentice-Hall, pp. 148–149. See also, Mark Krug. *The Melting of the Ethnics.* Bloomington, Ind.: Phi Delta Kappa Foundation, 1975, pp. 11–16.

37. Frederick J. Turner. *The Frontier in American History.* New York: Holt, Rinehart and Winston, 1920, pp. 22–24.

38. See especially U.S. Civil Rights Act, 1964.

39. G. Lerner. "Sarah M. Grimké," *Signs*, 1, 1975, pp. 246–256.

40. J. Freeman. *Women*, 3rd Ed. Palo Alto: Mayfield, 1984, pp. 519–532.

41. S. Wagner. "The World Anti-Slavery Convention of 1840," M, 12, 1984, pp. 35–41.

42. B. Blatt and Fred Kaplan. *Christmas in Purgatory: A Photographic Essay on Mental Retardation.* Boston: Allyn & Bacon, 1967.

43. J. Patton, R. Payne, S. James, and M. Beirne-Smith. *Mental Retardation,* 2nd Ed. Columbus, Ohio: Charles E. Merrill, 1986, p. 2.

44. Theodore Roosevelt. *An Autobiography.* New York: Scribners, 1913, pp. 470–471.

45. Joseph G. Rayback. *A History of American Labor,* New York: Macmillan, 1971, pp. 159–160.

46. Samuel Eliot Morison and Henry Steele Commager. *The Growth of the American Republic.* New York: Oxford University Press, 1962, p. 229.

47. Oscar Handlin. *Immigration as a Factor in American History.* Englewood Cliffs: Prentice-Hall, 1959, p. 16.

48. Don D. Lescohier. *History of Labor in the United States. Vol. III.* New York: Augustus M. Kelley Publishers, 1966, pp. 15–33.

49. John R. Commons. *History of Labor in the United States.* Vol. II. New York: Augustus M. Kelley, 1966, pp. 368–372.

50. "Preamble of the I.W.W." in Leon Litwack, *The American Labor Movement.* Englewood Cliffs: Prentice-Hall, 1962, p. 42.

51. Manuel A. Garcia, union organizer and coal miner, United Mine Workers of America, Secretary-Treasurer, Local 7989. Personal interview, July 2, 1973, Raton, New Mexico.

52. David Gordon, Richard Edwards, and Michael Reich. *Segmented Work, Divided Workers.* Cambridge: Oxford University Press, 1982, pp. 121–137.

53. W. Lloyd Warner. *Social Class in America.* Chicago: Science Research Associates, 1949.

54. Myrdal. *American Dilemma.*

55. Peter McLaren. *Life in Schools.* White Plains, New York: Longman, 1989, pp. 1–110; see also, Saul D. Alinsky. *Reveille for Radicals.* New York: Random House, 1946. Bernard J. Siegel. "Conceptual Approaches to Models for the Analysis of the Educative Process in American Communities," in George Spindler, *Education and Cultural Process.* New York: Holt, Rinehart and Winston, 1974, p. 43.

56. Horace Kallen. *Americanism and Its Makers.* New York: Bureau of Jewish Education, 1944, p. 8.

57. Hector St. John Crevecoeur. "Letters from an American Farmer," in Grodon, *Assimilation in American Life.* New York: Oxford University Press, 1964, p. 116.

58. John Quincy Adams. *Niles Weekly Register,* v. 28, April 29, 1820, pp. 157–158.

59. Abraham Lincoln, quoted in Benjamin Thomas, *Abraham Lincoln.* New York: Knopf, 1952, pp. 163–164.

60. Jesse Chickering. *Immigration into the United States.* Boston: Little Brown, 1848, pp. 79–80.

61. John Adams, quoted in Ahlstrom, *A Religious History of the American People,* p. 262.

62. Thomas Jefferson quoted in Gilbert Osofsky. *The Burden of Race.* New York: Harper & Row, 1967, p. 55.

63. Madison Grant. *The Passing of the Great Race.* New York: Scribner, 1916, p. 92.

64. Ricardo Garcia.

65. Alexis de Tocqueville, *Democracy in America,* p. 267.

Chapter
3

Schools as Community Affairs

Key Terms:

academic freedom
Brown v. *Topeka Board of Education*
Equal Educational Opportunity
Indian Education Act
in loco parentis
Lau v. *Nichols*

Education For All Handicapped
  Children
power elite
Title IX
school communities

In communities throughout the United States, people go about the business of making a living unaware of the communal ideologies upon which they operate. Most people conform to the laissez-faire, individualistic ethos of the American Creed and are more absorbed by pursuing their self interests than by any type of community interest. Consequently, they do not consciously act any of the communal ideologies discussed in Chapter 2. In other words, most people do not consciously think of a communal ideology, then on the basis of its assumptions, design their daily living practices. Communal ideologies are inferred from the social behavior of people within their communities. Most people unconsciously practice their unique renditions of the ideologies as they conduct their daily affairs. Within any community, if enough like-minded people express their communal ideology, and if they form an informal consensus of what the communal ideology should be, then the school's programs and educators' attitudes will to some degree reflect the prevailing communal ideology or ideologies. In short, the school will reflect a consensus about what makes a good community. Because every school district lies within a local human and geographic community, the school is affected by much of what is within its region, the country, and the world. What happens in a classroom on any given day in a U.S. public school is to some degree influenced by events in the many loosely interconnected communities that impinge upon the school, its teachers, and curriculum. Students thus acquire some of their culture through the school, as its teachers—through their cultural sieves—transmit and interpret the events of the outside communities for the students.

In the United States, public schools are a community affair. The schools are made up of children from the community surrounding the school and, with minor exceptions, public schools reflect their human communities. As commonsensical as these words may sound, their significance should not be ignored. Because schools are community affairs, they represent and reflect the prevailing community values and beliefs in their locales, just as children will reflect the values and beliefs of their parents. Therefore, what is taught and what is learned in any classroom is tremendously influenced by the community's values and beliefs. Teaching in a New York City ghetto neighborhood, for example, and teaching in a rural Wyoming school district are vastly different experiences because the schools' communities differ.

Just what is a "community"? Elsewhere in this text (see Chapter 10) a distinction is made between a "human" and a "civil" community. Here it is sufficient to define a community as a group of people living under the same government in the same locale. In a small, rural school district the school's community is easy to define. But in large cities—Houston, Los Angeles, Kansas City, Boston, to name a few—the school's community is not so easily defined. Due to school desegregation and busing pressures as well as more traditional changes and shifts in populations, urban communities tend to change continuously. Nevertheless, schools still serve human communities.

BASIC STRUCTURE OF THE PUBLIC SCHOOL

The basic governing structure of a public school is its district. A school district is a geographic construct; within the district are facilities for schools, maintenance and storage, a board of education, and central administration. Some districts have acreage for agricultural activities such as tree farms, livestock, and dairy barns, or for vocational training facilities such as auto mechanics and machine shops. Some districts have postgraduation vocational training programs; most districts coordinate their pregraduation programs with local vocational and technical institutes or community colleges. The district's land boundaries are usually the same as its town or city of residence. Some districts are organized by counties, especially those located in remote, rural areas. Generally, the county districts operate elementary and perhaps junior high schools; busing transportation for high school attendance in nearby towns and cities is provided for rural students. In some districts, the certified personnel in the schools—teachers, counselors, administrators—are the highest paid workers in the town or city. The educators are consulted for various reasons other than strictly school matters. Assisting with income tax forms, reading and interpreting legal documents, and sundry other services are provided by the educators at no cost to the people in the district. In other districts, the certified personnel are members of the genteel poor classes teaching students who have travelled more and further than they, and who often have better automobiles than they do. In some urban districts, the educators commute from the suburbs to teach in the inner city.

American school districts are variegated: in some respects, they differ, and in other respects, they are quite similar. Every school district has a broad community base, drawing students whose parents engage in various occupations, such as professionals, white-collar workers, blue-collar workers, mechanics, and many service occupations. In smaller towns and rural areas, the district and the community are often one and the same, and school activities such as Friday night basketball games, graduation ceremonies, or school plays are communitywide activities. In the broadest sense of the word, a school's "community" consists of varied social groups who interact with each other, developing cooperative and interdependent networks of relationships. The net result of these relationships is the functional operation of the school. In other words, people work together (cooperation) because they need each other's skills and talents (interdependence) to make a living. This cooperative, interdependent venture also helps provide the community's children a school (through taxation, school bonds, mill levies). Community interdependence and cooperation dispute the myth that our society is essentially competitive. We really live in a cooperative society as far as schooling is concerned.

Within a school district, which is a geographic and a demographic construct, several communities may coexist. In fact, most urban school districts are stratified, with coexisting ethnic and socioeconomic subcommunities. In most urban districts the subcommunities are readily visible because of neighborhood patterns. The very rich and the very poor live in the oldest parts of the city. The very rich often occupy the older homes, the so-called heritage area of the city. The very poor often live in the oldest industrial areas which are close to their jobs. White ethnic groups usually live in city areas traditionally relegated to them. While segregation ordinances are prohibited, ethnic minorities are often compelled by economic and social pressure to stay in the neighborhoods relegated to them. Often when ethnic minorities attempt to move from their neighborhoods to traditionally White neighborhoods, Whites move to the city's rim or suburbs—the "white flight" phenomenon—thereby perpetuating segregated neighborhoods.

Within most communities there exists what sociologists call a *power elite*. The power elite are the people within a community who control its basic economic activities. These people consist of bankers, lawyers, business executives, corporation officials, landowners and others (large ranch and farm owners in some communities) who influence how people make a living. The power elite is not an official or formal group. Instead, it consists of powerful individuals who legally control different parts of the community's economic system. Their decisions on issues involving, for example, who gets a loan to establish a business or who buys a certain house in a certain neighborhood affect the community's economic and social relations. The key point is that all school districts are in some way accountable to the power elite and the various subgroups in their districts. *Large and small districts alike—and the schooling therein—are community affairs.*

The fundamental reason for our public schools is to provide students with skills, knowledge, and attitudes to enable them to live and work in a democratic society. Deciding on appropriate skills, knowledge, and attitudes is the responsibility of the people in the school's community. This tradition of local control over the school has been diluted over the years, but as an ideal condition, the notion of local control is deeply embedded in the general American democratic value system. Members of the school's local community elect individuals to serve as their representatives on the school board. The school board, as a lay board (theoretically any member of the local community can be elected to the school board), determines the school's policy. The policy includes statements about appropriate survival skills, knowledge, and attitudes, based on the values of the individual board members and the community at large.

Teachers who are thought to be compatible with the school district's policy and its underlying values are hired to implement the policy. The essential decisions about what should be taught are made by school board members. They are not made by teachers, college professors, administrators, or any other persons. Teaching in a public school is not as simple as this may sound. The school board may represent the wishes and concerns of certain powerful community groups only, or it may acquiesce to the superintendent, allowing the superintendent to determine policy. The board may not be unified in its views about what should be taught, or who should teach. School board members are elected because of the value system they represent. Some communities are content with a strong superintendent, one who has become a tradition of sorts, and elect a school board to give him or her free play with the school system. Urban communities may elect school board members who represent "antibusing" positions, or "back to the basics" positions, or other popular views. Many communities don't really think much about who is elected for the board. The school has fulfilled its traditional functions over the years, and as such, the community expects it to continue to do so.

THE SCHOOL'S COMMUNITIES

School boards and the schools they oversee do not exist in a vacuum. Federal, state, and community laws influence the day-to-day operations of a school. The value systems of people in the local, state, regional, national, and international communities influence what is taught in the school. The school and its teachers must respond to legal, political, economic, religious, and social forces that exist outside the local community while simultaneously responding to the values and aspirations of the local community. To understand the value dynamic of teaching in the public schools, consider how the school exists in the context of at least five communities: the local, the state, the regional, the national, and the international community. Each community is not homogeneous. Indeed, each to some degree is pluralistic, but each community in some manner influences what is taught in school. Each community, and subgroup of a community, operates on the assumption that its values are the fundamental, critical values that will enhance the student's survival. The questions of whose view is correct, when it is correct, and for whom it is correct are not easy to answer, but teachers, as implementers of educational policy, must respond to and work with these competing value systems (see Figure 3.1).

Each community has either political power or political influence which is used to affect teaching and learning. The local community has the most direct influence and power to determine school policy. The local community elects members of the school board, and, theoretically, any citizen of the local community can be elected. However, in reality extreme members of a community, especially those who are leftist or Marxist, are not likely to be elected. The local community can also choose to raise or lower the taxes used to operate its school system. The powers to elect board members and to raise or lower school support taxes give the local community considerable power over the school district. Yet school board members are considered to be state officials who are

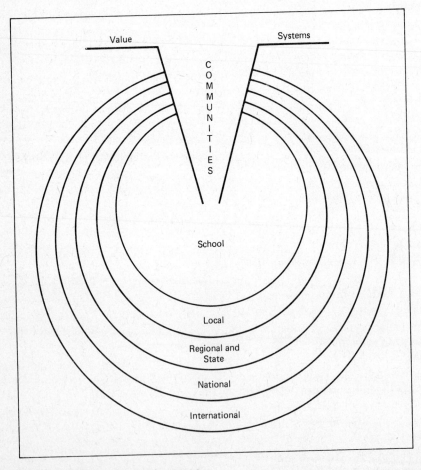

Figure 3.1 School and its communities

responsible to the state government. Usually the school board officials are responsible to the state's department of education, which in turn is responsible to the governor's office or the state legislature. The state has legal power and sociocultural influences over the local school. Each school district must be in compliance with its state regulations and laws.

STATE AS A COMMUNITY

Public school education is considered a state function, and the state is ultimately responsible for providing a free public education for all of the children residing in the state. Education must be provided equally throughout the state: that is, equal access to a free public education must be provided. "Free" education means the state must use the revenue that is raised through taxation of individuals, industry, and business to pay the education costs. Tuition charges and other types of charges to attend school are prohibited. While the expense to send children to school should be kept at a minimum, because of weaknesses and loopholes in most state educational finance systems, parents are asked to help defray costs by paying for certain items, such as the cost of hot lunches, fees for rental of musical instruments, or materials to be used in a woodworking shop or home economics class. Also, because some communities can afford to pay the taxes for better school facilities, most states have unequal school facilities. Within some school districts, it is apparent that the more affluent neighborhoods have the new buildings, more equipment, more paraprofessionals, and other resources when compared to the schools in less affluent neighborhoods.

THE NATIONAL COMMUNITY

School districts are locally controlled and responsible both to their local constituents and their state laws and regulations. Public schooling is viewed as the legal responsibility of the state. Likewise, educational practices in each state must be in compliance with the U.S. Constitution and other federal laws and regulations. School districts are required to provide all students with equal educational opportunities in nonsegregated schools; this is a federally mandated educational policy.

The bottom line to equal educational opportunity is that school boards, administrators, and teachers must be committed to providing equal educational opportunities. While the equal opportunity laws mandate, they cannot insure that students will be given equal opportunities. Adults in charge of schooling are the people who can insure that equal opportunity happens. Laws, in and of themselves, cannot guarantee equal educational opportunity, but committed people can.

REGIONAL AND INTERNATIONAL COMMUNITIES

The *regional community* has no legal or political power over schools, per se. What the regional community has are the values, customs, and attitudes which have evolved in different geographic regions of the United States. For example, schools in the southwestern United States are influenced by the pervasive cultural forces of the Anglo, Mexican American, and Native American peoples in that region. In the South, schools are influenced by the pervasive cultural forces of various peoples: the "hill" people, the French and Cajun peoples, African-Americans, Native Americans, and at one time the Spanish. What is important to understand is that the school exists within the context of a regional community and is influenced by the region's cultural and social forces. The state school system and its districts are ultimately responsible to and governed by the Constitution, Supreme Court decisions, the laws enacted by Congress, and the regulations promulgated by various federal cabinet offices which are administrative branches of the president's office, particularly the Department of Education.

The *international community* does not have political or legal authority over public schools either. However, political, economic, and social forces and circumstances have an impact on the public schools. For example, after the U.S. government's involvement in the Vietnam war ceased, thousands of Vietnamese refugees emigrated to the United States. Within months, schools throughout the United States were enrolling Southeast Asian children. Most of them spoke no English; all of them had a distinctively different cultural background than their new teachers and classmates. Schools had to redesign language and cultural programs and arrange for Southeast Asian teacher aides, translators, and curriculum materials.

The effects of other forces in the international community may be much more indirect but just as pervasive. Take, for example, the economic and political pressures on the United States from so-called third-world, oil-rich countries. Their actions have changed the way business, labor, industry, and educational leaders perceive them, and have made us all aware of the critical interdependence of nations throughout the world. Certainly, these changes have been reflected in the classroom. Table 3.1 summarizes the complexities of the relationship between the school and its communities.

THE NATIONAL POLICY OF EQUAL
EDUCATIONAL OPPORTUNITY

Schools operate as community affairs under the legal aegis of the state government. Schools are agents of the state and reflect the state's policies; when a school implements a policy, in effect, the school is implementing a policy of the state. Consequently, local school policies and practices must be in compliance with the U.S. Constitution. Starting in the 1950s, the federal government

Table 3.1   RELATIONSHIPS BETWEEN SCHOOL AND COMMUNITIES

Community	Authority	Influences
Local	Elects school boards, determines educational policies through school board, raises and lowers local taxes for school revenue.	Local religious, ethnic, economic, political groups express concerns and apply pressure to influence policies and practices.
State	Education is legal function of the state. State constitution, laws, State Department of Education regulations basis of educational policy.	State religious, ethnic, economic, political groups exert pressure to influence educational policy, laws, and regulations at the state level.
National	U.S. Constitution and federal laws, Supreme Court decisions pertaining to students' civil rights.	National religious, ethnic, economic, political groups exert pressure to influence policy at the federal level.
International	No legal authority, but considerable influence and impact on the U.S. through economic, political, military events.	

established a policy of equal educational opportunity for purposes of protecting the constitutional rights of students.

In 1954, the U.S. Supreme Court in *Brown* v. *Topeka Board of Education*[1] prohibited school districts from deliberately segregating schools on the basis of race. Prior to the 1954 *Brown* decision, ethnic minority students were formally or informally segregated from white students. (Formal, or de jure, segregation was mandated by state law; informal, or de facto, segregation was caused by neighborhood residential patterns and dominant antiintegration attitudes.) The segregated schools were justified on the legal grounds of an older Supreme Court decision, *Plessy* v. *Ferguson*, which allowed states to maintain segregated facilities, including schools, so long as they were "separate but equal."

In *Brown* the Supreme Court found enough tangible evidence, as well as psychological and educational testimony, to support the argument that segregated, separated schools were inherently unequal. The segregated schools were viewed by the Supreme Court as inherently unequal because they resembled an educational caste system in which the African American schools were viewed as inferior schools, thereby causing African American students to think of themselves as inferior. The segregated schools were the last vestige of de jure racial segregation.

Provisions under the U.S. Civil Rights Act of 1964[2] require school districts to comply with the school desegregation orders that emerged from the *Brown* case. The U.S. Office of Civil Rights has the authority to investigate charges of school discrimination and other forms of unequal educational treatment. If a school district is found in noncompliance with the various equal opportunity regulations, it faces loss of its federal financial aid. The U.S. Civil Rights Act put teeth into the federal policy of equal educational opportunity by prohibiting discrimination in educational practices and policies based on race, color, creed, national origin, and gender. The Act's Title IX[3] specifically focused on the rights of females to equal educational opportunities and treatment in the public schools which served to break down barriers erected in traditionally perceived masculine areas. Female students can no longer be excluded from participation in school athletic teams, or from school subjects formerly considered for male students only, such as industrial arts and auto mechanics classes. Schools must make an effort to eliminate segregated subjects once considered the domain of female students, such as home economics, typing, and clerical skills classes. Last, counselors must carefully interpret standardized exams, aptitude instruments, and any career counseling they provide to insure that gender biases are not influences on the counselors' perceptions about their female students.

Equal educational opportunity must be provided for students who (1) may not speak English, (2) may have limited English-speaking abilities, and (3) may live in homes where a language other than English is the dominant mode of communication. Authority to require school districts to alleviate inequities based on a student's language background came from the *Lau* v. *Nichols*[4] decision. The *Lau* v. *Nichols* suit was a class action on behalf of Chinese-speaking students who attended the San Francisco schools. In the lawsuit, the students presented facts that revealed that Chinese students were expelled from school more often, dropped out of school more often, and were low achievers more often than non-Chinese students. This was seen as evidence that the school district's English-only policy placed Chinese-speaking students at a disadvantage. The school district defended its English-only policy, arguing that Chinese American students were provided an equal opportunity to a free public education because they were provided the same textbooks, in the same language (English), and were taught by equally qualified English-speaking teachers. The Supreme Court ruled in favor of the students. The court's decision was based on the notion that the same program for all students in the same language was no guarantee of an equal opportunity to learn, especially when the students didn't speak or understand English. Consequently, the court ruled that schools must provide special language programs for students who don't understand or speak English.

For Native Americans, who were granted U.S. citizenship as late as 1924, the Indian Education Act of 1972[5] provides federal assistance for equal opportunities in schools and universities. The significance of the 1972 Act is that Indian tribes can receive direct assistance from the U.S. government without the bureaucratic interference of the Bureau of Indian Affairs. In the past on nonallotted Indian Reservations (reservations not parcelled into lots and distributed to individual family members under the Dawes General Allotment Act of 1887), the Bureau of Indian Affairs controlled the reservations' tribal government and educational systems. The Bureau implemented a policy of assimilation intending to transform the Native American students into "Anglo Americans." To accomplish the goal, all vestiges of "Indianness" were prohibited in the schools' curriculum and in the classroom. Students were prohibited from speaking their mother languages and dressing in their tribal costumes. The content of the curriculum was much like the content one would find in Midwest U.S. schools except that a stereotypic "Dick and Jane" vision of Anglo Americans was taught. Teachers and administrators were hired by the Bureau fully aware of the schools' assimilation mission. Turnover among these educators was quite high primarily because the teachers and administrators were soon frustrated by their very own misguided policy. On the surface, it is difficult to argue against integration of Native Americans; they are and should be considered an integral part of American communal life. How could real integration of Native Americans occur when the students were deliberately isolated from Anglo students and the curriculum was based on an unrealistic, stereotypic vision of Anglos? It is easy to argue against the Bureau's assimilation policy, especially when the Bureau publicly acknowledged in late 1988 that its policy had failed to meet the needs of Native Americans. The 1972 Act gives Native Americans the power to run their own schools; they operate much like any other public schools; while they must adhere to the accreditation and certification requirements of their respective states, Native Americans can elect their school boards who then determine the curricular content of the local schools as well as determine who will be hired to teach or administer the schools. Specific educational policies for the local schools are under the control of the school board rather than the Bureau of Indian Affairs. The opportunity exists for Native Americans to develop schools which are culturally relevant and sensitive to the needs of their local populations.

"Equal opportunity" to a free public education also means that schools must provide equal, nonsegregated facilities and educational experiences for physically and mentally handicapped students. In other words, handicapped students can no longer be segregated all day in "special" education classes. Under Public Law 94–142, Education for All Handicapped Children,[6] handicapped children must either be mainstreamed in regular classes or placed in the "least restrictive environment." Specific requirements are: an individualized education plan (IEP) must be developed for each handicapped child; the plan must state specific goals, objectives, activities, and evaluation methods; parents must be involved in the development, and any subsequent changes made, in the plan; any decisions made about placement in remedial classes, resource rooms, or any other "special" placements, must involve the parents. The intent of PL 94–142 is equal educational opportunity of handicapped students which can only be achieved through full integration of handicapped students in the regular classroom. The IEPs assure that the handicapped student has an opportunity to learn in the regular classroom.

ACADEMIC FREEDOM IN THE SCHOOL'S COMMUNITY

Schools as community affairs place teachers in the role of *in loco parentis,* that is, teachers act in place of the parents during the school day. Teachers are viewed as extensions of the parents in the community and are expected to reflect parental values. To ensure compatibility between the values and beliefs taught in school with those of the community, school boards control the content of the curriculum. The state legislature, through a policy board such as a state board of education, enacts general curriculum guidelines for school accreditation stipulating the subjects to be taught, qualifications for teacher certification, and other operations and safety regulations. The more specific curricular content is the province of local school board members who are elected, theoretically, to represent the values and beliefs of the community.

With the power to determine specific curricular content comes the power to censor. School boards can determine that a particular topic, say "contraception" for example, is offensive to prevailing community standards and disallow the topic in health classes. The same applies to all subject matter taught within the school's curriculum; the school board is the guardian of morality for the school district. In the U.S. Supreme Court decision, *Hazelwood School District* v. *Kuhlmeier,*[7] the court ruled that principals, as agents of the school board, could censor student-written articles in a school sponsored newspaper. At issue were two articles written for the May edition of the Hazelwood East High School paper, *Spectrum,* that described experiences associated with the pregnancies of three students and the impact that divorce had on some members of the student body. The principal objected to the contents of the articles because the students and families discussed could be easily recognized; parents of these families had not given consent to the student reporters to use the facts in the articles, a privacy rights argument. The principal deleted the articles from the paper on the grounds that the paper was produced in a second period journalism class; thereby, it was a part of the school curriculum, and as an agent of the school board, he was empowered to determine the content of the school's curriculum. The Supreme Court held in favor of the principal.

The *Hazelwood* decision overturned a number of precedents regarding students' rights initially established in the *Tinker* v. *Des Moines School District*[8] decision in which the Court ruled that students' had the same first amendment rights as other citizens. At issue were black armbands that Des Moines, Iowa, students and some parents decided to wear as a silent, nonviolent protest to the Vietnam War. When school officials heard of the silent protest, they adopted the policy that "any student wearing an armband to school would be asked to remove it, and if he refused he would be suspended until he returned without the armband."[9] Three students, John and Mary Beth Tinker and Christopher Eckhardt, wore their armbands to school; they were suspended. At the Supreme Court level, the students' right to wear the armbands was upheld. The Court ruled that the students were protected by the first amendment guarantee of freedom of expression. In the words of the majority opinion, ". . . it can hardly be argued that either students or teachers shed their constitutional rights to freedom of speech or expression at the schoolhouse gate."[10]

The *Tinker* decision applies to teachers as well as students. Teachers and students have fundamental constitutional rights; the *Hazelwood* decision limited the students' rights of expression in favor of the rights of the school to determine the contents of its curriculum. For example, in *Pickering* v. *Board*,[11] the Supreme Court ruled that a school board could not fire a teacher, Pickering, solely because he wrote a letter to the local newspaper criticizing his superintendent and school board for some of their spending decisions. Since Pickering's letter had not disrupted the educational process, his right to freedom of the press outweighed the school's desire to punish Pickering for using his rights. Yet, in *Mt. Healthy* v. *Doyle*,[12] the Court ruled that teachers cannot hide behind First Amendment rights when reasons for dismissal go beyond exercise of the rights. At issue was Doyle's claim that the school board dismissed him for telephone calls aired over a local radio station criticizing the school. The board demonstrated that Doyle was dismissed for a variety of reasons, such as altercations with students and other teachers, making an obscene gesture to a female student, and the telephone calls. With teachers and students—as with all citizens—constitutional rights are not absolute. Generally, the Supreme Court uses a balancing test to determine whose rights prevail with any constitutional issue. With teachers the balancing test is between the rights of the individual teacher and the rights of the school board to conduct school business. Because each case is taken on its individual merit only general statements can be provided to guide teachers in their exercise of constitutional rights, especially First Amendment rights:

1. There must be a compelling reason to suppress First Amendment rights; school boards that desire to suppress First Amendment rights must show that without suppression the educational process will be disrupted or that the health and safety of students are jeopardized; or, boards must show that the rights of others will be violated, as was the argument in *Hazelwood*, that the privacy rights of the parents discussed in the news articles were jeopardized since they had not given consent to publication of the articles.

2. School boards are empowered to develop policies governing curricular content, school activities, dress codes, health and safety concerns, and issues pertaining to libel, slander, and obscenity.

3. With most issues, teachers are insured the broad protections of the Fourteenth Amendment, i.e., equal protection of the law and due process, as well as First Amendment rights of expression, assembly, petition, and religion. These protections provide teachers with a modicum of academic freedom. "Academic freedom" refers to the teachers' need to teach the truth of their disciplines. At times, the academic content of a certain subject may contradict the values and beliefs of certain parents. The issue is, whose rights should prevail: the teachers' rights to teach? The students' rights to know? Or, the parents' rights to believe as they wish (freedom of conscience)?

Recall the evolution versus creation science issue discussed in Chapter 2.

Evolution is the theoretical basis of all biological sciences. Without knowledge about evolution, teachers cannot teach and students cannot learn even basic principles of biological sciences, which are the sciences used in all areas of medicine and health. With knowledge about evolution, Christian fundamentalists contend, their belief that God, an omnipotent being, created the earth as described in the Old Testament is contradicted; with knowledge of evolution, their children are taught a false religious belief; consequently, they argue, their version of creation should be given equal time in the curriculum with evolution to which they are entitled under the First Amendment (religious freedom). With this issue, the Court ruled (*Edwards* v. *Agguillard*) in favor of the teachers' rights to teach and the students' rights to know.

Academic freedom is not a constitutional right; rather, academic freedom is a folkway unique to the teaching profession. During the development of colleges and universities in medieval Europe, scholars were often criticized, persecuted, or imprisoned by government or church officials for expressing beliefs that contradicted official policy or dogma (such was the case with Copernicus discussed in Chapter 1). To protect the scholar's need to investigate and search for the truth, scholars were granted the license to investigate, research, and publish freely regardless of official church or government policies. Without the license, the scholar could not legitimately pursue the truth, which in the final analysis, would destroy a culture; new knowledge leads to changes which can improve the status quo; without new knowledge comes cultural decadence and demise.

In the United States, college and university professors are granted tenure after a probationary period; tenure provides professors academic freedom by protecting their positions when they express unpopular views or report research findings that are contradictory to governmental policies. During the Red Scare era of Senator Joseph McCarthy, however, very few professors expressed left-wing, Marxist beliefs for fear of political retribution as a "red" or a "communist." Public school teachers have academic freedom but it is not synonymous with the academic freedom granted professors. First, colleges and universities function as a free marketplace of ideas; all ideas can be hawked; theoretically, the ideas bought are the best current ideas, but they can be replaced by better ideas. The fundamental purpose of the marketplace is to provide a site where new knowledge can be produced and published. Public schools by design serve broader economic, social, and political purposes as discussed in this chapter. Second, the participants in the free marketplace of ideas, colleges and universities, are consenting adults who choose to be exposed to varied and often divergent ideas. The participants in public schools, students, are neither there by consent nor are they adults. The students are legally compelled to attend school; they did not elect to be exposed to the ideas advanced in the schools. Rather, their parents, by complying with compulsory attendance laws, have chosen to expose their children to the ideas, but the parents have not chosen to relegate to schools control over their children's values and beliefs. As the parental admonition goes, "so long as you kids live in my house, you will believe as I believe. When you are on your own, you can believe what you want!" Teachers are expected to act *in loco parentis* and school boards are expected to act as guardians of beliefs and values. Here's the rub for classroom teachers: they must teach the truth of their disciplines and they must respect the beliefs and values of students and their parents.

By *respect*, I refer to acknowledgment and not to acquiescence. Acknowledgment implies that teachers build a trust relationship with students and their parents premised on the understanding that rational people often disagree, rationally; or, that "we should agree that we may disagree from time to time." The student's task is to "winnow the chaff from the wheat," or to evaluate the views of teachers and parents. Understand that not all parents can agree to disagree and not all parents can agree that students should be allowed to decide for themselves the merits of the beliefs and values espoused by adults. Total acquiescence to parents would impede genuine teaching, a disservice to students, to parents, and to the human community.

Several Supreme Court cases provide guidelines for teachers to exercise their academic freedom. In *Keefe* v. *Geanakos*,[13] a high school English teacher distributed an article from the *Atlantic* that contained radical ideas about social protest and some vulgar words. Students were told that if the article offended them, they could choose another to read. Parents lobbied the school board to stop Keefe from using the article in class. Keefe refused and was threatened with dismissal. He sued, contending his First Amendment right was violated by threat of dismissal. The Court ruled in his favor because: (1) the article was directly related to an educational objective of the school curriculum; (2) the students were quite aware of the vulgar words in the article and were given the option to read another article should they consider the article offensive; (3) Keefe was hired to teach the subject and topic under question and should be allowed latitude to exercise reasonable judgment about the educational appropriateness of the materials selected, that is, parents should not be allowed to be the sole judges as to what is proper.

In *Brubaker* v. *Board*,[14] three eighth-grade teachers of French, English, and industrial arts, were dismissed for distributing "Woodstock" pamphlets condoning the use of drugs and sexual promiscuity, expressed with an abundance of vulgar words. The teachers sued, contending a violation of their First Amendment rights. The Court ruled in favor of the school because (1) the materials distributed were not directly related to an educational objective within the school curriculum; (2) the materials were inappropriate considering the age and immaturity of the students, that is, the teachers did not use reasonable judgment for selection of materials; (3) the teachers were not hired to teach the specific subject matter at issue. With *Brubaker* the Court supported the school board's power to determine the content of the curriculum; with *Keefe* the Court supported the teacher's right to teach (academic freedom) because he exercised reasonable judgment in selection of the materials which were directly related to curricular objectives and to the specific subject he was hired to teach. What follows are guidelines for exercising the right to teach, academic freedom:

1. Establish a trust relationship with your students and their parents based on the understanding that disagreement is basic to teaching and learning; agree to disagree.
2. Exercise reasonable judgment when selecting discussion topics and materials: (a) they should be directly related to educational objectives of the curriculum; (b) be appropriate for the students' maturation levels; (c) be related to the subject you've been hired to teach; (d) use discretion.
3. Provide alternative exercises for topics or materials that might be offensive or in violation of First Amendment rights; have options.

A discussion of academic freedom, and the guidelines above, have the potential of quashing good teaching practices. If teachers develop a trust relationship with students and their parents based on the understanding that reasonable people disagree, reasonably, then teachers need not fear parental conflict. Teachers should express their opinions on most issues if asked by students and if the teachers feel an answer is appropriate. Here, though, prudence is the greater virtue.

We live in an era of litigation. Laws that pertain to teaching and learning are ever expanding. Supreme Court decisions and federal laws that pertain to teaching in a pluralistic society are dispersed throughout the text, scratching the surface of school law. There are several very good texts on the topic,[15] but most have difficulty updating due to constantly changing laws. Read the constitution and state codes regarding education in the state(s) in which you plan to teach.

STUDYING THE LOCAL SCHOOL COMMUNITY

"Good grief," you might exclaim, "I just want to teach kids how to read, or spell, or how to shoot a basket, or think like a mathematician, or. . . . Now you're telling me that I have to be a politician who tries to please everyone, and at the same time never pleases anyone." The political realities of teaching in the public schools require that you understand the cultural dynamics of the school and its communities so that you can adroitly manage your classroom experiences rather than be managed by political and social forces. You should be realistic about the local community, sensitive to its prevailing folkways and mores, and above all, knowledgeable about its socioeconomic base. You should study the local community as though you were an anthropologist trying to understand a different culture.

When studying a cultural group, anthropologists use an observation technique called participation-observation.[16] Simply put, the technique is to participate fully in the cultural group experience while attempting, at times, to observe discrete behaviors and attitudes within the cultural group. In the setting of teaching and learning, use of the technique is explained in the following scenario:

> You have been hired to teach in the Cottonwood School District. You move to Cottonwood, rent an apartment, find your school, and quickly are swept into the swing of events: teaching classes, meeting colleagues, attending school events and

professional meetings. Halfway through the year, you decide to stick it out another year if rehired. You've established home base, but now you've got to build your career on your teaching effectiveness, which relies on your knowledge of your specialty as well as your knowledge of the community. If you're deficient in your specialty, during the summer you can travel, take college courses, or read to alleviate deficiencies. Now how to study the community:

1. Begin with a blank slate. Try to erase all the gossip and grapevine folk wisdom you've heard about the community.
2. Join some nonschool related community group, such as a civic club, a church group, or a community action group.
3. Become involved in the group's activities and develop friends within the group. Listen to them as they share concerns and interests. Then share your concerns about becoming an effective teacher in the community. Listen to their advice. Their comments will reveal their value systems as well as their perceptions regarding the prevailing folkways and mores, the powerful business and social cliques—the so-called power structure—of the community.
4. Weigh and consider their perceptions with your feelings, values, and perceptions. Remember that you should not judge their perceptions; you should instead consider their reference so as to understand why they feel the way they do.
5. Survey the community. Get in your car and ride around. Contrary to public myth, most communities are stratified according to some broad categories, such as social class, professional and vocational class, religious, racial, or ethnic-group membership. Ride around the community. Visit stores and industries in the community and try to get a feel for the daily dips and curves of the community. Visit cemeteries and read the tombstones. Americans, especially those who can afford the costs, are particular about where they bury their dead. Others have no choice because they are poor, or because many cemetery owners discriminate against ethnic minorities. In the Southwest, clear lines are sometimes drawn to mark the cemeteries in which Mexican Americans are buried. The same is the case in other parts of the country, such as the South, where black and white cemeteries are still segregated according to race. Don't be reluctant to visit with local business, labor, and religious leaders. Get their opinions about the purpose of teaching and learning. Ask them why they are paying taxes for schools.
6. Visit with as many parents as you can. Get to know your students' homes and parental backgrounds. Walk to the homes, or if your students are bussed to school, take a bus to visit parents. Get a feel for the students' lives outside school. Maintain your respect for the parents and students, and maintain your self-respect. Remember that regardless of cultural, social class, or ethnic-group affiliation, the parents have in common with you concern for the welfare and education of their children. If they sense in you a genuine commitment to the teaching of their children, they will respond in kind by working with you to enhance their children's education.
7. Once having accomplished all of the above, you should have a good feel for the community if as a participant-observer you have kept an open mind about the community's people and cultural groups, if you have become genuinely involved in some community groups' activities, and if you have become acquainted with your students' parents and home environments. Also, keep in mind that people, communities, and groups change. Therefore, for as long as you teach in the community, you must continue the participation-observation role.

I share this scenario with you so that you may avoid the pitfall of becoming an alienated teacher in the community. Even though you may be a first rate scholar, ignorance about the local community can spell failure for a new teacher. Here I will digress to tell my war story about the time I attempted to teach an important lesson, but out of ignorance of the community, nearly failed and nearly lost my job.

In a southwestern United States small town, I took a job as an American literature teacher. I soon realized that my students could not appreciate contemporary American literature because they believed that social class and ethnic minority discrimination did not exist in the community, in spite of the facts that the poor people lived on the east side of the tracks, and Mexican Americans could only frequent certain stores and churches. I decided to sensitize my students to the anguish of poverty and racism through American literature. Consequently, I developed a unit on great American writers who had addressed the themes of poverty and racism. First, we read John Steinbeck's *The Grapes of Wrath*. No sooner than the second chapter, the school board demanded a meeting with me, my principal, and the superintendent. I attended the emergency meeting where a report was read about how my students' parents objected to *The Grapes of Wrath*. Why had I chosen *that* novel? When I explained my goals and objectives, the school board members praised my efforts to counter elitist and racist attitudes in the community. They also reminded me that fifty percent of the community were Oklahoma people who had lived in the Dust Bowl of Oklahoma, who had lost their land, and who had migrated west in hope of a better life. *The Grapes of Wrath* was so close to the truth that it hurt too much. Parents demanded my resignation, altruistic goals or not! I decided to visit the disgruntled parents, teach other novels (such as *The Adventures of Huckleberry Finn*, which is much more controversial since it deals with White racism, violence, and poverty), and learn better the community. I kept my job and achieved my goals. End of a nonfairy tale.

Moral: as a teacher you are hired to teach skills, knowledge, and attitudes considered by some community members as essential to the survival of their children. Because your students are not your children, you must consider the values, beliefs, and attitudes of parents when making decisions about teaching and learning. Consequently, you must be true to yourself and true to parents. You must have the courage of your convictions, and you must never allow yourself to be in a position where you only carry out orders. I am asking you to be a real professional, a person who acts on well-articulated assumptions, specific educational goals and objectives, and applies them in such a manner that students benefit from their implementation. I do not mean to paint a grim picture of incompatible forces. But teaching and learning activities, after all, are assertions of values. In fact, you will teach what you value, and for better or worse, your students soon sense what you value. How you resolve value influences of the school's communities which conflict with your values is a continuing process, a process which should always receive your most serious consideration.

Hold your judgments about the community and the schools in abeyance.

Discuss with experienced teachers and administrators your observations, but again, listen to these voices of experience with professional objectivity. Some teachers and administrators have biases about students and will share them with you, thereby creating a skewed picture of your teaching-learning situation. Some experienced teachers and administrators have commitments to excellence and can provide you with very helpful hints, resources, and ideas for dealing with your students *and* the school's community forces.

SCHOOLS AS A COMMUNITY AFFAIR

This chapter's recurring theme is that schools are a community affair. Like all human affairs, some fare better than others. Some teachers and administrators are very responsive to their communities; this is often the case in suburban school districts, where educators maintain constant communication with parents, informing them of school meetings and events. Parent-teacher organizations, such as the PTA (Parent-Teachers Association), although often controlled by the teachers or administrators, actively involve parents in school activities like fund-raising for new playground equipment. In other schools, teachers and administrators are aloof from their communities, and condescending toward parents and other community members. These educators view themselves as several notches on the social totem pole above the squalid clients they are supposed to serve. In particular, this second category of school people is most evident in urban lower-class or ethnic minority schools. When asked about their posture, these educators will assert that school and community relationships are a two-way street which the parents do not use. Parents, according to these educators, rarely attend meetings or teacher-parent conferences. When asked what the educators have done to improve the "two-way street" so as to pave the way for better relations, the gist of their answers is usually that they've done little or nothing. Instead, by their aloofness, these educators have antagonized or alienated their parent clients. In some rural districts, educators who are aloof from their communities may soon find themselves unemployed. In these communities, parents and community members place high stakes in the school and its activities. A Friday night basketball game is a major recreational event, and the school play is a primary cultural arts activity in their eyes. These parents expect cooperation from the educators. In other rural areas, the educators run the schools with an iron hand and parents and community members acquiesce. In the final analysis, schools exist because some community of people, through tradition or accident, are compelled under law to send their children to some kind of school.

Of course, there are a few small communities, such as the Amish people, who send their children to school for only part of their education, kindergarten through eighth grade. The Amish then educate their children in their socioreligious way of life. At times in the state of Utah, polygamist communities have chosen to provide schooling for their youth rather than send them to some of the local district's schools. These nonconforming communities must comply with local and state regulations by providing or allowing some education of their children because education is an important interest of the state. Even though these nonconforming communities may isolate their youth, they cannot completely shut out the impact of the state, national, and international communities.

SUMMARY

This chapter described the relationships that exist between the school and the loosely interconnected communities that influence teaching and learning within the classroom. Local public schools function as community agents serving the parents and children within their respective communities. The values of parents and influential people, dubbed the power elite, are generally reflected within school programs and policies.

The local school district serves its immediate community, but it operates under the auspices of the state and must be in compliance with state laws; state laws must be in compliance with federal laws and the U.S. Constitution. Since the 1950s, the federal government has played a key role in the development of laws or Supreme Court decisions that have had a direct impact on local school programs and policies in the areas of equal educational opportunities, censorship, and academic freedom.

Schools are ultimately community affairs. Students learn their cultures through their homes and families, and they learn their cultures from the communal living ideologies of their respective communities. They acquire additional cultural orientations through the schools and their teachers. The teachers and the schools serve as conduits that interpret the events of all the communities that have an impact on the school. Teachers are in the position of cultural ambassadors interpreting and explaining the outside world to their students. The teacher must support or counter local or regional biases which may or may not be congruent with his or her own biases or beliefs. Speaking out against local mores and folkways has cost a few teachers their jobs, but in the final analysis, teachers should keep the courage of their convictions, especially when they pertain to student growth and development.

STUDY QUESTIONS

1. Explain how the policy of equal educational opportunity evolved from concerns about school segregation to broader concerns about different types of students.

2. Explain the principles or doctrines enunciated by the following U.S. Supreme Court decisions or federal legislation: *Brown* v. *Topeka Board of Education*, Title IX, *Lau* v. *Nichols*, Indian Education Act-1972, Education for All Handicapped Children, *Hazelwood School District* v. *Kuhlmeier*, *Tinker* v. *Des Moines School District*, *Pickering* v. *Board*, *Mt. Healthy* v. *Doyle*, *Keefe* v. *Geanakos*, *Brubaker* v. *Board*.

3. Compare the legal authority vested in the local, state, and national "communities" in terms of how each community affects school curriculum.

4. Discuss how the international community affects the day-to-day routine of schools.

5. Identify the basic elements of conducting a "participation-observation" study of a school district.

6. The following incident is based on an actual situation. It deals with a variety of issues and reflects the delicate relationship that exists between teachers and parents. Read the incident. Then discuss the four questions that follow it. But link the incident to key concepts, such as *in loco parentis*, academic freedom, community. (You may have to refer to Chapter 4 for a discussion of local values, norms, and tolerable deviation.)

David Goliath taught American Literature and Composition at Midvale High School. In a unit on American ethnic literature he assigned a Native American creation myth. This is a shortened version:

> THAT WHICH KNOWS AND DOES EVERYTHING (WKDE) lived above the sky with a daughter. One day the daughter fell through a hole in the sky. An eagle caught her and placed her on the back of a large turtle. Other turtles gathered mud from the ocean bottom. Soon a great island with land existed. The eagle brought grass and twigs from far away. They grew. WKDE asked the daughter to return. She refused and said she wanted to stay on the ground. WKDE granted her wish. Then she had a son. Soon the whole island was filled with people. That is how the first Indians were created.

A group of parents objected to the assignment. They believed:

> —the story taught that there might be more than one God;
> —the story taught strange ideas about God, such as WKDE had no gender;
> —that WKDE created a woman before WKDE created a man;
> —and who was the father of the daughter's son?

Mr. Goliath could not respond to the parents' concerns except to say that this myth, like the myth about creation in the Bible, left a lot of questions unanswered. The parents informed Mr. Goliath that the story of Adam and Eve was not a myth; it was the truth. The Indian story was a "myth." Mr. Goliath told the parents that in the future, the Indian legend would be optional reading. The parents went away happy.

DISCUSSION:

(a) Would Mr. Goliath's "right" to academic freedom protect him in this incident? Why or why not?

(b) Whether you agree or disagree with the parents' interpretation of the Native American creation story, discuss what religious "rights" they have in this incident.

(c) The parents call the Native American story a "myth," implying that it is not true; they state that the biblical creation story is true. How do you respond to the comment? What is the difference between "myth" and "truth"?

(d) How would you handle this incident? Would you make the assignment optional? Would you develop a unit on myths and their use in most cultures? Would you play it safe by not discussing myths of any kind?

NOTES

1. *Brown* v. *Topeka Board of Education*, 345 U.S.972, 1954.
2. U.S. Civil Rights Act, 1964.
3. Title IX.

4. *Lau* v. *Nichols,* 414 U.S.563, 1973.
5. Indian Education Act, 1972.
6. P.L. 94–142: Education For All Handicapped Children, 1975.
7. *Hazelwood School District* v. *Kuhlmeier.* 108 S.Ct.562, 1988.
8. *Tinker* v. *Des Moines Community School Dist.* 393 U.S.503, 1969.
9. Susan Suiter. *An Historical Review of Court Decisions Related to Freedom of Expression for Students in Public Schools.* Unpublished Master's Thesis, Eastern Montana College, 1988, p. 8.
10. *Tinker,* p. 506.
11. *Pickering* v. *Board of Education.* 391 U.S.563, 1968.
12. *Mt. Healthy* v. *Doyle.* 429 U.S.274, 1977.
13. *Keefe* v. *Geanakos.* 418 F.2d.362, 1969.
14. *Brubaker* v. *Board of Education.* 502 F.2d.973, 1974.
15. Julius Menacher. *School Law: Theoretical and Class Perspectives.* Englewood Cliffs: Prentice-Hall, 1987.
16. Severyn T. Bruyn. "The Methodology of Participant Observation," In Joan I. Roberts and Sherrie K. Akinsanya, *Educational Patterns and Cultural Configurations.* New York: McKay, 1976, pp. 247–263; see also, Gerry Rosenfeld. "Shut Those Fat Lips." *A Study of Slum School Failure.* New York: Holt, Rinehart and Winston, 1971; see also, James P. Spradley and David W. McCurdy. *The Cultural Experience: Ethnography in Complex Society.* Chicago: Science Research Associates, 1972.

Chapter
4

Sociocultural Factors for Pluralistic Teaching

Key Terms:

culture
ethnic group membership
exceptionality
folkways
gender-role identity
handicapping conditions
learned helplessness
looking-glass self

mores
norms
religiosity
self-concept
self-efficacy
stigma of poverty
socialization
underclass

"Cultural relativism," you might say, "is such an ethereal view of the teaching-learning universe. How can I understand this view when I really don't know even more basic concepts, such as what a culture is?" This chapter will describe the fundamental sociocultural factors which impinge upon teaching and learning in a pluralistic society. My concern is that beginning teachers and, all too often, experienced teachers are unaware of the sociocultural forces which affect the classroom experience. In the many human relations and cultural awareness workshops and courses I have taught, I found that while teachers and student teachers are eager to make differences in the lives of their students, they are not prepared to analyze in any meaningful and thorough manner the impact of a pluralistic society on teaching and learning. Also, they are eager to jump across the sociocultural factors and dive into methods for pluralistic teaching. My feeling is that teachers cannot use such methods effectively without a firm grasp of the impact of sociocultural factors on teaching and learning. And, having gained an understanding of the impact of sociocultural factors, teachers need a rational conceptual approach to countering those which are pernicious. (Chapters 6–10 of this text provides such conceptual models and strategies.)

I have emphasized that teaching and learning in a pluralistic society require a posture of cultural relativism, which in turn requires understanding one's own culture and that of others. We are now ready to examine the fundamental sociocultural factors that affect the classroom. I am calling these factors "concepts." They are descriptive of social, group, and human phenomena, such as "culture" or "community." The concepts consist of generalizations about some social phenomena; subsumed in the generalizations are "elements" or "components" which can be verified empirically.[1] For example, one element of the concept of "culture" is a value and belief system. That a group of people who have a certain culture hold certain beliefs or values can be verified in a variety of ways, such as by examining the group's religious literature. Yet, when persons analyze their values and beliefs in order to understand their cultures, they experience difficulty as they attempt to verify their values and beliefs. Social concepts make distinctions and delineations among different people and groups, but people and groups, in the meantime, are organic—changing, diffusing, and emerging.

Social concepts are empirical frames of reference that enable us to analyze group phenomena; they are not eternal verities or truths. Rather, they are attempts to make sense of humans in groups, who as dynamic phenomena are in constant flux. Consequently, the concepts discussed below are generalized ideas about the interaction of humans in groups. The degree to which the concepts fit any individual's life experience is, in the final analysis, an assessment each individual must make. My concern is that individuals should consider how the concepts fit them rather than how they fit the concepts. Once understood, the concepts can be used to analyze the complex social dynamics of a pluralistic society and the impact these dynamics have upon teaching and learning.

CULTURAL GROUP MEMBERSHIP

People are gregarious. They like to live in groups. In a pluralistic society, people are members of many groups simultaneously. Some groups, such as racial groups, are biological and inherited. Other groups, such as religious groups, are inherited but people can voluntarily join or leave these groups. Other groups are temporary, for example, the freshman class. Others serve individuals as important reference groups, such as the Elks or the Mormons at certain times in their lives. During infancy and childhood, the family is the primary reference group for most people. During adolescence, peer groups come to share importance with the family and possibly also with a religious denomination. After adolescence the individual may develop a plurality of reference groups, including occupational groups, religious groups, civic groups, and ethnic groups. To the individual, some groups are more important than others. We are concerned with basic sociocultural groups that give students their fundamental values, attitudes, and beliefs. In other words, *How do people develop their individual cultures?*

For discussion's sake, the entire United States of America is construed as the *pluralistic* society and the macrogroup to which all students belong. The society consists of myriad occupational, cultural, religious, and social class groups that are loosely cohered by general ethical principles enumerated in the Declaration of Independence, the U.S. Constitution, and the state and federal legal systems. Here we will examine group membership in ethnic groups, gender groups, nationality groups, religious groups, and social class groups with the objective of better understanding the sociocultural forces that encroach on teaching and learning. (For a discussion of the American core culture, review Chapter 2.)

DEFINITION OF CULTURE

Every student has an individual culture. Every student belongs to some ethnic or cultural group. Without a culture or an ethnic group, a student could not exist; such group affiliation is essential to human survival. Twenty-five years ago it was popular to label students from ethnic minority or low socioeconomic backgrounds as *culturally deprived.* The cultural deprivation theories were based on the assumption that because ethnic minority and lower-class students did not exhibit in school the cultural characteristics of middle-class youngsters, they were deprived of a valid culture. Without a valid culture, the theories reasoned, it was difficult for these students to compete and succeed in school. Subsumed in the cultural deprivation theories was the notion that "culturally deprived" students were also linguistically deprived because they did not speak school English. Speakers of nonschool English were described as *a*lingual, that is, without a legitimate language, and their dialects were perceived as adulterations of school English. Using the jargon of behavioral modification, elaborate methods were developed to extinguish these so-called dialects; once cleansed of their deviant dialects, students were programmed with school English.

The cultural deprivation theories spawned myriad compensatory education programs. These programs attempted in various ways to provide the ethnic minority and lower class students the background, experiences, and replacement dialects necessary for succeeding in middle-class school English. Compensatory programs attempted to transform ethnic minority and lower class students into middle-class, school-English-speaking students. Some compensatory programs failed to improve educational achievement substantially. They were not successful because they were based on the faulty assumption that ethnic minority and lower class students have invalid languages and cultures. The programs ignored the reality of culture; they ignored the fact that ethnic minority and lower class students have cultures, languages, and ethnic group heritages that cannot easily be replaced by those of another culture.

We now realize that all students, regardless of race, creed, and social class affiliation, come to school as culturally whole persons with a culture and a language and concomitant values, attitudes, beliefs, and knowledge. What we now need to know is how to understand the student's cultural background and experiences so we may utilize them productively in the teaching-learning process.

One myth about culture that must be dispelled is that it is elitist. This belief views culture as a characteristic that only a few people attain, such as those who listen to opera or read only Shakespearian plays and poetry. While great poetry, plays, and operas are products of cultural activities, the elitist view of culture limits a culture to a small group of people. Another myth is that culture is esoteric. This belief views culture as a phenomenon that existed in the past or, if in the present, exists in the backwoods of dense jungles where exotic music and rites are performed. This view, like the elitist view, limits culture to a few groups of people. Both views ignore the reality that all people must have a culture in order to live and work. Ralph Linton classified these mythic views of culture that leads us to a workable definition. Culture, he wrote,

> refers to the total way of life of any society, not simply to those parts of this way which the society regards as higher or more desirable. . . . It follows for the social scientist there are no uncultured societies or even individuals.[2]

Anthropologists define culture as the totality of learned attitudes, values, beliefs, traditions, and tools shared by a group of people to give order, continuity, and meaning to their lives.[3] Culture is not merely an abstraction, nor is it a mysterious entity acting outside the realm of human existence. Rather, it is central to human and group existence; it is invented and transmitted by the individual in a group, and by individuals acting in a group. Individuals take action, influencing other individuals, and collectively these individuals internalize a pattern or system for daily activities. Because human action takes place in time, the past undoubtedly influences present action; each group has a history which percolates into the present, influencing perceptions, opinions, and, ultimately, decisions about how to live in the present. The total history of a group, combined with its present modes of living, coalesces to form its culture.

A group's culture can be defined as a distinctive way of life. This is a holistic definition; it includes the total group's history, current practices, traditions, material products, tools, and attitudes and beliefs. One of the earliest definitions of culture, written by anthropologist E. B. Tylor in 1871, stated:

> Culture . . . is that complex whole which includes knowledge, belief, art, law, morals, customs, and any other capabilities and habits acquired by man as a member of society.[4]

Much later, in 1929, the anthropologist Ruth Benedict wrote that a group's culture consists of "that complex whole which includes all the habits acquired by man as a member of society."[5] These two definitions are actually representative of definitions given by many other anthropologists, all of whom stress culture as the sum total or the totality of a group's past and present experiences. Culture, as conceived by these definitions, focuses on the accumulated products and experiences of a particular group.

LEVELS OF CULTURE

A culture is like an iceberg. Two-thirds of an iceberg is submerged and out of sight. The visible one-third is important because it signals the iceberg's location, but the mass of the iceberg is unknown, its overall shape, density, and volume hidden from view. Culture is much the same. The visible signs of a

culture, for example, costume, consist of about one-third of the culture's substance; the mass of the culture's substance is hidden; the unconscious, implicit
level of culture, like the iceberg, is really the culture's substance as well as the
part that can create problems. When cultural conflict occurs, it usually occurs
at the unconscious, implicit level where people tuck away their ideologies,
biases, beliefs, and attitudes that have been formed by their life experiences.
Social psychologists refer to the unconscious level of culture as one's *schemata*,[6]
i.e., a frame of reference that provides structure and organization for new
experiences and that one uses to interpret social interactions and social events.

A group's culture operates at two levels of reality, explicit and implicit. The
explicit level consists of overt, standardized ways of behaving, reacting, and
feeling. The implicit level consists of covert, unstated, and largely unconscious
values, attitudes, and assumptions. Verbal and nonverbal behavior and language mediate the culture for a group. For example, in one ethnic group direct
eye contact between individuals is a presumed signal of trust and respect, and
yet in another ethnic group such eye contact is presumed to be a signal of
defiance and disrespect. What is important to understand is that one must
carefully interpret the explicit actions of a group's culture from the group's
perspective, a perspective based on the implicit meaning the group gives certain overt acts. This requires knowledge, sensitivity, and an understanding of
the group's values, beliefs, and attitudes—all of which are affected by its history
as well as its current status and condition. In short, to really know a group's
culture, one must know it at the implicit level of reality.

From a strictly existential point of view, no one can truly know someone
else's culture primarily because an individual's culture is an aggregation of
largely unconscious experiences unique to the individual. It is difficult to really
know someone else's experiences. No one can know what it felt like when I was
a teenager who experienced discrimination because of my Hispanic group affiliation. Nor can I truly understand what it feels like to be a poor White in an
affluent society. What I can know are the generalizations about the poor White
group's history and current status (based on its explicit cultural components).
From these historical and current details and generalizations I can begin to
infer something of the group's implicit culture, keeping in mind that I must
perceive this culture from the group's vantage point.

Because of the importance of implicit culture, I would like to present
another illustration. Consider the ubiquitous western movie which shows the
"Injuns" attacking a wagon train of "harmless pioneer families." Why would the
Native Americans attack a group of pioneers who were crossing the land in
peace? The pioneers, one might say, were simply trespassing on Native American land. One is tempted to infer, on the basis of the Native Americans' explicit
acts, that they were in those days a violent and barbarous group. Yet, before
making that inference, consider the explicit action from the perspective of the
Native Americans. More than likely, the situation was that the Native Americans had signed with the U.S. government a treaty which defined this particular tribe's territorial boundaries. Further, the treaty prohibited any non-
Indian settlement or crossing on the land. Yet, as was the case with many

treaties between the U.S. government and Native Americans, pioneering expeditions were not informed of the treaty's settlement and crossing agreements. Some pioneers had already settled in the Indian territory and others crossed without obtaining permission. From the Native American perspective, an attack on the wagon train was necessary to defend the Native Americans' homes. The seemingly violent and barbarous attack on the wagon train was actually nothing more than people defending their own homes. What at first appears to be a morally reprehensible act, at second view appears to be the expected behavior of a rational group of people who are defending their homeland. In this example, a true understanding of the Native Americans' action necessitates recognition of the implicit beliefs and values of the Native Americans.

DISCRETE ELEMENTS OF CULTURE

A culture can be construed as an intragroup experience that has discrete components or elements. Of the various definitions which describe culture, that of anthropologist Franz Boas has withstood the test of time and explicit criteria:

> Culture may be defined as the totality of the mental and physical reactions and activities that characterise the behavior of the individuals composing a social group. . . . It also includes the products of these activities and their role in the life of the group.[7]

What is good about Boas's definition is its explanation of three discrete cultural components: (1) behavior of individuals in a group; (2) the individual's reactions or behaviors as influenced by customs; and (3) material or tangible products determined by the customs or habits. While the definition explicitly describes three cultural components, it does not mention the implicit aspects of culture—values, attitudes, beliefs. Under Boas's definition, the individual's mental reactions most nearly approach the implicit level of culture. Nevertheless, the definition establishes a basis from which culture can be understood. On the explicit level of cultural reality, it is the stuff of customs combined with the individual's reactions and products that tangibly reflect a culture.

In the United States there exists a core culture which revolves around the ethos of individualism (see Chapter 2 for discussion of American culture and its Creed). The core operates from basic beliefs about capitalism, free enterprise, liberty, and equality under the law. The English language, as spoken in the United States, is the core's basic language. Beyond the core American culture, individuals form their own cultural groups within the context of the general American society. As such, the cultures of the different groups within the society can be visualized as intricate webbings which provide the society an infrastructure. Likewise, the core culture is the frame to which the cultural subgroups of the infrastructure is attached. Each of the subcultural groups consists of discrete values and beliefs, behavioral patterns, and tools which synthesize into folkways and mores that reflect the culture's norms (Figure 4.1).

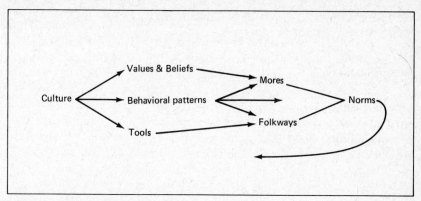

Figure 4.1 Discrete elements of culture

Cultural *mores* couch the attitudes, beliefs, values, and ideologies of the cultural group; they are implicit assumptions formed over time by group members. Cultural *folkways* couch the group's customs and traditions; folkways are the way people conduct their lives; the folkways are based on the implicit assumptions of the group's cultural mores. Cultural *tools* are the implements, machines, and material objects that people use to carry out their folkways. For example, early this morning I shaved the stubby hair on my face using soap and a safety razor (both the soap and the razor are tools). The tools allowed me to accomplish a simple folkway, shaving. Why did I shave? Now I probe my unconscious cultural assumptions and decide that I shaved because that makes my day more comfortable. Had I not shaved, then colleagues would wonder why I hadn't shaved. Was I ill? In a rush? Growing a beard? In other words, colleagues would apply a norm to my behavior—one should shave in the morning—and note a deviation from the norm. They would wonder why I deviated from the norm. Because my colleagues consider themselves liberals, they would allow some deviation from the norm. Nonetheless, they would inquire. So to prevent situations where I would have to answer many extraneous questions, I find it easier to shave; the day is more comfortable that way.

LANGUAGE AND CULTURE

Language is a cultural tool developed so that individuals can communicate with each other. It is the most natural and most essential tool developed by humans. As such, language and culture are inextricably bound. Culture is learned through both imitation and language. Through imitation of parents, siblings, and sometimes grandparents, uncles, and aunts, youngsters learn the family's or parents' culture. By imitation, youngsters assume attitudes, beliefs, and values about religion, politics, economics, and people. Further, the content of the culture is learned through the parents' language. The language youngsters inherit, imitate, and eventually speak serves to form perceptions and attitudes about their human and physical environments.

Language develops in youngsters at an early age. Exactly when language begins in infants has not been determined. However, by 2½ years of age, children exhibit streams of sounds and individual words which resemble the inflections of full, natural sentences. By age 4, most U.S. youngsters exhibit control over basic sentence patterns and most sounds of American English. When youngsters begin kindergarten or first grade (ages 5–7), they exhibit control over the fundamental rules, sentence patterns, and sounds of their parents' language. In short, youngsters begin school with basic control of their language.

The notion that some youngsters begin schooling speaking a substandard dialect or language is a misconception about their dialect. In fact, the language of their parents is the standard they have learned to imitate: black urban children, for example, who speak a form of Black English, adhere to the standards and rules of the language taught by their parents and family.[8] They do not enter school speaking a substandard language. Rather, they may enter school speaking a nonschool standard brand of English or a different standard of English. To take the position that these children speak a substandard brand of English is a blatant imposition of school English as the only standard brand of English capable of use for learning, which is an untenable, ethnocentric position unsupported by linguistic research. The natural language research of Labov,[9] Baratz,[10] Garcia,[11] has affirmed that dialects and languages are capable of abstract reasoning, mathematic reasoning, and human communications. In short, all language and dialects are valid systems of cognition and communications.

In American public schools, teachers have traditionally attempted to ignore or eradicate languages and dialects which deviate from the standard taught in schools. Rather than accepting the language of youngsters who speak different dialects and building from their language bases, teachers have attempted to remediate the language through behavioral modification and English-as-a-second-language techniques which have not been optimally successful. The attempt has caused the youngsters innumerable cognitive and emotional problems because of the disorientation caused by the language remediation thrust. Students have a right to their particular dialects, and teachers have a responsibility to use that language as a means to expand the students' perceptual, cognitive, and emotional development. The students' language, after all, is as intimate as their mother's love, and any educational practice that seeks to strip away this language is morally and humanly reprehensible. Yet, it is possible for students to learn how to speak, read, and write standard English if their teachers were to teach standard English literacy as the language of broader communication, necessary for survival in a highly technological and literate society. (Chapter 8 describes language education approaches that allow teachers to use the student's home language as a vehicle for learning standard American English. All students must develop full literacy in standard American English.)

TEACHING AND LEARNING A CULTURE

Culture is learned. Everyone is born into a culture, but the culture is not inborn, innate, or inherent. Rather, once born into a culture, the individual goes about the task of learning the culture. Family members, especially parents and siblings, go about the task of teaching the culture to the new member. Of course, this is not an overtly conscious effort. Instead, the parents and siblings simply do different things to protect and nurture the new child. The things that they do—for example, cuddle the child, feed the child, sing to the child—are habits and activities once learned and now transmitted to the child. Thus, the process of socialization begins.

Socialization is the process used by parents, siblings, and other significant persons to transmit their culture and prepare the new member for living. Some anthropologists prefer the term *enculturation* instead of "socialization." Both terms refer to the process by which persons are inducted into their cultures. Essentially, the new member of a group is taught the group's values, behaviors, and language(s). Socialization activities are not formal tasks taught to the child; they are just things parents and siblings do as a matter of course. What is important to understand is that socialization activities and tasks are not instinctive. Rather, they are tasks that have been taught in some way to the parents and siblings. In like manner, the new member catches many attitudes, values, and beliefs in the process of growing up in a family. The child is constantly catching attitudes and values by the tone of the voices, the vocabulary, and sundry other parts of the surrounding human environment.

Notice in this scenario how two young boys from different groups "catch" different attitudes about crisis management:

JIMMIE ECHOHAWK AND THE SNAKE

JIMMIE: Daddy!! Daddy!! There's a snake outside! Go kill it!
DADDY: What color is the snake?
JIMMIE: I don't know!
DADDY: Does it have rattles?
JIMMIE: I don't know!
DADDY: Jimmie, you must learn to look carefully at it.
JIMMIE: But daddy?
DADDY: If the snake has no rattles, or if it has no diamonds on its back, it's probably a bull snake.
JIMMIE: But, it's still a snake.
DADDY: No, Jimmie. Bull snakes never bite people. They eat rattlers. But even rattlers aren't bad. They will rattle and run from you unless you step too near them. Now go watch the snake carefully. Then, if it tries to get in the house, tell me.

JIMMIE MACNIGH AND THE SNAKE

JIMMIE: Daddy!! Daddy!! There's a snake outside! And . . .

DADDY: I'll get my shotgun! You watch it!

JIMMIE: But, Dad . . .

DADDY: You get over to the window and watch it! (Scurries to gun rack for gun). Now, I've got my gun loaded! Where's the snake?

JIMMIE: I tried to tell you, Daddy! Joe brought it over! It's dead!

DADDY: Oh, heck! Why didn't you say so?

JIMMIE: I did, but . . .

DADDY: Okay, okay. Let's forget about it.

In both scenarios the boys were excited about the snake. Jimmie Echohawk's father, who may have been equally excited, emphasized the attitude that snakes have a place in the ecosystem and that they are to be respected in that place. The father insisted that Jimmie learn to first observe the possible "crisis" and then act accordingly. Jimmie MacNigh's father took the "shoot and then ask questions" attitude. He reacted immediately by getting and loading his gun to kill the snake. He emphasized through his behavior that the snake was an enemy, part of the "untamed" wilderness that had to be tamed. Both sons caught different attitudes toward snakes, toward the human relationship to nature as well as the way to solve problems. Yet, neither father realizes that he is teaching and his son is unconsciously catching attitudes that reflect his respective cultural values.

Many of the prejudices about African Americans that children learn are "caught" rather than explicitly taught.[12] Parents transmit their attitudes, biases, and beliefs through their tones of voice or the unconscious connotations of their vocabulary. References to the color black as a negative or evil influence are replete in American English vernacular. Common conversational expressions, from "he was blackballed," or "he was blacklisted" to more subtle expressions such as "she's in a black mood," serve to transmit negative attitudes toward blackness and African American people. While the negative connotation of "blackness" is part of the American English vernacular, the use of black to connote evil and white to connote good has its origins in Christian theology and the *Holy Bible*. A negative bias toward black is easily caught given the long history of the bias.

The culture is taught by family members. As children grow, friends, teachers, rabbis, priests, ministers, and others teach their cultural roles. A child is taught to watch adults acting out, or living within, certain roles, and then by modeling after one or some of those roles, the child begins to learn a role in the cultural group. As one is taught a role in the cultural group, a self-concept develops—a global attitude and idea about who and how important one is.

FORMATION OF SELF-CONCEPT

As a child, everyone tells me who I am. As a teenager, I challenge everyone. As an adult I tell everyone who I am, sort of. A *self-concept* is a person's perception of self that forms through social interaction with others; a person's self-concept is a result of how the person perceives the responses of others toward him or her. Cooley[13] called this phenomenon the "looking-glass self," a social interaction process by which people define themselves by internalizing their perceptions of how they think others perceive them.

The self-concept serves to guide or influence a person's behavior. As the person's experiences expand and opportunities arise to experiment with different roles, the self-concept expands to incorporate the new experience and opportunities. The roles are learned by modeling or imitating adults, an interactive process by which a person perceives certain behaviors as appropriate or inappropriate for emulation. The adults serve as "significant others,"[14] signaling through nonverbal and verbal modes adult behavioral expectations. This is the "looking-glass self" notion of cultural group participation wherein the adults—who are viewed as significant by the person learning the roles—reflect and transmit their expectations and attitudes about the person learning the role. In other words we learn that others in a cultural group are like mirrors who reflect to some extent what we look like in a sociocultural sense. However, the mirror image is not an exact reflection of the attitudes and expectations of others. The mirror image is filtered through the person's attitudes and expectations. As a child, the question "Who am I?" is largely answered by significant others. As adolescents and adults, the question is also answered by the person asking. The individual, through maturation and the accumulation of experiences can develop the ability to evaluate the attitudes and expectations of others and thereby select those attitudes and expectations that best fit the person's desired perception of self.

Self-concept formation is a dynamic process. Much like a spiral beginning at birth, the self-concept expands with experiences and opportunities. As the experiences and opportunities cumulatively build upon each other, individuals form a mental picture of who they are and how powerful they are within their cultural group and their society in general. But, the mental picture can be modified by others or by the individuals. As children, adults tell us who we are. As adolescents we question the adults' perceptions; as adults, we tell ourselves who we are in reference to others. It is extremely important to know that a self-concept is malleable and that individuals can change how they perceive themselves; here reference is to *self-efficacy*,[15] the attitude that one can make changes in oneself and in one's culture.

Infants and young children have little conscious knowledge of their self-concepts. Imagine what happens to the self-concept of a Native American youngster. She is born into a Comanche tribe and taught the folkways and mores of the Comanche people. She notices that her brothers and sisters, parents, and grandparents are dark in skin color, have black hair and eyes. She learns the Comanche language; she learns rhymes and songs in the language. Then she attends an American public school. There she notices that the teacher speaks only English, and that her classmates are of different skin colors, but primarily they are off-white in color. She is taught that these off-white-colored people brought civilization and culture to the "untamed" wilderness, and that these same people had to fight against barbarous, savage dark-skinned tribes who did not want to be tamed. She notices that dark-skinned people, especially those whose tribes were rooted in Africa, had to be enslaved so they could be tamed and civilized. When she goes home at night, she again sees dark-skinned people, her people. Yet, it's true—they have language and beliefs like those people who resisted civilization, who were like the "untamed" wilderness. What kind of self-concept will this youngster learn? She is taught two opposite lessons: be a Comanche, but don't be a dark-skinned savage. But her parents and her teachers mean no harm. Her teachers are just teaching American history from the White colonial point of view.[16] Nevertheless, she experiences difficulty because there is no consonance between what the parents are teaching and what the teachers and the school are teaching. If the school's point of view prevails, she will develop a negative self-concept. Kenneth Clark, in his research on African American children who perceive rejection in school and by members of the larger, White society, concluded that:

> Since every human depends upon his cumulative experiences with others for clues as to how he should view and value himself, children who are consistently rejected understandably begin to question and doubt whether they, their family, and their group really deserves no more respect from the larger society than they receive.[17]

CULTURAL NORMS AND TOLERABLE DEVIATION

A culture is shared. People form a culture to enhance their survival. Then they share it with group members. Sharing a culture requires cooperation and interdependence among group members. When a member is not cooperative, or when he or she is deviant, the group applies certain sanctions. The sanctions range from mild physical punishment (e.g., spankings) to withholding of affection or ostracism from the group. The sanctions are based on *norms,* or what is considered normal behavior by the group. The norms spring from the behaviors valued by the group. They are couched in the group's mores and folkways which may or may not be codified in the group's civil laws. Generally, a group's mores and folkways have more power than the civil laws to control the behavior of group members. Most cultural groups do not expect total conformity to their norms; a certain amount of deviation from norms is tolerated. Individuals within a culture, or individuals who wish to assimilate into a culture must learn the degree or extent to which cultural group members will tolerate deviation from a particular set of norms. How do you react to the following incident?

> A new neighbor invites all his neighbors including you over for an outdoor picnic in his backyard. After eating the main fare, including punch, pop, coffee, barbequed ribs, corn, and apple pie, the group sat around exchanging jokes. When your new neighbor was asked to tell a joke about Korea where he was from, he said that he didn't know any. Then one of the guests stated that he really liked the ribs, asking "where did you get them?" "At the 'Mutt Canine Kennel' where they had some Siberian Husky pups on sale," he replied. "It's not often," he continued, "that you find pedigree Siberians on sale. They make especially good eating because of their natural fat."

This actually happened at a barbeque I attended with neighbors. We were appalled! Most of us had dogs who were a part of our families; we did not eat dogs; we incorporated dogs into our families. How would you react? Would it be easy to apply the principle of tolerable deviation and say, "after all, we do not expect total conformity to our norms?" I think not. At least, most middle-class suburbanites could not react calmly. After we sputtered our protests about the fact that we did not know that we were eating dog meat and that ordinarily we do not eat dog meat, we noticed that our host was bewildered by our comments. In his culture, dog meat is considered a delicacy, and in his case, he had purchased an expensive, healthy, and clean pedigree pup to serve as the main fare. He had noticed that rattlesnake steak and frogs legs were considered a delicacy in the United States; he had noticed that Americans are fond of chicken which to him was a dirty animal. Why, then, the uproar about the dog ribs? It became clear that our new neighbor did not understand our middle-class, suburban attitude toward dogs nor did he understand the norms we upheld regarding the kinds of meat we consume. Our new neighbor would have to learn, and we would have to teach him, the extent to which we could tolerate deviation from this particular norm.

People from different cultural groups may not apply the same norms to assess deviant behavior. A teacher may see as deviant a child who is acting normally within his or her cultural perspective. For example, in some Mexican American families a child is expected to show respect for elders and anyone in a position of authority. The youngster is also taught to think independently, but to think of the feelings of others, especially those who may be older and wiser. The child's teacher, on the one hand, may encourage all students to disagree with him as a way of learning to be independent thinkers. To the child, dis-agreeing with the teacher—like disagreeing with a grandparent—is deviant behavior, behavior not valued by the child's group; this child's attempt to show respect by refusing to disagree may confuse the teacher, who may think of the child as "passive," "introverted," or "disinterested" and "unmotivated" to learn. In this instance, the student and the teacher do not share the values of a common culture and unconscious cultural conflict occurs. The teacher means the student no harm, and the student means the teacher no disrespect. Neither is conscious that a basic cultural problem exists. For the student this unaware-ness is acceptable; for the teacher who is responsible for teaching and learning, it is unacceptable.

A culture is gratifying. In other words, a culture must fill certain biological and emotional needs of the group members. For example, every culture has a customary behavior for fulfilling basic biological needs. Every culture provides infants with some kind of family: adults whose major responsibilities are the care and feeding of the infants. Every culture has a customary behavioral pattern for fulfilling sexual drives. Courtship and marriage rituals determine how, when, and with whom sexual drives (along with other needs such as love, security) will be consummated. The culture is the mechanism by which polit-ical and economic as well as social needs are fulfilled. Systems of government and (ways to make a living) are developed by the people within the culture.

When a particular need is not filled, then individuals within the group look for ways to change their behavior so as to better fulfill the need.

As you can see, a culture consists of values, behaviors, and products which become manifest when humans organize a group to enhance their survival. Group members learn and teach each other their culture by sharing it, and when a particular aspect of the culture does not meet the group's needs, then a change is required. A culture, then, both preserves and conserves the group's values, behaviors, and products. Just as individuals acquire unique, individualized cultures, they can change their cultures when experiences warrant a change in ideologies, values, beliefs, or attitudes. When enough individuals make the same change, a basic cultural change occurs. The dynamics—the individual making personal changes which effects a chain reaction among others to change—is the process that causes cultural renewal, thereby keeping a cultural group vital. Cultures change because individuals will the change. Included here is the belief that individuals can make changes and effect outcomes within their personal lives and the lives of other members of their cultural group. Consequently, a culture is not an eternal verity, an absolute truth. Rather, a culture is pliable. The pliability of culture will take on greater importance when the impact of ethnicity, gender, religiosity, social class affiliation, and handicapping conditions is discussed.

ETHNIC GROUP MEMBERSHIP

Ethnic group identity refers to allegiance to a human group that is cohered by a sense of peoplehood. The sense of peoplehood, a subjective, emotional feeling or condition, is embodied in such factors as (1) shared symbols, customs, traditions, (2) common racial or kinship ties, (3) shared religion, folklore, myths, (4) common language, and (5) common geographic or national origin.[18] These factors combined constitute an ethnic group culture. The culture can be traced back many generations through ancestral ties.

Twentieth century American ethnic groups, especially those formed in Europe, originated as basic forms of social organization among the European peasantry. These primordial ethnic groups germinated in confined geographic regions, such as manor villages or valleys; the groups identified with the soil—it was their "land," or "territory." Group members were blood-kin related (family) to a greater or lesser degree. They had an economic purpose in common, such as farming; in pursuit of their common economic interests, the group members developed their culture which was rooted in a sense of peoplehood and a sense of place. When these primordial groups immigrated to the United States, they encountered another much larger form of social organization, the nation-state or American nationalism, which operated in a very self conscious, deliberate manner to transform their ethnicity into American nationalism. Using assimilation ideologies (see Chapter 2 for discussion of the ideologies), the ethnic groups were under pressure to transform their ethnicity into American nationalism. Some groups made the transformation almost completely. Others developed a first generation bi-ethnicity (ethnic group and American national-ism) which was often lost on the second generation.

Some of the early ethnic groups chose to sustain their ancestral identities indefinitely, such as the Amish, the Seventh-Day Adventists, and the Hutter-ites which show little desire to identify with the American mainstream. Other ethnic groups, because of segregation, racism, and social exclusion have main-tained a form of bi-ethnicity as is the case with racial minority groups: Asians, African Americans, Hispanics, and Native Americans. These groups have at-tempted at different times in American history to integrate into the American mainstream, but the resiliency of racism and social exclusion forced a bi-ethnic condition upon them.

Our latter-day twentieth century ethnic groups differ from their ancestral groups in important ways. Our twentieth century groups are dispersed through-out the United States rather than confined to one geographic region so that territoriality is not a critical factor, with the exception of Native Americans who have legally designated and marked land bases (the reservations). Harvard University's *Encyclopedia of American Ethnic Groups*[19] identified at least 106 existing American ethnic groups after combining the more than 170 Native American groups into one very large group. What is significant is that the percentage of White ethnic group members is on the decline while the per-centage of non-White (people of color) ethnic group members is on the in-crease.

Currently, these latter-day twentieth century ethnic groups are defined in cultural terms. Banks and Gay provide a contemporary definition of an ethnic group:

> A cultural ethnic group is an ethnic group which shares a common set of values, experiences, behavioral characteristics, and linguistic traits which differ substan-tially from those of other ethnic groups within the society.[20]

Banks and Gay are careful to point out that their definition of an ethnic group represents an ideal-type construct, and that in actuality ethnic-group members will exhibit in varying degrees the ethnic-group characteristics they have iden-tified.

In preindustrial, European societies the family or the primordial ethnic group transmitted the traditional skills necessary for group perpetuation. So-cialization began at birth and extended beyond puberty. At puberty, the indi-vidual was inducted into the group by some rite of passage. Cultural transmission was the education of youth; it was the family's essential function and the parents' primary responsibility after biological needs were met. In current western European societies and in the United States, the family has delegated educational responsibilities to other institutions. Education of youth is a responsibility shared with the church, schools, and mass media. We expect the teacher and other school personnel to act *in loco parentis* to the degree that we wish them to share in the technical and spiritual education of our youth; cultural conflict occurs in the schools when the teacher's and the ethnic group's socialization practices vary.

Is a nationality group the same as an ethnic group? In some cases, the two are the same. Technically, nationality is one's official country of citizenship. For example, anyone who is a legal citizen of Canada is a Canadian regardless of race, color, or religious creed. U.S. citizens, including citizens of the Commonwealth of Puerto Rico and other U.S. territories, regard their nationality as American. For some Americans, their sense of peoplehood, their allegiance and loyalty, is to their nationality rather than to a specific ethnic group. For other Americans, allegiance and loyalty to both the country as a whole (nationality) and to their ethnic group are not considered mutually exclusive. In times of national crisis, priority may be given to national considerations. In the United States, one can be an ethnic and a citizen of a pluralistic nation. One's ethnic group, as a human cultural group, is identified by race, religion, or national origin.

One's ethnic group in American society is not synonymous with one's language or nationality. In nineteenth-century Europe, a person's ethnic group was also his or her nationality. Many times, the ethnic, national, and language group was the same. A Spaniard (ethnic group) was Spanish (nationality) and spoke Spanish (language group). Yet, Jews in Spain were described as Sephardic Jews. They spoke Spanish and considered themselves Spanish Jews. Citizens of the United States call themselves Americans and perceive their national allegiance to be to the United States of America. One can have an American nationality, a particular ethnic group such as Greek American, and speak an American variety of English. Some people can trace their ethnic heritage to various national origins and identify as members of transnational ethnic groups; some members of transnational groups are not sure they have an ethnic group. Many will say they have no ethnic group and that they are "Heinz 57" variety, that is, of mixed national origins.

The latter-day twentieth century American ethnic group is a reference group; its importance to individual members is largely a function of families who may encourage weak or strong ethnic group affiliation or consciousness. In some families, ethnic group consciousness is very evident in the home, with the use of language, and the observance of ethnic group holidays and festivities. In other families where ethnic group consciousness is relatively weak, national or religious observances may replace ethnic group activities. Consequently, youngsters in school may or may not be aware of their ethnic group heritage which is largely dependent upon their respective family orientations toward ethnicity (see Chapter 7 for approaches for teaching students their ethnic heritage).

SEX AND GENDER-ROLE IDENTITY

Just as all students have a culture, all students have a sex and gender-role identity. While culture is entirely learned, sex and gender-role identity have both a biologic and sociologic basis. We know that boys and girls differ in academic and social behavior in elementary grades. Maccoby and Jacklin[21] reviewed more than 1,500 students and reported that boys and girls differed significantly in elementary grades. Girls performed verbally better than boys; boys performed better in mathematics and visual-spatial activities, and boys were more aggressive than girls.

The causes for the differences have been attributed to genetic differences and to socialization practices. Prevailing folk wisdom has been that girls are more socially oriented and boys are more task oriented which leads some to the specious conclusion that girls are naturally (genetically) more verbal and boys are naturally more mathematic than girls. Whether sex differences are largely determined by innate biological structures or by socialization practices is an unresolved issue, but current thinking is that socialization is the key force for shaping gender-role identities. Maccoby and Jacklin,[22] for example, did not discount the possibility that genetic factors may partially explain the causes for the differences between the girls and boys reported in their analyses of research studies. The key here is that genetic factors may "partially" explain sex differences in school behaviors. Sociobiologist Wilson in *On Human Nature* posited that:

> modest genetic differences exist between the sexes; the behavioral genes interact with virtually all existing environments to create noticeable divergence in early psychological development; and the divergence is almost always widened in later psychological development by cultural sanctions and training.[23]

Wilson goes on to say that the modest at birth differences can be cancelled by training and planning, which means that while there may be a genetic reason for gender differences there is also a cultural way for eliminating the differences through socialization practices.

We know that children become aware of their sexual identity early in life by the way their parents hold them, talk to them, and in some instances, dress them. As soon as children learn the words "boy" and "girl" they quickly label themselves correctly as a boy or a girl. Children learn their sexual identity quickly. Children learn their gender-role identity more slowly as they are socialized by parents and significant others. Kohlberg describes the formation of a gender-role identity as an interactional process, that is, children form their gender identification based on their experience with their own bodies and within their cultural contexts.[24]

After an analysis of the research on gender-role identity, Honig concluded that ". . . biology, socializing forces, and the developing cognitive capacities of a child all play a vital and complex role in the development of gender identity."[25] Gender identities, or gender-role identities, are ideal mental constructs pertaining to behaviors considered appropriate for men and women; gender-role identities are culturally defined; how females and males are supposed to act within any given situation is culturally defined.[26]

Gender-roles first form as a result of the division of labor within families. All cultures have some kind of division of labor based on gender. The division of labor reflects the economic function of the family. Historically, in hunting cultures, females tended the home and family while males hunted for food away from the home and children. This basic division of labor was linked to the biological function of females as childbearers. Because females could not hunt while pregnant, and because males were physically bigger and stronger than women, men became the hunters and women became the homemakers. But not all cultures developed a hunting, economic base. Over the centuries, cultures developed economic bases with crop raising, livestock tending, and in our times, industrial capitalism. The division of labor based on gender manifested itself differently as economic bases diversified, causing variations in gender-roles. Draper's ethnographic research[27] among the *Kung* illustrates how economic relationships foster gender-roles. Among traditional *Kung* bands, both women and men gathered food and water for the home. While the women foraged for food, they also gathered information about game which they passed on to the men. Men always shared the meat they hunted with the entire band; women did the same with the food they foraged. Because of the interdependency of males and females within the traditional *Kung* bands, there existed an egalitarian ethos between the genders. When the men were home, they tended to the home and cared for the children. Draper also studied nontraditional *Kung* bands who worked for wages, herded livestock, raised crops, and lived in settled villages. These bands did not forage for food and game; the men were the primary producers of food. They raised the crops, tended the herds, and worked for wages. In these *Kung* bands, there existed a less communal, interdependent relationship between men and women. The men developed a stratification system that ranked families based on the size of the herds, houses, and the number of sons each had. Men, as the primary producer of food, valued sons over daughters because sons could produce more wealth for the family. The role of women was to work in the home and care for the children. Females and their work were devalued. Draper's study of the *Kung* bands demonstrates how gender-roles change as the economic relationships between men and women within families change.

In the United States, gender-roles are presently in a state of flux. The nuclear family is experiencing dramatic changes as single-parent families increase. Clearly, both boys and girls should be guided by sensitive teachers and parents to develop gender-role identities consistent with the individual's proclivities and inclinations. Blanket acceptance of traditional gender-role identities serves only to suppress individual creative expression and discourage the development of full human potentials. Surely the world would be impoverished if Mozart's parents had taught him that playing the piano is for "sissies and women," or if Margaret Thatcher's parents had taught her that "girls only keep house" rather than be head of the British government.

RELIGIOSITY AND IDENTITY

Religion is a pervasive factor in all societies. Emile Durkheim, the sociologist who studied the sociology of religions throughout the world, concluded that religion was a foundation of all societies and cultures.[28] Durkheim's study of

Australian aborigines revealed that the aborigine group shared principles and beliefs that cohered the group; the principles and beliefs derived from the group's religion. Durkheim found a similar pattern in more complex societies; members of the societies had reached a consensus about the principles that would serve to cohere the societies. Without the consensus, there could be no social life. Yet, all of the religions also contained a personal, private dimension.

Just what is religion? Durkheim separated the religious world into two domains, the "sacred" and the "profane." The domains are polarities; the sacred domain provides answers about the unknown and about the meaning and purpose of life; the sacred domain is often called "spiritual," and in our society, is considered private. The profane provides beliefs, morals, and norms which serve to cohere the religious group; the profane domain is considered public because it deals with the daily and mundane but still ethical relationships of the members within the religious group. The profane domain is considered the "law and order" function, and the sacred domain is considered the "meaning and purpose" function of religion. As polarities, the domains intersect somewhere in the middle which means that what is sacred and what is profane is decided by the particular group defining the domains. The group also defines practices and beliefs which serve to unite the group into what Durkheim called a "moral community" or "church." By church Durkheim referred to the idea of solidarity of group purpose couched in moral terms. To Durkheim, a church was much more than a building; it was a moral community of like-minded people who united around certain ethical principles. A church is a group's way of thinking and believing. Earlier in the chapter we examined how a culture on an implicit level consists of commonly held values and beliefs that cohere a group, and how an ethnic group coheres through mores and folkways commonly held. Members of the ethnic group usually develop a consciousness of kind or a sense of peoplehood. The story of the Hebrews of the *Old Testament* is largely a story about "the chosen people" (a sense of peoplehood) held together by common beliefs (e.g., The Ten Commandments), common traditions (observing the Sabbath), and common practices (Kosher foods). The Hebrews were a moral community—a "church" in Durkheim's definition—and an ethnic group whose cultural core was religious.

In a pluralistic society, a religious group provides an important communal function by giving meaning and purpose to existence as well as membership in a human group. As with the Hebrews, we can see that religion can provide a value and belief system to a cultural group. Lenski's study[29] of religious affiliations in Detroit reported that church attendance served a communal function by providing people with personal meaning, group membership, and the sense of belonging to a group.

Now we shift from the personal, private aspects of religion to the more public, social functions of religion in the United States. The idea that ethnicity and religiosity are linked—if not synonymous—is not unique. What is unique to pluralistic societies such as the United States, formed by large-scale immigrations of peoples representative of many cultures, languages, and religions, is a type of religious pluralism that spawns denominations, of which membership is voluntary and individualistic. The nation was founded with the conscious effort to maintain a separation of church and state by creating a secular (non-religious) government. Religion was to be a private rather than a public matter. The national, state, and local governments, and their agencies, such as the public schools, were to be religiously neutral secular institutions. However, because schools are housed with students and teachers who live within local neighborhoods and to a large extent are members of the local culture, schools have difficulty remaining neutral. Here we are concerned with the relationship between religion, denominational membership, and identity. For many individuals, denominational religions provide the function of an ethnic group: denominations provide guidelines for living, structures that explain the meaning and purpose for living, and a reference group for identification.

A denomination is a nuclear religious organization which is a subcomponent of a larger, more generalized church. The specific denomination serves as the reference group of first recourse for many people. As such, the denomination becomes the crucial factor for identification and self-concept. Other factors, race, national origins, social class, language preference, or gender may play a part, but the denomination, if it is the reference group of first recourse, sets the basic structure for identification and self-concept formation.

Movement between denominations is provided by the attitude that all denominations are part of a larger, generalized church. Herberg described this phenomenon as "denominational aggregation,"

> something that pertains primarily to Protestantism and to a lesser degree to Judaism; both have more or less organized denominations which . . . form the religious community. Catholicism . . . has no such overt inner divisions, but American Catholics readily understand the phenomenon . . . Denominations are felt to be somehow a matter of individual preference, and movement between denomination is not uncommon.[30]

Denominations serve the functions of providing the individual with a specific religious group for membership and communal participation, i.e., communion. For example, one may attend the Congregational Church as a youth. As an adult, living in a community where there are no Congregational denominations, the person identifies as a Protestant and may attend any church, depending upon personal preference. While Roman Catholics do not have organized denominations, their parishes often reflect one dominant ethnic group, so that in times past, the individual attended church in a parish that reflected the individual's mother language and culture. For example, as a youth I attended a Catholic Church that was predominantly Hispanic in culture, including the use of Spanish for church services. As an adult, living in communities where the Catholic parishes are ethnically non-Hispanic, I am still a Catholic and may attend any Catholic Church. I've attended masses, funerals, and weddings that were ethnically Polish, German, Italian, and Pueblo Indian.

What emerged from the denominational phenomenon is what Herberg called a religious "triple melting pot" of Protestants, Catholics, and Jews which have amalgamated into a ". . . 'common faith' of American society . . . standing for the same 'moral ideas' and 'spiritual values'. This conception . . . is in fact held, though hardly in explicit forms, by many devout and religiously sophisticated Americans."[31]

While switching denominations is possible within the triple melting pot, it is not a common occurrence with some denominations. Kluegel indicates that adults tend to identify with their childhood denominations. His study[32] provides these data on adults who remained with their childhood denominations: Jews, 87%; Catholics, 85%; Lutherans, 77%; Baptists, 74%; Presbyterians, 62%; Episcopalians, 64%; United Church of Christ, 64%; Methodists, 64%; Disciples of Christ, 64%.

Current demographic data[33] on church membership show that church attendance is at a steady state with attendance represented by most major religions, Buddha, Christian, Hebrew, Hindu, and Islam (or Muslim) especially in

Table 4.1 RELIGIOUS BODIES AND CHURCH MEMBERSHIP, 1960 TO 1983, AND NUMBER OF CHURCHES, 1983 (MEMBERSHIP IN THOUSANDS, EXCEPT AS INDICATED)

Religious Body	Membership						Number of churches 1983
	1960	1965	1970	1975	1980	1983	1983
Total	114,449	124,682	131,045	131,013	134,817	140,816	338,244
Members as percent of population[a]	64	64	63	61	59	60	X
Average members per local church	359	382	399	393	401	416	X
Buddhist Churches of America	20	92	100	60	60	70	100
Eastern Churches	2,699	3,172	3,850	3,696	3,823	4,034	1,656
Jews[b]	5,367	5,600	5,870	6,115	5,920	5,728	3,500
Old Catholic, Polish National Catholic, & American Churches	590	484	848	846	924	1,150	436
The Roman Catholic Church	42,105	46,246	48,215	48,882	50,450	52,393	24,260
Protestants[c] Miscellaneous[d]	63,669	69,088	71,713	71,043	73,479	77,254	307,147
			449	372	161	188	1,145

[a] Based on Bureau of the Census estimated total population as of July 1.

[b] Estimates of the Jewish community including those identified with Orthodox, Conservative and Reformed synagogues or temples.

[c] Includes non-Protestant bodies such as Latter-Day Saints and Jehovah's Witnesses.

[d] Includes non-Christian bodies such as Spiritualists, Ethical Culture Movement, and Unitarian-Universalists.

Note: X = Not applicable.

Source: National Council of the Churches of Christ in the United States of America, New York, NY, Yearbook of American and Canadian Churches, annual.

major urban areas. The National Council of the Churches of Christ provided the data in Table 4.1 on church numbers and membership: Notice that overall church membership has increased in the decades of the 1960s and 1980s with some fluctuations with some of the religious bodies. Table 4.1 is a composite and does not show the counterculture religious groups such as Zen, TM, Hare Krishna or so-called secular religions such as est, Synanon, and Scientology.

THE SOCIAL CLASS CHALLENGE

All societies have stratification systems reflective of their economic and political divisions of labor. In the U.S. three social classes exist: upper, middle, and lower. Lines between the classes are diffuse because the middle class continually expands in both directions, shrinking both the upper and lower class. In theory, upward or downward mobility between the classes is fluid. Upward mobility—central to the American Creed—is purportedly possible through such efforts as getting a good education, changing religions, or working hard. The ideology of the common school movement (see Chapter 3) centered on schools as funnels through which students, especially lower-class students, could raise their social class status, what Horace Mann meant when he spoke of schools as the "Great Equalizers."

Social class membership is a slippery concept. Members of traditionally considered middle-class groups, teachers, nurses, social workers, some college professors, cannot afford to buy a home lest 40 percent of their take-home pay be used for monthly mortgage payments. The American ideal of owning a home has become an out-of-reach ideal for many young, middle-class families. What is happening is expansion from the center. The middle class is expanding in both directions so that an increasing number of people are included in the middle class. This is especially the case with the service industries which spread across a wide range of occupations, for example, from waitress to computer operator. But the wages of these new members of the middle class are exceedingly low.[34]

While the middle class is expanding, the bottom of the lower class is crystallizing into what some scholars fear is a permanent underclass. The idea is not new. An *underclass* is synonymous to a "pariah caste" which is locked into a life-cycle of destitution with no hope of escape for its members. Medieval European serfs and seventeenth century American slaves are classic examples of the "pariah caste." Sharecroppers, migratory agricultural workers, and some urban beggars approximate pariah castes in our contemporary society.

The noted educator, Clark Kerr, reported in a Carnegie Foundation study[35] that one of every three youths is ill-employed, ill-equipped, and ill-educated to succeed in the United States, causing Kerr to infer that without vast educational improvements the country faces the danger of producing a permanent underclass. This study was the precursor of the educational reform studies that flurried in the 1980s, and when one contemplates that underclasses are the forces of revolution—the Bolshevik and French Revolutions—the motives underlying the studies are easily understood. While our nation may not face an incipient revolution of the underclass, the development of a permanent underclass would grievously wound the American Creed and plant the seeds of revolution; educational improvements can stymie the development of an underclass—I do not believe that poverty is inevitable in any society— knowledge can deter poverty; education can be a liberating force in the lives of people. Knowledge, after all, is the fuel that drives the pursuit of self-interests.

Wilson's study identified elements of an American underclass: (1) structural unemployment in declining manufacturing industries is relegating older workers to a life of permanent unemployment because their job skills are obsolete in a technologically advancing postindustrial service economy; and (2) the upward mobility of some members of inner-city communities due to opportunities created by civil rights and affirmative action policies. The remaining individuals have few or no role models to emulate. Rather, they are surrounded by other poor people, holding poverty in common.[36]

LOWER-CLASS STUDENTS AND EDUCATIONAL ACHIEVEMENT

We have experienced a plethora of educational reform reports. They call for a multilateral war on mediocrity at all levels of public and higher education. Some of the reports are outward statements of opinion with little supportive data. Others reflect careful collection and analyses of data. All hold in common the belief that schools, colleges, and universities have succumbed to mediocrity and that the solution exists with academic reform (see Adler, *The Paideia Proposal;*[37] Boyer, *High School: A Report on Secondary Education in America;*[38] Goodlad, *A Place Called School;*[39] National Committee on Excellence in Education, *A Nation at Risk*[40]).

The reports emphasize academic reform for the benefit of all students eschewing the issues of cultural differences, institutional racism and sexism, and poverty. Will the academic reform movement affect lower-class and minority youth negatively? The academic records of African American, Hispanic, Native American and lower-class White students, when compared to their middle-class peers, generally fall below expected norms. The reasons for the disparity have been attributed to such factors as cultural and linguistic differences, institutional racism, and poverty. Academic reform need not have a negative impact on minority and lower-class youth. Rather, the hope is that the reform movement will elevate the academic performance of all students.

That lower-class students do not do well in schools is not new. The revisionist critique of American public education describes the schools as sorting machines which perpetuate the nation's social class structure. Screening practices such as ability grouping and tracking that place lower-class students in low academic ability classes or groups serve to destine lower-class students to blue-collar vocations and middle-class students to white-collar professions (see

Greer, *The Great School Legend;*[41] Katz, *Class, Bureaucracy and the Schools;*[42] Bowles and Gintis, *Schooling in Capitalistic America*[43]).

Another perspective places blame on the lower-class student's "poverty culture." The *culture of poverty* concept was developed by anthropologist Oscar Lewis. After conducting extensive ethnographic studies of lower-class people, he identified attitudes and values developed by poor people to adapt to their impoverished conditions, such as ". . . feelings of not belonging, marginality . . . and the feeling that the institutions of the larger society are not there to serve the interests of these people."[44] Using the culture of poverty as an explanation, educators assume that the poverty culture of lower-class students inhibits their ability to take advantage of school opportunities. From this belief, the lower-class students do not perceive schools as acting in their best interests; the students are not willing to delay gratification for a job and salary until after graduation. Hence, they drop out of school. The notion encouraged some educators to take the attitude that nothing could be done for lower-class students.

The culture of poverty concept has been examined and evaluated by social scientists.[45] Empirically, parts of the concept proved to be untrue for most people. Theoretically, the concept tended to blame the poor for being poor, a new form of the old argument that "poor people are lazy and that is why they are poor" (Wilson, *The Truly Disadvantaged: The Inner City, the Underclass, and Public Policy*[46]). The attacks on the concept did not deny the existence of poverty and its effects upon the education of some lower-class youth. The circumstances of impoverished parents can debilitate their ability to provide their children with an appropriate academic support system at home.

What are the data on lower-class people? U.S. Bureau of the Census figures[47] show that in 1983 poverty was not distributed evenly among the population. Whites constituted the highest number of poor people, approximately 24 million, while Blacks constituted only 9.9 million. The 24 million poor White population equals 12.2 percent of the total White population, but 9.9 million poor Blacks equals 34 percent of the total Black population. Figures on Hispanics indicate a similar pattern; 27 percent of the total Hispanic population are poor. Poor people live primarily in rural areas with about one-fourth of the nation's population living in rural areas. Last, the majority of breadwinners from poor families work full- or part-time and are not perennial recipients of unemployment compensation.[48] The U.S. Census data reveal that the highest number of poor people are White, but poverty is distributed highest among racial minority groups, including Asians and Native Americans. Poor people are distributed highest in rural areas, and the majority of poor people work for a living.

Lower class students reflect the broader demographic pattern. The greatest number of lower-class students are White, but poverty is distributed highest among racial minority students. Further, lower-class students drop out of school at a much higher rate than their middle-class peers. According to surveys conducted by the National Center for Educational Statistics,[49] 22 percent of lower-class students compared to approximately 11 percent of the middle-class student population, i.e., twice as many lower-class students compared to the middle class drop out of school. But the dropout rate is distributed unevenly with a disproportionate percentage of dropouts comprising lower-class minority students. By race, 13 percent of the dropouts are White, 17 percent are African American, 19 percent are Hispanic, and 22 percent are Native American, and 26.5 percent are Southeast Asian students.[50] Another demographic trend: racial minority students are concentrated in urban areas (Native Americans are the exception) while lower-class Whites are distributed in both rural and urban areas. There exists at least 27 major urban school districts in which non-White students comprise the majority of the student population. Yet, the problem of poverty in American life and the challenges for public schools to serve the children of the working poor are not racial or ethnic problems. They are human problems that affect every racial and ethnic group. They are problems that must be solved.

Rumberger[51] examined a large body of data regarding why students drop out of school. The primary reasons the students reported for dropping out of school were school-related, such as poor performance or reading difficulties. Personal reasons were second, such as being pregnant or getting married. The least-cited reasons for dropping out of school were economic, such as needing a job to help the family. In an earlier study *High School and Beyond*,[52] the National Center for Educational Statistics reported correspondent reasons. In both studies, lower-class students rarely dropped out of school for economic reasons. Neill[53] reported that the dropouts in his study were usually one or two years below grade level in reading and mathematics. Academic deficiencies were cited as the primary reasons for dropping out. More than a third of the dropouts blamed their own grades or dislike of school. Only one in five dropped out because they could not get along with their teachers and only 13 percent were expelled.

Lower-class students, African Americans, Hispanics, Whites, were disproportionately represented among the dropouts. Overall, these students made lower grades in school (when compared to their middle-class peers), scored lower on standardized tests, completed less homework, and created more discipline problems in school. The dropouts came from homes with parents who both worked and who were less involved in both the out-of-school and in-school activities of their children. Some dropouts were from single-parent families.

Why do lower-class students experience academic difficulties in school? What follows are five explanations that describe causes for the poor academic performance of lower-class students. Each explanation has a data base, but the empirical research on the impact of poverty on academic achievement is meager. Much more empirical research is needed so that educators can reduce, if not eliminate, the negative effects of poverty on academic achievement.

1. Stigma of Poverty. This is a social interaction explanation that operates between members of an in-group (the haves) and members of an out-group (the have-nots). A *stigma*[54] is an attitude held by members of an in-group that members of an out-group are not quite normal, that is, the stigmatized person is perceived as being "not quite human." The effect of being stigmatized is that the stigmatized persons often believe the stigma to be true. Or, the stigmatized persons believe that they have the "not quite human" features attributed to them. Lower-class children are easily identified in elementary grades by their clothing, their grammatical usage, and lack of familiarity with such things as colors and shapes. Teachers, who may pity or dislike these "not-quite-normal" students, will protect the lower-class children from embarrassment by not asking them to recite, waiting less time for them to answer questions, or paying less attention to their answers.[55] This type of interaction between the teacher and lower-class students conveys an attitude that lower-class students are not as bright compared to their middle-class peers. When students internalize the stigma, they believe that, in fact, they are not as bright; they develop a low academic self-concept which triggers a self-fulfilling prophecy (see Chapter 5 for a description of the self-fulfilling prophecy). The stigma of poverty—that lower-class students are not quite normal academically—when believed by teachers and students alike causes the lower-class students to think of their academic abilities as not quite normal epitomized in the convoluted logic: "Poor folks ain't smart, that's why they's poor."

This is a problem of teacher prejudice compounded by other social forces that teach lower-class students that they are not quite as capable as others. As facile as this may sound, teachers must not allow their own biases regarding lower-class people to influence their interactions with lower-class students. Teachers need to be on guard for any manifestations of social class prejudices in their classes (see Chapter 5 for a discussion of elitism and classroom interaction).

2. *Learned Helplessness.* This is a conditioning theory referring to the negative feedback that teachers give to lower-class students. Studies[56] have been conducted (with dogs as well as humans) in which the subjects were given goals to achieve. As they attempted to achieve the goals, the subjects were frustrated so that goal achievement was not possible. Eventually, the subjects would "give up" in their attempts to achieve the goals. They had been conditioned to be helpless. Under this theory, lower-class students who continually experience failure in school, "give up" in their efforts to learn. Continually frustrated by lack of academic achievement, they lose their motivation to try harder. They have been conditioned to fail and helplessly accept failure as normal to them.

Instructional approaches that continually frustrate lower-class students must be discontinued. John Dewey's notion that children learn through their experiences upon which they build and transform into even newer experiences provides nonfrustrating instructional bases. Simply put, teachers need to build upon the experiences that lower-class children bring to class rather than decry the fact that lower-class children may not exhibit the experiential backgrounds of middle-class students.

3. *Resistance Culture.* This is a social interaction theory in which the out-group (lower-class students) rejects the in-group's culture as a means of self-preservation. In schools, the theory refers to the phenomenon Ogbu[57] calls "acting White" in which lower-class Black and Native American students be-

lieve that "making it" in school requires them to act White, i.e., speak standard English, cooperate with teachers, and make good grades. The price of acting White is costly: the loss of lower-class minority identity as well as abandonment by other lower-class minority students. The Resistance Culture is based on an attitude that high academic achievement is synonymous with being middle class and White. By resisting what the school has to offer, lower-class minority students retain their identities and group affiliation. A study by Willis[58] reports similar Resistance Culture behavior by lower-class White, English boys. The "lads," a name they call themselves, perceive high grades, speaking the Queen's English, and cooperating with teachers as a threat to their identities. As a youngster in school, I recall similar pressures from a few Hispanic peers who felt that I was "abandoning the fold" especially since I liked acting in plays. What the Ogbu and Willis studies imply is that some lower-class students are waging a social class battle in the schools, a battle that will be won by the middle class.

Here the students see the school as their enemy. Teachers and principals cannot address the Resistance Culture alone. They should seek the help of community persons who have "made it." Ask these persons to visit the school to discuss with students how "making it" in life is much like "making it" in school. The idea here is to reduce the perception that schools are only for middle-class Whites, and that lower-class students can use what schools have to offer to "make it." This approach was the basic thrust of Operation PUSH led by the Reverend Jesse Jackson in the 1970s.

4. *Academic Socialization.* An instructional process theory, Academic Socialization refers to differential instruction for lower- and middle-class students. Anyon[59] reported in her study of instructional approaches used in lower-, middle-, and upper-income middle schools that teachers teach the same subjects to all the students but that lower-class students are taught to consume (memorize) knowledge while the middle- and upper-income students are taught to think (process) with the knowledge. Under this theory, lower-class students are academically socialized to be passive consumers of purportedly static knowledge. Middle- and upper-income students are socialized to be active users of purportedly dynamic knowledge, i.e., middle- and upper-income students are taught how to use knowledge to draw inferences and make decisions while the lower-class students (with the same knowledge) are programmed merely to receive the knowledge without learning how to manipulate it. Consequently, the academic socialization of lower-class students prepares them to be passive, docile workers; the academic socialization of middle- and upper-income students prepares them to be active, initiating managers, thereby perpetuating the community's social class stratification. I have always been surprised to hear of the "higher-level thinking skills" that are taught in classes for the gifted and talented students mostly because these same skills were always a part of the regular activities in all of my English composition courses regardless of the student's giftedness or lack of it.

Here teachers need to strive toward the same goal for all students—critical thinking. Lower-class students, as well as all others, need to be taught how to use knowledge to draw inferences, make predictions, and reach conclusions that are rationally sound. Teachers should strive for full literacy at three levels. (See Chapter 8 for a discussion of Language Education.)

a. Functional literacy refers to the ability to speak, read, and write standard English; this includes the ability to read basic technical literature which entails an understanding of rudimentary mathematics and science concepts.

b. Cultural literacy refers to an expansion of functional literacy; it refers to a knowledge of the literature, history, and grand traditions of the culture of the United States, including major scientific accomplishments. It also refers to knowledge about a person's ethnic or cultural heritage. While it is important that students know the details of the core U.S. culture, it is equally important that they know the details of their ethnic or cultural heritage. The latter should not be sacrificed in the name of "assimilation" or "Americanization" ideologies.

c. Critical literacy, the highest form of literacy, refers to the ability to think critically and creatively. Specific abilities here are the abilities to analyze, synthesize, and evaluate what one hears and reads as well as the abilities to use data and knowledge (scientific, mathematic, literary, historical) for purposes of making inferences, predicting outcomes, and drawing valid conclusions. Teachers should resist the notion that critical literacy is the province of gifted students only.

5. *Lower-Class Home Environment.* This is the oldest of explanations for the poor academic achievement of lower-class students.[60] It refers to the inability of lower-class parents to provide adequate reinforcement and academic support for their children at home. When both parents work (or the one parent in a single-parent home) parental quality time spent at home with the children may be minimal.

The stereotypic, middle-class home environment with plenty of reading materials, with parents who read to their children, and where children develop study habits reinforced by parents (who are involved in what the children are studying) may not characterize the lower-class home. Some lower-class students may go home from school to an environment where there are no parents present (latchkey kids) or where parents are too tired or feel inadequate to help their children with schoolwork. It's highly possible that the children are not told as many bedtime stories nor are they "read to" by their tired parents. Often, because the parents may have unpleasant memories about their own school experience, they may not provide altogether positive encouragement about school to their children. As the children grow older and they experience one or more of the above explanations—stigma of poverty, learned helplessness, resistance culture, academic socialization—they may develop an attitude that school learning is of little consequence.

These explanations require that teachers and principals work with parents of lower-class students. The parents need to be taught how they can provide their children with an academic support base at home. Such a base will require that the parents allocate a certain amount of time to discuss with their children various aspects of schoolwork. Primarily, parents can be taught activities such as using television viewing for creative and critical thinking or responding to their children's homework in a supportive and authentic manner. (Further suggestions for working with parents are given at the end of this section.)

The above explanations do not address the physical and psychological effects of poverty. Students who do not have enough food to eat, or whose diet is not wholesome, will not function normally in school. Also, students whose day-to-day experience is tentative due to their parents' low wages, unemployment, or domestic strife, cannot function normally in school. The explanations do shed light on a socialization process that leads to academic failure and its consequences, dropping out.

What probably happens to dropouts begins in the elementary grades where they are not able or simply do not keep pace with other students. No doubt their academic disparity is known to teachers and principals. When the dropouts move to junior high or the middle school, the disparity should become more pronounced as students are scheduled into classes that are formally or informally tracked by ability. Again, the students' academic disparity is known to teachers and principals. By the time the dropouts reach the upper grades, their academic deficiencies become sources of frustration, anxiety, and embarrassment. Trapped in what must be an academic whirlpool pulling them deeper into academic failure, the students may elect to resist learning (resistant culture) or give up on learning (learned helplessness); either choice is self-defeating. Teachers in elementary schools located in lower-class neighborhoods should be assisted with the identification of potential dropouts. Also, teachers in these schools should be made aware of social class biases which may cause them to lower their expectations for lower-class students. Teachers and principals have, at times, been known to lower their academic expectations for lower-class students which then triggers a self-fulfilling prophecy.[61] By expecting less from lower-class students, teachers actually get less out of the students. Lower expectations can trigger lower performance, which if repeated throughout the elementary grades, will produce students who in fact perform at a lower academic level than their middle-class peers.

Parents of at-risk students can be trained to provide in-home academic support for their children. They can be taught to use such devices as reading the student's homework, writing comments on it to the teacher, sending the comments with the homework to the teacher who then returns the parents' comments with the teacher's added comments, establishing a home-school dialogue. Parents can be taught to use television watching as a tool to teach analytical and reflective thinking. Parents can watch with their children situation comedies or dramas; then parents can query the children about the program's basic theme (thesis), conflict, and conflict resolution. Commercials can be used to discuss persuasive techniques. And, with some creativity, basic mathematics lessons could be devised! These suggestions are based on the data that the parents of dropouts often do not feel adequate to provide an academic support system for their children at home. Basically, the parents can be taught how to develop such a support system. At-risk students deserve a system of individualized planning much like the IEP (Individualized Educational Plan) used for handicapped students. The IEP specifies an individualized educational program complete with goals, objectives, and evaluation approaches; parents are involved in making the plan, modifying it, and monitoring it.

HANDICAPPING CONDITIONS AND SPECIAL NEEDS STUDENTS

Individuals who experience handicapping conditions in their lives that require special or unique educational attention have always existed. Their existence has been begrudgingly acknowledged in spite of the fact that handicapped individuals from all the sociocultural categories discussed in this chapter—ethnic, gender, religious, and social class groups—have always existed. In general, handicapped individuals have experienced the poor relative treatment, i.e., handicapped individuals have been shut away from the view of society so that awareness of them emerged only as awareness of their institutionalization manifested itself.[62] Passage of P.L. 94–142: Education for all Handicapped Children in 1975 did much to heighten awareness of the special needs of handicapped students. As discussed in Chapter 3, handicapped students are entitled to equal educational opportunities within the least restrictive environments.

Who are the special needs or handicapped students? And how many currently attend school? Students labelled as *exceptional* are students whose learning abilities or physical attributes are not within the normal range of students and require an individualized education program. *Disabilities* or *handicaps* are reduced bodily or mental functions or losses of bodily parts which serve to hinder the student's efforts to learn in the classroom. While all students differ as individuals due to such factors as social class, ethnicity, religiosity, and gender, handicapped students differ in ways that schools typically are not prepared to treat. Schools are structured, and teachers are trained to provide educational experiences to normal students. *Normal* here refers to students who fall into the middle range of a broadly based norm. On a bell-shaped curve, most students would fit somewhere in the middle range of the curve, but some students fall at either extreme of the bell-shaped curve. These students are labelled as *exceptional;* they consist of students who are intellectually gifted and require specially enriched educational programs as well as students who are physically or intellectually disabled and require specially designed educational programs. The latter students, the physically or intellectually disabled, experience a physical or cognitive impairment which limits the students' ability to function within the normal context of a classroom. These students are not handicapped, as such, unless their disability creates problems that limit their ability to take advantage of the educational experiences within a normal classroom. For example, I have had students who were totally deaf, but because of their ability to read lips, these hearing impaired students functioned quite well in my classroom, setting the curve in some classes. It was only later that I discovered they were hearing impaired. Of course, had these students experienced difficulty reading my lips, for any reason, they would have been handicapped. In other words, the environment may serve to handicap students making critical the identification of students who are disabled so that teachers and the environments they create do not serve to handicap the disabled student.

How many disabled students currently attend school? The question defies an answer because of the differing criteria used by the federal and state governments as well as the criteria used by many schools. According to the U.S. Department of Education's Office of Special Education and Rehabilitation Services, the following data describe students served in special education programs during the 1984–1985 school year:

- 90% of all students in special education programs are "mildly" handicapped;
- "Mental retardation" (16%), "learning disabilities" (42%), "speech and language impairments" (26%) are the three largest categories of students treated in special education programs;
- 4.3 million students, ages 3–21, received instruction through special education programs, which is about 11% of the total school population in the United States.[63]

Identification of disabled students is a complex procedure that should be highly individualized. The effects of labelling a student as "handicapped" or as a "special needs" student can be extremely debilitating or unproductive depending upon how the identification process is handled. (See Chapter 5, subsection on handicapping conditions and stereotyping for discussion on the effects of labelling.) Current practices require a team effort for identification of handicapped or special needs students; identification teams consist of regular and special education teachers, school psychologists and other trained specialists, principals, and parents of the students under review.[64] Categories of educational handicaps are: (1) behavioral and emotional disorders, (2) hearing impairments and visual impairments, (3) learning disabilities, (4) mental retardation, (5) speech and language disorders, (6) other—multiply handicapped, physical or health impairments, severe disorders.[65] The six categories are broadly conceived; the identification team looks for the specific conditions that cause a particular student to be handicapped within a regular classroom environment. Once the specific handicapping conditions have been identified, then the team must assign an IEP (Individualized Educational Plan) that focuses on approaches to ameliorate the specific handicapping conditions as identified. The IEP must be implemented in the least restrictive environment, which means that in most cases, the IEP should be implemented within the regular classroom.

SUMMARY

Culture is central to all human activities, including learning. Acknowledging that all students have a valid culture places emphasis on the notion that all students are learning beings who have learned and will continue to learn a culture. As such, all students are educable. A student's culture provides a means to function within different groups and in the greater society. While culture is not innate or inborn, it is learned and transmitted so unconsciously that students consider their culture as the "natural" way of perceiving and believing. Students learn their cultures within a circular socialization process. As they are learning their cultures, they are forming self-concepts. Through a multiplicity of references—ethnicity, gender, handicaps, race, religiosity, and social class—they are informed of the options available to them for the formation of their self-concepts and their unique rendition of a culture. As adolescents, and later adults, they can be empowered to use their self-concepts to change their culture when it does not enhance their survival. The power to change one's culture—self-efficacy—is the voice students have by which they can influence their fates. While none of us are ever the complete masters of our destinies, we at least can have a say about our destinies if we know that our individualized cultures are transmutable. Social interaction forces within the social milieu into which one is born, reared, and thrust also influence the formation of self-concept. These are the forces of ethnocentrism and other pernicious isms, which are the subject of the next chapter.

STUDY QUESTIONS

1. Compare and contrast the elements of the concepts of: (a) culture and (b) ethnic group membership. Explain why the elements are so similar.

2. Define the following key concepts: folkways, mores, norms. Connect them to the notion of "tolerable deviation." Then fill in the following questionnaire. Keep in mind that it is not a valid measure of anything, but that your responses (individually or as a group) can be used as a point of discussion regarding norms and the principle of tolerable deviation. As you discuss each question, you may need to look ahead to the next chapter for definitions of ethnocentrism and stereotyping and look back to Chapter 1 for a definition of cultural relativism.

   Answer questions 1–14 as follows: 1 = strongly agree; 2 = agree; 3 = neither agree nor disagree; 4 = disagree; 5 = strongly disagree.

    1. Swearing in public school classrooms should be prohibited._____
    2. Students with body odor are unclean._____
    3. Unwanted pregnancies should not be aborted._____
    4. Interracial marriages (Black/White) usually end in divorce._____
    5. Cohabitation is an acceptable alternative to marriage._____
    6. There are more male than female scientists due to innate intellectual differences between the sexes._____
    7. People with strong religious convictions make good marriage partners._____
    8. I would feel uncomfortable if a member of my gender made a sexual advance toward me._____
    9. Single parent status should be limited to females only._____
    10. Political extremists (e.g., John Birchers or Marxists) should not be allowed to teach in the public schools._____
    11. People with body odor are unhealthy._____

12. Surrogate mothers have no rights to the children they bear as surrogates.

Now that you've answered the questions, analyze each to get an idea about which topics you are open-minded about (cultural relativity?), closed-minded about (ethnocentrism?), and which you have a "I can take it or leave it" attitude (tolerable deviation?). Then discuss your analysis with classmates, if you are comfortable discussing these topics in public.

3. Describe the basic processes involved in (1) self-concept formation and the looking-glass self, and (2) gender-role identity and self-efficacy.

4. "Folkways are stronger than legalways" is a generalization that can apply to teaching in a pluralistic society. Read the following incident which is based on an actual situation. Then discuss the questions listed and any other issues that arise as you discuss the incident.

> The following is a true incident (names are fictional):
>
> Ms. Fonda Henderson was a successful fourth-grade teacher in Mite Elementary School. She had taught for two years at Mite. In January of her second year, she attended a pro-abortion rally held in Chicago. Several photographs of the rally were published in local newspapers. Ms. Henderson could be identified in the photographs. In April of that year, Ms. Henderson was told by the school board that her contract to teach for the next year would not be renewed. They believed that "she was an inappropriate role model for young children, as evident with her attendance at pro-abortion rallies." In most states, tenured teachers can be dismissed on grounds of immorality, incompetence, or breach of contract which the school board must demonstrate. Nontenured teachers have less legal protection from dismissal. Ms. Henderson was not rehired.

Discussion:

(a) What assumptions did the school board make about Ms. Henderson's attendance at the rally? Since they may have been operating from an implicit level of culture, what might be their "schemata" regarding the rally?

(b) If Ms. Henderson's behavior was triggered by implicit assumptions she held, discuss what some of those assumptions might be.

(c) Discuss which was more potent: legalways or folkways. Then discuss how beginning teachers might deal with any conflicts between legalways and folkways.

NOTES

1. Talcott Parsons. *The Structure of Social Action.* New York: McGraw-Hill, 1937, pp. 27–36.
2. Ralph Linton. *The Cultural Background of Personality.* New York: Prentice-Hall, 1945, p. 30.
3. Al Kroeber and Clyde Kluckhohn. *Culture, A Critical Review of Concepts and Definitions.* Cambridge, Mass.: Peabody Museum of American Archeology, 1952.
4. E. B. Tylor, quoted in Kroeber and Kluckhohn, *Culture,* p. 43.
5. Ruth Benedict, quoted in Kroeber and Kluckhohn, *Culture,* p. 43.
6. Robert A. Baron and Donn Byrne. *Social Psychology: Understanding Human Interaction,* 4th Ed. Boston: Allyn & Bacon, 1984, p. 89.

7. Franz Boas, *The Mind of Primitive Man*. New York: Macmillan, 1938, p. 159.
8. Janet Catro. "Untapped Verbal Fluency of Black School Children," in Eleanor Leacock, ed., *The Culture of Poverty, A Critique*. New York: Simon and Schuster, 1971; see also, Martha Word. *Them Children: A Study in Language Learning*. New York: Holt, Rinehart and Winston, 1971.
9. W. Labov. "The Logic of Nonstandard English." In F. Williams, ed., *Language and Poverty*. Chicago: Markham, 1970, pp. 153–189.
10. J. Baratz. *Language Abilities of Black Americans—Review of Research: 1966–1970*. Unpublished manuscript, Washington, D.C.: Education Study Center, 1973.
11. Ricardo Garcia. *Identification and Comparison of Oral English Syntactic Patterns of Spanish-English Speaking Hispanos*. Unpublished dissertation, University of Denver, 1973; see also, Carolyn Kessler. *The Acquisition of Syntax in Bilingual Children*. Washington, D.C.: Georgetown University Press, 1971.
12. Kenneth B. Clark. *Prejudice and Your Child*. Boston: Beacon Press, 1962, pp. 29–31.
13. Charles Cooley, "Looking-Glass Self" in Jerome Manis and Bernard Meltzer, *Symbolic Interaction*, 2nd Ed., Boston: Allyn & Bacon, 1967, pp. 231–234.
14. John W. Kinch, "A Formalized Theory of the Self Concept," in Jerome G. Manis & Bernard W. Meltzer, eds., *Symbolic Interaction*, Boston: Allyn & Bacon, 1972, pp. 245–252.
15. Albert Bandura. "Self-Efficacy Mechanism in Human Agency." *American Psychologist*, 37, 2, February 1982, pp. 122–147.
16. Jack Forbes. "Teaching Native American Values and Cultures," in James Banks, *Teaching Ethnic Studies*. Washington, D.C.: National Council for the Social Studies, 1973, pp. 201–205.
17. Kenneth Clark, *Dark Ghetto*, New York: Harper & Row, 1965, p. 64.
18. J. A. Momeni. *Demography of Racial and Ethnic Minorities in the United States*. Westport, CT.: Greenwood Press, 1984.
19. *Encyclopedia of American Ethnic Groups*. Cambridge: Harvard University Press, 1975, p. vi.
20. James Banks and Geneva Gay. "Ethnicity in Contemporary American Society: Toward the Development of a Typology," *Ethnicity*, 1978, 5: 244.
21. E. E. Maccoby and C. N. Jacklin. *The Psychology of Sex Differences*. Stanford, CA: Stanford University Press, 1974.
22. Maccoby and Jacklin, *The Psychology of Sex Differences*.
23. Edward O. Wilson. *On Human Nature*, New York: Bantam Books, 1979, pp. 133.
24. Lawrence Kohlberg, "A Cognitive-Developmental Analysis of Children's Sex-Role Concepts and Attitudes," in E. E. Maccoby and C. N. Jacklin, *The Psychology of Sex Differences*, 1974.
25. Alice S. Honig, "Sex Role Socialization in Early Childhood," *Young Children*, September 1983, p. 59.
26. N. Eisenberg, "Social Development," *The Child: Development in a Social Context*, ed. C. B. Kopp and J. B. Krahow, Reading, Mass.: Addison-Wesley, 1982, pp. 226.
27. Patricia Draper, "!Kung Women: Contrasts in Sexual Egalitarianism in Foraging and Sedentary Contexts," in Rayna Reiter, ed. *Toward an Anthropology of Women*, New York: Monthly Review Press, 1975, pp. 283–308.
28. Emile Durkheim. *The Elementary Forms of the Religious Life*. New York: Collier Books, 1961.
29. Gerhard Lanski. *The Religious Factor*. Garden City, NY: Doubleday, 1963.

30. Will Herberg. *Protestant-Catholic-Jew*. Garden City, NY: Anchor Books, 1960, p. 87.
31. Herberg, p. 87.
32. James R. Kluegal. "Denominational Mobility: Correct Patterns and Recent Trends," *Journal for the Scientific Study of Religion*, 19 (1980) 26–39.
33. Reported in the U.S. Bureau of the Census Statistical Abstract of the United States, 1986, 106th Edition. Washington, D.C.: U.S. Government Printing Office, p. 50.
34. *Monthly Labor Review*, September 1984, p. 63.
35. Clark Kerr. "Giving Youth a Better Chance: Options for Education, Work, Service." *A Report of the Carnegie Foundation for the Advancement of Teaching*. Berkeley, CA, November 1979.
36. Wilson, Julius. *The Declining Significance of Race*. Chicago: University of Chicago Press, 1980, pp. 156–158; see also, Robert H. Lauer. *Social Problems and the Quality of Life*. Dubuque, Iowa: Wm. C. Brown, 1986, pp. 257–262.
37. Adler, Mortimer. *The Paideia Proposal: An Educational Manifesto*. New York: Macmillan, 1982.
38. Boyer, Ernest. *High School: A Report on Secondary Education in America*. Boston: Houghton Mifflin, 1984.
39. Goodlad, John. *A Place Called School*. New York: McGraw-Hill, 1984.
40. National Commission on Excellence in Education. *A Nation at Risk: The Imperative for Educational Reform*. Washington, D.C.: U.S. Government Printing Office, 1983.
41. Greer, Colin. *The Great School Legend*. New York: Basic Books, 1972.
42. Katz, Michael. *Class, Bureaucracy and the Schools*. New York: Praeger, 1976.
43. Bowles, Samuel and Gintis, Herbert. *Schooling in Capitalist America*. New York: Basic Books, 1976.
44. Lewis, Oscar. "A Puerto Rican Boy." In *Culture Change, Mental Health, and Poverty*. J. C. Finney, ed. New York: Simon & Schuster, 1969, pp. 149–154.
45. Valentine, Charles A. *Culture and Poverty*. Chicago: University of Chicago Press, 1968.
46. Wilson, Julius. *The Truly Disadvantaged: The Inner City, the Underclass, and Public Policy*. Chicago: University of Chicago Press, 1987.
47. U.S. Bureau of the Census. *Current Population Reports*. Washington, D.C.: U.S. Government Printing Office, 1984, p. 3.
48. ———. *Statistical Abstracts of the U.S.* Washington, D.C.: U.S. Government Printing Office, 1984, p. 476.
49. National Center for Educational Statistics. *Percentage of Students Who Drop Out of School By Race, Ethnicity, and Socio-Economic Status*. Washington, D.C.: U.S. Government Printing Office, 1985.
50. David Brand. "The New Whiz Kids," *Time*, August 31, 1987, p. 49.
51. Rumberger, William. "High School Dropouts: A Review of Issues and Evidence." *Review of Educational Research*, 57, 1987, pp. 101–121; see also, Calabrese, Raymond. "The Structure of Schooling and Minority Dropout Rates." *The Clearing House*, 61, 1988, pp. 325–328.
52. National Center of Educational Statistics. *High School and Beyond*, 93–221b. Washington, D.C.: U.S. Government Printing Office, 1985.
53. S. B. Neill. *Keeping Students in School: Problems and Solutions*. Arlington, Va.: American Association of School Administrators, 1979, p. 31.

54. Erving Goffman. *Stigma*. Englewood Cliffs, N.J.: Prentice-Hall, 1963, p. 5.

55. Thomas Good. "Which Pupils Do Teachers Call On?" *Elementary School Journal*. January 1970, pp. 190–198.

56. Martin E. P. Seligman. *Helplessness: On Depression, Development, and Death*. San Francisco: W. H. Freeman, 1975.

57. John Ogbu. "Class Stratification, Racial Stratification, and Schooling," in L. Weis (Ed.), *Race, Class, and Schooling*. 17, 1986. Special Studies in Comparative Education, Faculty of Educational Studies, State University of New York at Buffalo, p. 22.

58. Paul Willis, *Learning to Labor*. Lexington: D. C. Heath, 1977.

59. Jean Anyon. "Social Class and the Hidden Curriculum of Work." *Journal of Education*, 162, 1, Winter 1980, pp. 67–92.

60. Daniel Levine and Robert J. Havighurst. *Society and Education*. 7th Ed. Boston: Allyn & Bacon, 1989, p. 262.

61. H. M. Cooper and T. Good. *Pygmalion Grows Up: Studies in the Expectation Communication Process*. New York: Longman, 1983; see also, J. E. Brophy and T. Good, "Teacher's Communication of Differential Expectations for Children's Classroom Performance." *Journal of Educational Psychology*, 61, 1970, pp. 365–374.

62. B. Blatt and Fred Kaplan. *Christmas in Purgatory: A Photographic Essay on Mental Retardation*. Boston: Allyn & Bacon, 1966.

63. U.S. Office of Special Education and Rehabilitation. *Eighth Annual Report to Congress for the School Year, 1984–1985*. Washington, D.C.: U.S. Government Printing Office, 1986.

64. R. L. Burgdorf. *The Legal Rights of Handicapped Persons*. Baltimore: Brookes Publishers, 1980.

65. William L. Heward and Michael D. Orlansky. *Exceptional Children*, 3rd Ed. Columbus: Merrill, 1988, p. 4.

Chapter 5

Ethnocentrisms: Causes, Consequences, Prescriptions

Key Terms:

cultural pride
cultural degradation
cultural chauvinism
elitism
handicapism

ethnocentrism
stereotyping
self-fulfilling prophecy
racism
sexism

If students acquire their culture in their homes, communities, and schools, where do they acquire biases and stereotypes about different kinds of people?

Students acquire their biases through the attitudes of their parents and siblings as well as the prevailing attitudes expressed in their communities and schools. Most teachers do not consciously teach biases against ethnic minority, female, handicapped, or lower-class students. Rather, they may fail to counter the biases that penetrate their classroom walls, biases endemic to U.S. communal living. This chapter describes the sociocultural forces of ethnocentrism and its chauvinistic manifestations: elitism, racism, sexism, and stereotyping based on culture, race, social class, gender, and handicapping conditions which are linked to the self-fulfilling prophecy. The intent is to clarify ethnocentrism and its manifestations as they are common in American communal living but are not often understood and discussed in reference to teaching and learning.

ETHNOCENTRISM AND CULTURAL RELATIVISM

The *raison d'être* of cultural relativism in the classroom is to allow students to benefit equally from the schooling experience irrespective of their backgrounds. It is now axiomatic that ethnic minority and lower-class students do not benefit equally from public schooling when their academic success rates are compared to those of middle-class students; this can be attributed in part to the strong middle-class bias of most U.S. public schools. We find that cultural relativism alone is not enough. Its effects can be neutralized by extreme forms of ethnocentrism—racism, sexism, stereotyping, discrimination—that occurs outside the classroom, especially if they are allowed to slip into the classroom through unconscious attitudes and beliefs of teachers, other educators, and students. To proactively counter these extreme forms of ethnocentrism, educators need to understand not only the nature but also the types of ethnocentrisms that can be dealt with in the public school classroom.

Extreme ethnocentrisms are unpleasant realities. They take their toll in the daily conflicts of intergroup, interethnic relations of American society. Racism, sexism, stereotyping, elitism are loaded with negative connotations; in ostensibly polite company, these negative social phenomena are not discussed, but this only serves to intensify their tenacity. Therefore, it is critical that we discuss the terms from as objective as possible a point of view. Admittedly, objectivity is not easy. I will define the terms broadly and then discuss each as pertinent to group relations in American communal life.

ETHNOCENTRISM, CULTURAL PRIDE, CHAUVINISM, AND DEGRADATION

The universal attitude of pride in one's own ethnic or cultural group is known as *ethnocentrism*. Ethnocentrism serves the function of providing a group with solidarity and unity. An ethnic or cultural group is solidified by a pervading sense of peoplehood, as in the phrase "We, the People," of the Constitution. The sense of peoplehood is felt with differing degrees of intensity by its members. As such, ethnocentrism is a dynamic social force that can be cohesive or corrosive in a society. When ethnocentrism causes bigotry and intolerance, or whenever ethnocentrism causes alienation and social dejection, it is corrosive; whenever it causes group and individual self-esteem, it is cohesive.

Ethnocentrism appears within a society in at least three variegated forms which can be placed on a continuum (Figure 5.1). The ethnocentrism contin-

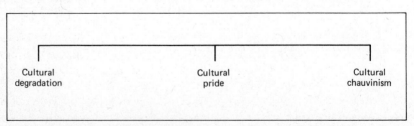

Figure 5.1 Degrees of ethnocentrism

uum ranges between two extremes with a center. The two extremes are anti-social and destructive; the center is socially cohesive and constructive.

Cultural pride pertains to the satisfaction people take in their ancestral, cultural heritage as well as their current group affiliation, whatever that group might be: a nationality, an occupational group, a religious denomination, an ethnic group. For example, in many western states people take great pride in the many generations they have homesteaded and worked a ranch. And cultural pride pertains to the much maligned virtue of love of country expressed by singing its anthems and celebrating its holidays.

Cultural pride is a positive form of ethnocentrism. In this context, cultural pride refers to self-respect or self-esteem for one's ethnic or cultural heritage. It is necessary for positive group identity and is essential to group solidarity. It is also helpful in the development of positive self-identity for individual group members. When group members are allowed to grow in the awareness that their group has a rich heritage reaching back over centuries of cultural development, they can experience a sense of roots in the past and continuity in the present. By taking pride in their group's heritage, the members can develop self-esteem, and they can continue acting within their group's tradition to contribute to the overall society.

Ethnic groups in the United States have been allowed to develop cultural pride so long as the groups have also espoused beliefs in the core national ethos, such as "freedom and justice for all." Knowledgeable of the dual responsibility to country and to ethnic group, ethnic groups have achieved highly commendable wartime records as demonstrated by the World War II crack fighting units of Japanese Americans or the fact that more Mexican Americans have been awarded Congressional Medals of Honor than any other group.

Cultural chauvinism is a negative form of ethnocentrism. As the antonym of cultural pride, cultural chauvinism refers to attitudes of superiority about one's own in-group (ethnic group, nationality, social class, race, religion, gender) and opposing attitudes of inferiority toward other out-groups. This type of group pride is similar to the ancient Greek notion of *hubris*, or pride, that denoted arrogance.

Cultural chauvinism is an antisocial, destructive form of ethnocentrism. During World War II, for example, Japanese Americans were dispossessed of their property, most of their constitutional rights, and imprisoned in concentration camps throughout the interior United States. These people, like many other ordinary citizens, were loyal to the United States government as attested by their excellent combat record in the European theatre during World War II. Justification for this act of cultural chauvinism was the fear that Japanese Americans were plotting against the U.S. government and collaborating with the Japanese government after war had been declared following the Japanese bombing of Pearl Harbor in Hawaii. In 1989, the U.S. Congress officially admitted that the sabotage and collaboration charges were not true and that the U.S. government had been wrong to imprison and confiscate the property of Japanese American citizens.

Cultural degradation is a destructive, corrosive type of ethnocentrism gen-

erally caused by cultural chauvinism, i.e., cultural degradation is usually a reaction or a defense mechanism to cultural chauvinism. Because of such forces
as Americanization movements and discrimination some groups have been
made to feel that their cultures are inadequate, backward, or inferior. When
a group experiences cultural degradation, some of its members respond by
developing low self-esteem and self-rejection. Goodman's[1] study on race
awareness in young people reported that when White and Black children
were asked if they preferred to play with dolls that were colored white or
black, the White children selected the white colored dolls; the Black children, without knowing which color the White children had selected, also selected the white dolls. In short, the Black children rejected the doll that was
the same color as they were, a manifestation of self-rejection caused by cultural degradation.

Often degradation is not caused by deliberate acts of prejudice or discrimination. Sometimes degradation is caused by acts of omission, silence, or in the
case of history-telling, by ignoring the existence of a particular group. While
some group members who experience degradation respond by self-rejection,
others respond by developing hostile attitudes and intolerance toward the
groups who practice cultural chauvinism, furthering intergroup conflict, and at
times, outright violence.

Biases and prejudices usually spring from chauvinism rather than cultural
pride. Cultural pride, while a mild form of ethnocentrism, is necessary for
positive group identity and is essential to cultural group revitalization. Cultural
chauvinism, a corrosive form of ethnocentrism, is not necessary for group
survival and not essential for cultural group revitalization.

The distinction between group pride as a cohesive form of ethnocentrism
and cultural chauvinism and degradation as corrosive forms of ethnocentrism is
made to respond to the often heard accusation that ethnic groups are currently
indulging in "nationalism" and "reverse prejudice." It's true; many white ethnic groups and minority groups are currently attempting to revitalize their
group cultures, and in the attempt are rekindling pride in their cultures. These
revitalization efforts would not now be necessary if the impact and potency of
the Americanization policies that existed in the first half of this century had not
so thoroughly stifled their ethnic-group languages and cultures. In actuality,
ethnic revitalization is perceived by many ethnics as a necessary, human reaction to the excessive cultural chauvinism and degradation precipitated by na-
tivistic U.S. policies and laws during the early twentieth century.

There will be critics who will say that cultural group pride is doublespeak
for chauvinism. My only reply to these critics is that if they had ever experienced great feelings of inferiority because of their ethnicity, or if they had ever
felt the humiliation and economic loss of racial and cultural discrimination,
they, too, would be advocates of their self-esteem. If these critics have never
felt ethnic and racial discrimination, they perhaps can never understand these
words. If they have felt ethnic and racial discrimination, they cannot help but
admit that these words do not adequately express the rage, humiliation, and
indignation caused by cultural chauvinism and degradation.

DISSECTION OF CHAUVINISM

Cultural chauvinism is the attitude that one's in-group culture and people are superior to others and that people from the out-groups are devoid of the traits that make one's in-group purportedly superior. There is a tendency for persons who foster chauvinistic attitudes to perceive members of out-groups as categories of people rather than individuals who may more or less be members of a particular group. In other words, chauvinists are "lumpers"; they lump people into groups and forget that groups are aggregations of individuals. As the term is used here, cultural chauvinism encompasses a number of other isms, such as:

- Elitism: the attitude that one's social class is superior to all other classes; also called "classism";
- Creedism: the attitude that one's religious denomination, or general religious affiliation, is superior to others;
- Handicappism: the attitude that physically or mentally handicapped individuals are "less human" than "normal" people;
- Homophobism: the attitude that homosexual individuals are perverted or mentally ill;
- Racism: the attitude that one's race is superior to other races; because of the resurgence of racism in American life, a case study analysis of racism is presented later in this chapter;
- Sexism: the attitude that one's gender is superior and should dominate the opposite gender;
- Nationalism: the attitude that one's country is superior to others to the extent that its ways should be imposed on other nations;
- Groupism: the miscellaneous ism, includes the attitude of superiority about one's ethnic group, occupational group, etc.

All of the isms have in common an attitude of superiority toward an in-group; each of the isms focuses on a different group, and if the manifestations were attitudes of superiority only, then there would be little to fear. The following is an examination of one form of chauvinism, racism in American life, that reveals much to be feared. Racism, as a manifestation of chauvinism, is an attitude held by some people within some groups rather than "traits" held by all members of a particular group.

RACISM: THE MORAL DILEMMA

The moral dilemma of racism in American life is that Americans have espoused ethical values of human equality while at times practiced unethical beliefs of racial and cultural superiority, thereby contradicting the widely professed values of human equality.

Katz, in a thorough study of racism in American life,[2] concluded that racism exists because of a serious cleavage between White American beliefs and actions; while some White Americans believe in equality and human rights, they act upon racist assumptions about people of color or racial minorities. According to Katz, the moral cleavage between beliefs and actions is rooted in American social, political, and economic history. In short, White racism is endemic to the American experience:

> The reality is: racism exists. It has been a part of the American way of life since the first Whites landed on the continent. Although the United States prides itself on its ideologies about human rights and particularly on its philosophies of freedom and equality, the bleak reality is that, both historically and presently, this country is based on and operates under a doctrine of White racism.[3]

Myriad studies support the Katz thesis. On a national scope, the Myrdal study,[4] the United States Commission on Mental Health Report,[5] and the Kerner Presidential Commission Report[6] all support the thesis.

How could racism evolve in a society based on Judeo-Christian precepts of brotherhood and equality? In *Race and Racism, A Comparative Perspective*,[7] van den Berghe developed the thesis that current racism in the United States exists because of a complex dynamic of group conflict which evolved over a long period of our history. Basically, racism has served an economic function for White groups and individuals who have benefitted from the exploitation of and discrimination against racial minority peoples. While some White Americans have professed a belief in equal opportunities irrespective of race, ethnic, or social class affiliation, they have not practiced these beliefs when their economic interests were advanced through racial and ethnic-group discrimination.

Racism—as does chauvinism—serves the function of providing an in-group defense against other out-groups by building racial group allegiances and maintaining a rigid caste-like system between a powerful, dominant, in-group race and other subordinate, powerless racial out-groups. In the antebellum South a racial caste-like social system evolved as a means for southern plantation owners to dominate Blacks. A myth of White racial superiority and Black racial inferiority evolved to rationalize White dominance. Racism served an economic function in that it provided White southerners beliefs that supported an economic system based on the free slave labor of Blacks.

Racism is the attitude that one racial group is inherently superior to another.[8] Racist attitudes reflect the prevailing norms of a racial in-group toward a racial out-group. When racist attitudes are carried out into behaviors, they result in expressions of ridicule and hate, in acts of exclusion and discrimination, and in genocide against the alleged inferior out-group. An example of biological racism carried to the degree of mass genocide is the Aryan race theory Adolf Hitler described in his autobiography *Mein Kampf*.[9] The theory, and its ideology of Aryan racial superiority, provided Nazi officials with a rationale for exterminating European Jews who were blamed (scapegoat theory) for the economic problems of Europe during the decades between 1920 and 1940.[10] Nazi officials conducted propaganda campaigns (expressions of ridicule and hate), practiced private and official discrimination against Jews regarding property ownership and employment opportunities (acts of discrimination), and exterminated more than 6 million Jews in the Nazi concentration camps (mass genocide). Ironically, Jews are not a racial group, per se; Jews can be described more accurately as an international religious-ethnic group with a membership consisting of most known human races living on all of the major continents of the earth. While Jewish Americans were allowed to enter military service in the U.S. Armed Forces to fight against the Nazis, many of them were concurrently prohibited entrance to some American colleges and universities.[11] In the decades between 1920 and 1940 antisemitism was not exclusive to German society; it was practiced in the form of exclusion and discrimination in American society by educated U.S. citizens against American Jews.

Racism is past history, one might argue. In particular, biological racism— the attitude that one's race is genetically superior to others—has been discredited internationally, especially in the scientific community. Even the Ku Klux Klan, the epitome of biological racists, changed its focus from biological racism to White, Protestant chauvinism during the 1920s and 1930s so that Jews and Catholics (irrespective of race) along with African Americans bore the brunt of their hatred. Clearly, biological racism is not a creditable scientific theory or a viable political ideology. It is past history. Further, one might argue that desegregation of the armed forces and public schools, the Civil Rights Act, increased numbers of interracial marriages, all these and many other examples tend to refute the existence of racism in contemporary U.S. society. It's true: antidiscrimination laws exist; some degree of interracial marriages and school and military desegregation exist. Most official racism has been banned by federal laws and U.S. Supreme Court decisions. But, poorly enforced and meekly supported as they are, these laws and court decisions cannot in themselves change racist attitudes. What remain are racist attitudes and beliefs which have their roots in the folkways of U.S. society. Racist attitudes and beliefs persist in contemporary society because, as with traditions and folkways, they are deeply ingrained in the minds and consciences of many Americans. Racist attitudes perish slowly.

The preceding discussion on racism focused on the collective racism of White Americans. However, just because White racism was and is a real group social force in American life does not mean that all White Americans are racists in belief or behavior. Rather, it's important to consider that while collective racism can exist in a society, not all members of the society will be racists. Conversely, individual racism can exist in the absence of formal, collective racism. Consequently, it's possible that some nonsouthern, White Americans may believe and behave as White racists even though their region of the country never formalized a system of collective racism like that in the antebellum South.

CAUSES OF INDIVIDUAL CHAUVINISM

There are many reasons why a person may harbor chauvinistic attitudes about another person's race, gender, social class, religion, or handicap. Causes for individual chauvinism are learned attitudes acquired by individuals through the same process of social interaction individuals undergo when learning their cultures. Acquired chauvinism should be attributed to multiple causes since they are as complex as the humans who harbor them. Social and behavioral scientists[12] have isolated various human experiences which catalyze chauvinistic attitudes. Theories pertaining to single causes for chauvinism range considerably with varying anthropologic, sociologic, historic, and psychologic emphases. I have categorized these theories into eight types:

ignorance

negative traits

xenophobia

unpleasant experiences

folkloric wisdom

pathological personality

scapegoating

economic competition

These eight types are listed in order of complexity from the simplest type to the most complex type of chauvinism. The simpler types—ignorance, negative traits, xenophobia—refer to individual orientations; the more complex type— unpleasant experience, folkloric wisdom, pathological personality, scapegoating, economic competition—are complicated because they are inherent in the dynamics of the social structure, making them more difficult to manage when compared to the simpler types which are individual orientations. Actually, the more complicated types are unmanageable in the classroom. Table 5.1 lists and describes the causes of chauvinism in society.

If the cause of cultural chauvinism can be isolated, then a prescription to counter the cause might be possible. Table 5.2 presents the causal theories, briefly describes them, and provides change strategies to counter the origins. As you will quickly note, only five of the causes can be countered by teaching-learning approaches because of their nature. All of them require fundamental changes in the economic and political structure of our society.

These types of chauvinism can be countered in the classroom: Ignorance, Negative Traits, Unpleasant Experiences, Folkloric Wisdom, Xenophobia. These types of chauvinism cannot be countered successfully in the classroom because they require changes in the social structure which are beyond the reach of the classroom teacher: Scapegoating, Economic Competition. The Pathological Personality requires competent psychiatric care and is also beyond the limits of the classroom.

GROUP STEREOTYPING

Generic psychological descriptions for chauvinist attitudes and actions are not so difficult to identify. Research studies report that a chauvinist personality

Table 5.1   THEORIES AND ETIOLOGIES OF CHAUVINISM

Theories of Chauvinism	Etiologies of Theories
Ignorance	Chauvinism and prejudicial attitudes and actions are caused by ignorance; a person does not know the out-group and is acting on limited or biased data pertaining to the individual's out-group.
Negative Traits	The chauvinist person imputes traits considered obnoxious by his or her group as characteristic of all members of an out-group; a stereotype exists for many ethnic groups: e.g., "the tight Scot, the greedy Jew, the sneaky Mexican, the Latin lover."
Xenophobia	Chauvinistic attitudes and actions are rooted in a dislike of strangers or a discomfort with persons or groups who are "strange" to the xenophobic person. The aversions felt toward a gay person—homophobia—for example, reflect a discomfort or dislike toward an unconventional gender preference group.
Unpleasant Experience	The chauvinist person has had unpleasant experiences with members of the out-group and generalizes the unpleasant experiences as characteristics of the whole group, e.g., an Anglo boy is beaten up in a fight with a Mexican American boy; the Anglo boy then dislikes all Mexican American boys because they are all "mean."
Folkloric Wisdom	Chauvinistic attitudes and actions are caused by conformity to traditional norms and roles learned through socialization. A theory of lowered life expectations, folkloric wisdom (a manifestation of cultural degradation) describes learned norms and roles that impute low caste status to a person. For example, lower-class White youngsters may conform to the role of being "poor White" because from their perspective "everyone they know has always been poor," and therefore, "we will always be poor."
Pathological Personality	This places extremely chauvinistic persons into a category in which they have a chronic personality disorder. According to this theory, persons with delusions of grandeur and paranoic and sadistic tendencies may hold chauvinistic attitudes, and practice violent crimes, against members of an out-group. This type of person is a genuine hater, is often the leader of a hate group, and while very dangerous, is not very common among the general lot of chauvinists.
Scapegoat	The chauvinist person's prejudices are symbolic of the person's own fears, hopes, aspirations: e.g., the unsuccessful businessman blames the Jews in the community for his lack of success. Subconsciously the chauvinist may fear that he is the cause of his failure, but rather than accept the blame, he transfers it to the out-group.
Economic Competition	In times of rapid changes, economic depressions, or other social or political crises when competition for land or basic resources is intensified, chauvinistic attitudes and actions against an out-group increase, thwarting the out-group's economic advancement. A social dynamic theory, the economic competition theory describes the motive that undergirds the chauvinism that may prevail. The motive is to stymie the economic advancement of the out-group so as to increase the economic advancement of the in-group. The Jim Crow laws enacted after the Civil

Table 5.1 THEORIES AND ETIOLOGIES OF CHAUVINISM (continued)

Theories of Chauvinism	Etiologies of Theories
	War, for example, were intended to hold African Americans down by segregating and otherwise limiting their full participation in Southern society, e.g., poll taxes and literacy tests for voting, which in turn allowed Whites to maintain the political and economic advantages they held before the Civil War.

exhibits tendencies toward dogmatism and authoritarianism. The chauvinist personality structure is rigid, manifesting categorical thinking and/or insecure feelings with people who are culturally different.[13] Chauvinist attitudes and feelings revolve around the axis of fear of cultural differences; in other words, cultural differences, and the people who exhibit them, pose a felt threat to the racist. To alleviate the fear and remove the insecurities caused by contact with racially and culturally different people, the prejudiced person will tend to avoid and exclude the "different" people from his or her social circles, neighborhoods, and schools. This kind of avoidance pattern, when practiced by enough members of a group, leads to social and neighborhood exclusion and segregation of racial outgroups.[14] Isolated and segregated away from the out-group, the in-group members substitute misconceptions, myths, and stereotypes about the feared group for the more authentic traits that contact might actuate. Do teachers unconsciously transmit biases? And, do teachers discriminate against students? Answers to these questions are "yes," "no," and "sometimes." Traditionally, classroom teachers have been expected to represent a high degree of moral and ethical standards. At one time, teachers were forbidden to smoke, court in public, swear, or use obscene language. In other words, teachers were expected to be the epitome of respectability. Now it is clear that these expectations were unrealistic, and teachers (especially those in urban areas) have much more ethical and moral latitude. In fact, few if any teacher certification requirements address the question of teachers' morality. An avowed racist and an avowed sexist could with almost equal ease achieve certification in most states, because the questions of a person's attitudes and ethnocentrisms are simply not raised in the process of teacher certification. Yet the problem with attempts to assess teacher discrimination is that chauvinism can be transmitted to students without deliberate acts of discrimination. Amorphous human factors, such as tone of voice, innuendo, and other translucent acts can nevertheless transmit bias. Cultural and group stereotyping addresses this point.

There is much truth in the adage, "birds of a feather flock together." Or, the group one is in, the company one keeps, and the social circles one circulates in, all can teach chauvinism. It is not surprising to find college-educated White Americans who have stereotypic notions about African Americans—stereotypes

Table 5.2   CHANGE STRATEGIES AGAINST CHAUVINISM

Theory	Cause of Chauvinism	Change strategy
Ignorance + Xenophobia	Poor understanding of different peoples.	New data; new knowledge about different peoples. (Ethnic Studies Model)
Unpleasant Experience	Bad experience with certain groups.	Positive experiences with certain groups, preferably on a one-to-one basis. (Intergroup Relations Strategy)
Negative Trait	Same as Ignorance, but stress on stereotypes about groups.	Same as for Ignorance, but stress frontal attack on stereotypes. Do not replace stereotypes with "positive" stereotypes; rather, study groups from the groups' perspective. (Ethnic Studies Model/Intergroup Relations Strategy)
Scapegoat	Chauvinism and prejudice with a purpose. They represent something more basic, such as desire to maintain class/caste system in which out-groups remain second-class citizens. Frustrations ostensibly caused by out-group; thus, chauvinist hostile toward members of the group.	Reason with students about how democracy cannot function with tyranny of the majority, which is self-defeating, or with a second-class citizenship class/caste system. Appeal to universal human rights. (Human Rights Strategy)
Economic Competition	Economic and political change provokes fears and insecurities in chauvinist, who benefits from the status quo. Thus, chauvinist attempts to block progress of cultural/racial group.	An economic and political problem which requires political and economic solutions, such as fundamental changes in government and financial system.
Pathological Personality	Chauvinism a pathological syndrome of deeply repressed fears, anxieties, and other emotional disorders.	Competent psychoanalysis or therapy.
Folkloric Wisdom	Manifested cultural degradation; out-group members conform to in-group's chauvinistic expectations.	Work with families to raise expectations and lower self-limitations.
Economic Competition	Economic and political changes provoke fears and insecurities in chauvinists who benefit from the status quo; thereby, they try to block progress of the out-group.	Requires basic change in the social structure.

taught them by their respective groups. Having had little contact with African Americans in the public schools or in colleges, and having only their group's folk wisdom knowledge about African Americans, these college-trained individuals know very little about the largest minority group in the country. Neither is it surprising to meet college-trained minority people who have a variety of stereotypes about White Americans, especially since stereotyping is the result of limited and distorted information about some out-group. We now turn our attention to the concept of stereotyping.

What motivates stereotyping? Economic gain? Social gain? Domination over a particular group? Or simply human insensitivity to others? All of these, perhaps? Understand that in normal human interactions *social typing* is necessary.[15] Social typing is what people do in the course of daily events: that is, we make assumptions about the way certain types of people should act, and then we act on those assumptions, treating the person according to our assumptions, and thereby providing that person a role in our relationship. For example, we assume that a lawyer will be meticulous and thorough about our legal problems. We expect a lawyer to ask all types of minute questions so as to become thoroughly informed about our legal problems. We expect the lawyer to tell us whether we really have a case, or whether, in the lawyer's opinion, the law would support our case. We also type people by stigmatizing them on the basis of physical characteristics such as deformities, weight, and height; we are all familiar with such stigmatizations as the "jolly fat person," or the "agile midget."

A group stereotype is a kind of social type.[16] A stereotype is an in-group's oversimplified conception of members of an out-group. The conception is devoid of traits valued by the in-group and is loaded with traits devalued by the in-group. Consider a stereotype about Mexican Americans in the southwestern United States. There exists a southwestern Anglo conception about Mexican Americans: an image of a Mexican slumped against a cactus plant, a tequila bottle in one hand, taking a siesta. This image is supposed to reflect Mexican American cultural values: they are lazy, sleep in the middle of the day (they lack industry!), and get drunk on tequila. Notice that the stereotype is devoid of the Anglo values of the work ethic and sobriety; rather, the image is loaded with traits devalued by the Anglo group such as drunkenness and laziness. In other words, in-group members develop exaggerated perceptions about some out-group largely because the in-group has little data or contact with the out-group or because the stereotype serves to support the material or economic interests of the in-group. Depicting Mexican Americans as lazy serves to vindicate the low wages Anglo farmers pay Mexican American migrant workers. High wages would only be paid to hard workers! Then the in-group commences to treat members of the out-group on the basis of the stereotype. By assigning the out-group a stereotypic social role, the in-group can treat out-group members in such a manner that many out-group members come to believe they actually have the assigned stereotypic traits. A self-fulfilling prophecy is effectuated.[17] A person who is treated as inferior by enough people will eventually believe he or she is inferior. Once the beliefs of inferiority take hold, such a person will act inferior in relation to others, and other people will reciprocate by treating the person as inferior. Such people perceive themselves, and are perceived by others, as inferior.

STEREOTYPING AND THE SELF-FULFILLING PROPHECY

Students tend to live up to (or live down to) the expectations of their teachers. When teachers convey to students expectations based on stereotypes, the results can be potent. Rosenthal and Jacobson's well-known studies on the effects of teachers' expectations of students' academic performance illustrates the point. In their book, *Pygmalion in the Classroom*, Rosenthal and Jacobson tell of their experiments with an academic potential stereotype.[18] A group of youngsters, academically at various ranges of skills and knowledge, were identified as late bloomers. Their teachers were told that these students were tested with new types of intelligence tests, and that these tests revealed the youngsters to be exceptionally bright. Overtly, the teachers did not treat the "late bloomers" differently. However, through such subtleties as facial expressions, tone of voice, and a general ambiance of acceptance conveyed to the late bloomers, the teachers conveyed to the students that they were exceptionally bright. By the end of the experiment, the youngsters were exceptionally bright according to standardized tests. The point is that the teachers treated the youngsters on the basis of a stereotype, and the youngsters reciprocated by assuming that role; the rest became a self-fulfilling prophecy.

The Rosenthal and Jacobson study was criticized for experimenter bias, i.e., the researchers allegedly created the situation that effected the study's results, implying that the self-fulfilling prophecy was created by the researchers' design rather than caused by the actual relationships between the teachers' expectations and the students' responses. In response to the criticism, Rosenthal and Rubin conducted a meta-analysis of the self-fulfilling prophecy. The examined studies were taken from nonclassroom settings and dealt with such variables as reaction time, interpretation of ink blots, and laboratory interviews. Based on their assessment of the 345 experiments, Rosenthal and Rubin concluded:

> The reality of the phenomenon is beyond doubt. . . . the effects of interpersonal expectations were as great, on the average, in everyday life situations as they were in laboratory experiments.[19]

Good conducted a meta-analysis of at least 18 studies that dealt with teacher expectations and the self-fulfilling prophecy. Good concluded that for the most part, teachers are unaware that they ". . . vary their behavior toward high- and low-achieving students. . ."[20] to the detriment of low achievers. Good also identified the 12 ways that teachers vary their behavior toward high and low achievers. The 12 ways are summarized thus:

1. Teachers tend to praise low achievers less than high achievers when they risk answering questions of which they are unsure;
2. Teachers tend to criticize low achievers more for making inaccurate responses to questions;
3. Teachers tend to provide fewer details and less precise feedback to low achievers;
4. Teachers tend to communicate less (and call upon less frequently) with low achievers;
5. Teachers tend to provide low achievers less time to respond to questions and less eye contact when teachers do call upon low achievers;
6. Teachers tend to demand less homework and less effort from low achievers.[21]

What happens to ethnic minority students when teachers treat them on the basis of the stereotype that they have low academic abilities? The U.S. Commission on Civil Rights conducted a study[22] analyzing the verbal and nonverbal interaction of teachers and students in the public schools of Texas, New Mexico, Arizona, and California. The study investigated the kind and amount of verbal and nonverbal interaction which actually occurred between teachers and Anglo and Mexican American students. The study reported:

> Mexican American pupils . . . received considerably less of some of the most educationally beneficial forms of teacher behavior than did Anglos in the same classroom.[23]

In the 429 classrooms that were observed, the study verified that teachers spoke less often and less favorably to Mexican American students than to Anglo students. Anglo students were praised more and challenged intellectually more often than were Mexican Americans. But, the teachers verbally scolded or disciplined the Mexican American students more often than Anglos. In both quality and quantity of verbal and nonverbal interaction, teachers tended to favor Anglo over Mexican American students. The teachers in this study unconsciously assumed that Mexican American students were more unruly and required more discipline. Also, the teachers assumed that the Mexican American students were less bright than the Anglo students. The Anglo students were asked the more difficult questions and were praised more for their responses than were the Mexican American students. If these teachers continue to act on their stereotypes about the Mexican American students in their classes, the students will internalize the stereotype as role expectations to which they must conform. Eventually, standard instruments and deportment reports will reveal that these Mexican American students are less bright and more unruly than their Anglo counterparts. It's important to understand that in the southwestern United States there is a stereotype about Mexican Americans which attributes to them violent characteristics, the characteristics of the *bandito*. Also, the stereotype attributes to them a low level of intelligence and a poor command of English. The teachers in this study were simply transferring the stereotype to their Mexican American students, assuming they would be more unruly and less bright than their Anglo counterparts. They treated the students according to their expectations, and the self-fulfilling prophecy held true.

These teachers were not bigots bent on suppressing minority students. Rather, they were both from the Anglo and Mexican American groups, and yet they all treated the Mexican American students inequitably. But because they were unaware of the impact of group ethnocentrism, chauvinism, and the consequent stereotyping that occurs in most communities, they operated on folk wisdom data they had acquired in the southwestern communities. We must also remember that teachers can harbor stereotypes about a variety of other kinds of students: the "spoiled WASP," the "jiving black," the "dumb Polack," the "smart Oriental," "giddy females." One only has to visit enough teacher lounges to hear comments like "those kinds of kids," or "you can't expect much from their kind" to understand how easily teachers fall into the trap of stereotyping and labelling their students.

One last point about stereotypes. They change as the nature of intergroup relations changes. Consider the way stereotypes about Native Americans have changed. I analyzed 15 different American history books which had been written between 1890 and 1930. These books were written with college students in mind. Original accounts in the history books describing events prior to the westward expansion of the colonists referred to the Native Americans as "Noble Savages." The Iroquois nation was used as the model. The Native Americans were considered innocent, courageous, and honest, but because they chose to live in the forests and chose not to adopt the Christian religion, they were considered savages. During the period of westward expansion, when Anglo pioneers were dividing the continent and when Native Americans were being removed or crowded farther and farther west, the original accounts of Native Americans described them as "savages." Because of the intense conflict between the Native Americans and the government, they were described as having lost their nobility. No longer innocent and good, the Native Americans were portrayed as uncivilized warriors. The Sioux tribes were used as the model. After the intense conflict ceased, especially after the last Native American battle for survival, the Battle of Wounded Knee, the accounts of Native Americans referred to a "conquered savage." The Cherokee tribes were used as the model. The accounts portrayed the Native Americans as an almost extinct group who had reached the end of the trail. Because they were now subdued, and because some had taken up the ways of the pioneers, the stereotype portrayed them as conquered, defeated, and almost civilized. But, because many of the tribes chose to retain their religion rather than abandon it for Christianity, they were considered somewhat savage, or without Christian souls.

GENDER-ROLE STEREOTYPING

Gender-role stereotypes are the result of socialization practices. They are based on culturally defined ideal behaviors and roles for men and women within a society. In Chapter 4 sex and gender-role identities were defined as learned attitudes. Youngsters first learn their sex and gender-role identities through interaction with their parents and other family members.

The weight of the evidence is that the environment, and the socialization practices therein, have the greatest impact on gender-role stereotyping. In fact, the classroom environment often reinforces gender-role stereotypes. Gender-role stereotyping in the classroom is the result of folkloric wisdom by which male and female students are expected to conform to traditionally derived gender roles.

Myra and David Sadker observed student and teacher interactions in more than a hundred fourth-, sixth-, and eighth-grade classes in four states and Washington, D.C. Based on their observations, they concluded

> Teachers behave differently, depending on whether boys or girls call out answers during discussions. When boys call out comments without raising their hands, teachers accept their answers. However, when girls call out, [without raising their hands] teachers reprimand. . . .[24]

The Sadkers inferred that the teachers, both men and women, conveyed a subtle but potent message that boys should be ". . . academically assertive . . . girls should act like ladies and keep quiet."[25]

Teachers need to keep in mind that they are "significant others" who play a key part in the socialization process of their students, especially as the students develop an academic self-concept. Gender-role stereotyping, as with any form of stereotyping, limits the student's opportunities to grow and develop in directions which differ from the gender-role stereotypes. Teachers, once aware that they are operating upon the basis of gender-role stereotypes can modify their behavior so that both female and male students can benefit in the classroom.

HANDICAPPING CONDITIONS AND STEREOTYPING

Now that handicapped students are mainstreamed into regular classes, they are experiencing a reception similar to the one first experienced when Black students were bussed to White schools for desegregation.[26] When the Black students were shunned (as they often were in the early stages of desegregation), they reacted by resegregating, i.e., coming together into all-Black cliques in the White schools.

When handicapped students are mainstreamed into regular schools, they often come from schools especially designed for them.[27] The students in the regular schools have little or no history of contact or interaction with the handicapped students. In the regular schools the handicapped students appear "strange" or different which may trigger a xenophobic reaction in the regular students. Consequently, the regular students may avoid contact with the handicapped students, which is a subtle form of shunning. At times, academic and social interaction between the handicapped and regular students is hindered within the regular school by the practice of placing the handicapped students in special classrooms, a form of resegregation that lessens opportunities for the students to interact socially and academically.

Social acceptance of handicapped students appears to be a greater problem than academic acceptance. Van Bourgondien[28] reported that regular students reacted positively to peer tutoring activities in which the regular students tutored the handicapped students. Yet, social rejection of handicapped students persists. In a 1972 study[29] students with disabilities were regarded unfavorably by their regular peers; in a 1982 study[30] similar negative perceptions were held by regular junior high students toward their handicapped peers.

Social rejection of handicapped students by regular students may be rooted in ignorance, xenophobic, or negative trait stereotyping. A generic stereotype that all handicapped students are not very bright is based on ignorance as there are many kinds of handicaps ranging from the physical to emotional, or cognitive aspects. Or, when regular students stereotype handicapped students, the regular students may be using the stereotype as a defense mechanism to conceal their fear of someone who appears to be different, a xenophobic reaction. And, the stereotype may be a function of imputing negative traits of regular students into the behavior of handicapped students. The key to lowering social rejection of handicapped students may be in the area of academic interaction and acceptance. In programs where regular and handicapped students are integrated, both academic achievement and social interaction patterns are improved for all students involved,[31] which supports the contact thesis of cooperative learning discussed in Chapter 9. Cooperative learning activities, and the necessary academic interaction, promises to reduce stereotypic responses and thinking among students.

Stereotyping and discriminatory behaviors against handicapped students may not fit this chapter's definition of *chauvinism*. The Council on Interracial Books for Children defined stereotyping and discrimination against handicapped individuals as *handicapism*. The Council defined handicapism as any attitude or practice that causes unjust treatment of people with disabilities; stereotypes about the handicapped present them as helpless, strange, odd, or fearsome.[32] In children's literature, and in movies and television programs for children, the villains are often portrayed as handicapped, such as the one-legged or one-eyed pirate; less-than-normally bright characters are portrayed as being speech disabled, such as stuttering or lisping.

In Chapter 4, six broadly conceived categories of disabilities were presented. Care should be taken so that the categories are not used to label and thereby stereotype a handicapped student. For example, experience with Down syndrome students shows that they are not all alike. Down syndrome is the most prevalent type of mental retardation and consists of a combination of birth defects including an enlarged tongue, smaller than normal ears and a shorter stature, and oval-shaped eyes. The degree of mental retardation varies among Down syndrome children ranging from mild to moderate retardation, according to the National Down Syndrome Society. Rather than relying on categories or labels as a means to perceive handicapped students, Lovitt[33] provides some very practical and nonstereotypic labels for handicapped students; what follows are Lovitt's labels and a paraphrase of what he meant by them:

1. *Slow Academically*. Some handicapped students have trouble with basic skills, especially reading;
2. *Poorly Motivated*. These are the handicapped students who can do classroom work but they just do not want to do it! The Poorly Motivated is simply not interested in the classroom materials either in general (doesn't like school work), or in specific terms (doesn't like multiplication problems, for example).
3. *Naughty Behavior*. These are the handicapped students who lie, cheat, fight, or misbehave in other ways. Often, they really have no handicap; rather, before mainstreaming, teachers found it convenient to send unruly students to the "special education room." Yet, there will be some handicapped students who misbehave.
4. *Poor Endurance*. Some handicapped students are able to handle the academic subject matter of their classes; they are generally well behaved, but are unable to sustain their attention on one activity. Rather, they tend to move from one activity to another as they are easily distracted so that they rarely totally complete any given assignment.
5. *Special Equipment*. Because of impairment(s), some handicapped students require special equipment simply to accomplish the academic tasks of the classroom. Otherwise, the students are much like the regular students.

Lovitt's descriptors of the majority of handicapped students portray the handicapped person as a human who happens to be different; the differences manifested by the handicapped students do not vary greatly from regular students who can also be slow academically, poorly motivated, naughty, and easily distracted. To avoid stereotyping handicapped students, teachers should think of and treat handicapped students just as they would treat their regular students:

1. *Three-dimensional humans*. Handicapped students are not cartoon caricatures with unidimensional personalities; rather, they are like other humans; they are complex and capable of the full range of emotions known to humans.
2. *Self-actualizing humans*. Handicapped students are in the process of becoming, growing, and developing into adulthood; they must wrestle with all the challenges and obstacles that adults have created as a part of one's rite of passage into adulthood. Consequently, handicapped students do not need their teacher's pity; rather, they need their teacher's sensitive guidance.
3. *Social-interaction humans*. Handicapped students are not unlike their regular peers regarding the need for love, affection, companionship, competition, success; in short, they need to interact with others.

THE PERVASIVE SOCIAL CLASS STEREOTYPE

In 1986 the New World Foundation reported that ". . . school failure for lower income and minority students has reached epidemic proportions. . . . The taproot of this failure is in the chronic inequality . . . in the ways that learning is stratified and structured."[34] How students learn is a function of where they happen to go to school. In Chapter 4, explanations for the low academic achievement of lower-class students were presented. Here we reexamine the thesis that schools, and the teachers therein, play a significant role in perpetuating a pervasive stereotype that lower-class students are not academically inclined.

Goodlad's impressive 10-year study of 1,016 classrooms, 1,350 teachers, 8,624 parents, and 17,163 students reported in *A Place Called School* that the junior and senior high schools studied made two distinctively different academic tracks available to students in which either college preparatory skills or utilitarian skills were taught. For example, in the college preparatory track, English lessons consisted of reading established standard literature, creative, expository and persuasive theme composition, and grammar for language analysis. In the utilitarian track, English lessons consisted of functional literacy (reading newspapers, magazines, filling out job applications, language mechanics, and reading simplified forms of writing). Goodlad concluded:

> High track classes devoted more time to relatively high level cognitive processes— making judgments, drawing inferences. . . . Low track classes devoted time to rote learning and application of knowledge and skills.[35]

The high track classes, in the Goodlad study, taught students how to think with knowledge; the low track classes were taught how to consume knowledge; the middle track classes were more like the high track classes.

Academic tracks, now quite common in most middle, junior, and high schools, are not based solely on academic ability. Rather, the low and high track academic tracks are directly linked to social class levels. Lower-class students are found in disproportionate numbers in the low, utilitarian track and upper- and upper-middle class students are found in the high academic, college preparatory track.[36]

Anyon conducted an ethnographic study of fifth-grade classes of schools in low-, middle-, and high-income neighborhoods. Anyon observed teacher performance, classroom materials, and the classroom environment. Within each school, all the fifth-grade teachers (usually 2 to 3 per school) were observed teaching. Anyon reported:

> In the working class schools, work is usually mechanical, involving rote behavior and very little decision making or choice.[37]

In the middle-class schools, work consisted of getting the correct answers with some emphasis on decision making about which answers were correct. In the upper-income neighborhood schools

> work is developing one's analytical, intellectual powers. Children are continually asked to reason through a problem, to produce intellectual products.[38]

The Goodlad and Anyon studies reveal a socialization process that is preparing lower-class students for occupational roles relegated to the blue-collar, working class while upper-middle and upper-class students are being prepared for occupational roles in the white-collar, managerial class. Other scholars (Bowles and Gintis[39] in the United States, Basil Bernstein[40] in England, Jim Cummins[41] in Canada, Tove Kangas[42] in Denmark have advanced a similar thesis that schools are social role allocators that provide their students with the skills necessary for survival within their respective social classes, which is what is meant by the educational slogan of "meeting the needs of the students." When the American public school system was in its formative stages, advocates such as Horace Mann argued that the emerging public school system would serve as the "great equalizer" or that the public school system would ameliorate social class stratification by providing all students with a common body of knowledge. The lower class would especially benefit as it could be elevated through hard work and diligence within a common academic curriculum. All students would have equal access to a common body of knowledge, and all students would have equal access to methods for utilization of the common knowledge.

Some 140 years after the birth of the common schools in Massachusetts, the notion that schools would be "great equalizers" has been replaced by the notion that schools are role allocators. The pervasive social class stereotype—practical knowledge for the lower class and decision-making skills for the middle and upper classes—portends a society highly divided between the "knows and the know-nots." The implications for teaching are quite clear. Teachers should teach all students how to use knowledge to make decisions, thereby empowering their students to think independently and critically. *Analyzing, inferring, predicting, synthesizing, evaluating;* these are the verbals of cognition, of thinking that treats knowledge as the fuel that drives judgments and decisions.

The practice of ability grouping should be discontinued. Other countries, Sweden and the Soviet Union for example, report high literacy rates as well as continued scientific and technologic developments without ability grouping in their schools.

Tracking and ability grouping practices have a negative influence on the school's intergroup relations because these practices tend to isolate students along cultural, racial, or economic lines, and thereby perpetuate in-school segregation and unequal educational benefits. Ability grouping has the effect of segregating lower-class students within the school and dooming them to failure. Once placed in a low track, rarely do they advance to a higher track. These students are deprived of the academic experiences and skills that would prepare them for college entrance and a consequent professional career. Also, tracking and ability grouping deprive middle- and upper-class students of positive relationships with lower-class students. The negative consequences of tracking and ability grouping—stereotyped attitudes toward lower-class students and predetermined academic failure for minority students—far outweigh whatever administrative expediencies tracking and ability grouping practices provide. Both tracking and ability grouping should be abandoned and replaced by heterogeneous grouping, individualized instruction, peer tutoring, and cooperative learning experiences (to be described in Chapter 9). Last, counselors and teachers have tended to advise lower-class students to pursue nonacademic, nonprofessional advanced training. Counseling lower-class students to enter certain programs based on single-interest inventory instruments, biased achievement tests, or stereotypic career aspirations will tend to relegate lower-class students to vocational programs. These counseling practices, compounded by tracking and ability grouping, are clearly discriminatory.

PRESCRIPTION FOR CHAUVINISM

The novel *Don Quixote de la Mancha* by Miguel Cervantes is about a knight, Don Quixote, whose goal in life is to eradicate all the injustices he encountered on his journeys. Sadly, he came to be viewed as a fool not to be taken seriously. Eventually, he returned to his home, a beaten, disillusioned man who discontinued his quest for justice. Don Quixote's heart was in the right place but he was not selective about the social windmills he encountered, and because he was not selective, he finally was defeated by them. Teachers can learn from Don Quixote to challenge the social injustices that appear in their classrooms, but unlike Don Quixote, teachers must be selective about the social windmills, i.e., the types of chauvinisms they challenge to insure that the encounter is successful, benefitting their students and their communities.

Teachers should work toward the reduction of chauvinism in their classrooms but they should keep in mind that only certain kinds—ignorance, negative traits, xenophobia, unpleasant experiences, folkloric wisdom—are manageable. The latter kinds—pathological personality, scapegoating, economic competition—require major changes in the social structure and are beyond the reach of the classroom teacher. Further, chauvinism effectively challenged requires that the entire school be analyzed for chauvinistic biases.

One analytical approach that shows promise for reduction of chauvinism in entire schools is dubbed the "Effective School Movement." The Effective School Movement reflects an empirical study of schools that is effective with any type of student population. The U.S. Department of Education[43] reports the following attributes as characteristic of effective schools:

- effective schools have high expectations for student success;
- effective schools have a clear sense of their educational mission and purpose;
- effective schools have principals who provide strong leadership;
- effective schools have a safe and orderly school environment;
- effective schools emphasize the learning of basic skills;
- effective schools make students accountable for their own learning and regularly monitor their progress;
- effective schools involve parents and the local community closely in the educational process.[44]

In 1985, the Northwest Regional Educational Laboratory reported that schools based on the attributes identified for effective schools, with some modifications, were successful in Native American populations.

SUMMARY

In Chapters 6 to 10, strategies and approaches for challenging different kinds of chauvinism are described. The strategies and approaches are based on the assumption that teachers can and will foster the desire in every student to excel in school. A particular way to effect this assumption is by teaching for full literacy at three levels: (1) functional literacy, (2) cultural literacy, and (3) critical literacy. Here teachers need to strive toward the same goal for all students—critical thinking—through achievement of full literacy at the three levels:

1. *Functional literacy* is the ability to speak, read, and write standard English; this includes reading basic technical literature which entails an understanding of rudimentary mathematics and science concepts. (See Chapter 8 for Language Education.)

2. *Cultural literacy* is the expansion of functional literacy and refers to a knowledge of the literature, history, and grand traditions of the culture of the United States, including major scientific accomplishments. It also refers to knowledge about a person's ethnic or cultural heritage. While it is important that students know the details of the core U.S. culture, it is equally important that they know the details of their ethnic or cultural heritage. The latter should not be sacrificed in the name of "assimilation" or "Americanization" ideologies. (See Chapter 7 for Cultural Education.)

3. *Critical literacy,* the highest form of literacy is the ability to think creatively and critically. Specifically, it is (a) the ability to analyze and evaluate effective oral and written expression, including the ability to identify a speaker's or writer's biases; (b) the ability to quantitatively reason with mathematics; (c) the ability to draw inferences and reach conclusions regarding written materials, the ability to examine relationships and extend concepts to new situations, the ability to interpret and to make deductions from graphic and experimental data; (d) the ability to form research experiments, to form hypotheses and predict their outcomes, to examine the generalizability of experimental data and results, and to evaluate scientific theories in relationship to empirical data; and (e) the ability to understand the disciplined routines or forms used by artists to express an idea or emotion, or to produce a desired result, in the fine and performing arts. Teachers must resist the notion that critical literacy is the province of gifted students only.

STUDY QUESTIONS

1. Define the concept of "ethnocentrism" by explaining the continuum that ranges from cultural degradation, to cultural pride, to cultural chauvinism.

2. Explain how "negative traits" or "unpleasant experiences" as causes of chauvinism can be linked to sexism or handicapism.

3. Explain how the self-fulfilling prophecy and stereotyping are interrelated.

4. Describe why racism in American life is viewed by scholars as a moral dilemma. Discuss how racism in our current times has manifested itself.

5. Describe and discuss the origins of gender-role stereotypes; how do gender-role stereotypes limit the life options of both boys and girls?

6. Explain the pervasive social class stereotype especially as it affects lower-class students. Then discuss how attributes of the effective school movement, if implemented in schools, might reduce the impact of social class stereotyping.

7. Define the term *handicapism*. How does the term appear to differ from *ethnocentrism* or *chauvinism*?

8. Explain the difference between academic and social acceptance of mainstreamed handicapped students. What are the limitations of the categories of handicaps listed in Chapter 4 and referred to in this chapter?

9. How might the guidelines provided for perceiving handicapped students be used for perceiving most students?

NOTES

1. M. E. Goodman. *Race Awareness in Young Children*. New York: Collier Books, 1973.
2. Judy H. Katz. *White Awareness*. Norman, Okla.: University of Oklahoma Press, 1978.
3. Katz. *White Awareness*, p. 4.
4. Gunnar Mydral. *An American Dilemma*. New York: Harper & Row, 1944.
5. U.S. Commission on Mental Health. *Joint Commission on Mental Health*. Washington, D.C.: U.S. Government Printing Office, 1965.
6. Kerner Commission. *National Advisory Commission on Civil Rights*. New York: Bantam, 1968.
7. Pierre L. van den Berghe. *Race and Racism, A Comparative Perspective*. New York: Wiley, 1967, pp. 21–26.
8. R. Daniels and H. H. Kitano. *American Racism: Exploration of the Nature of Prejudice*. Englewood Cliffs, N.J.: Prentice-Hall, 1970, p. 2; see also, Kurt Lewin. *Resolving Social Conflict*. New York: Harper & Row, 1948, p. 85.
9. Adolf Hitler. *Mein Kampf*. Boston: Houghton Mifflin, 1943, p. 654.
10. William Shirer. *The Rise and Fall of the Third Reich*. New York: Simon & Schuster, 1960, pp. 231–234; see also, Nora Levin. *The Holocaust: The Destruction of European Jewry, 1933–45*. New York: Schocken Books, 1968, pp. 3–24.
11. President's Commission on Higher Education. *Higher Education for American Democracy*. New York: Harper & Row, 1948, vol. 2.
12. James Lynch. *Prejudice Reduction and the Schools*. London: Nichols Publishing Company, 1987.
13. T. W. Adorno. *The Authoritarian Personality*. New York: Harper & Row, 1950.
14. Andrew Greeley. *Why Can't They Be Like Us?* New York: Dutton, 1971, p. 156.
15. Peter Berger and Thomas Luckmann. *The Social Construction of Reality*. New York: Doubleday, 1967, pp. 32–34.
16. Roger D. Abrahams. "Stereotyping and Beyond," in Abrahams and Rudolph C. Troike, *Language and Cultural Diversity in American Education*. Englewood Cliffs, N.J.: Prentice-Hall, 1972, pp. 22–23.

17. Charles P. Loomis. *Social Systems: The Study of Sociology.* Cambridge, Mass.: Schenkman, 1976, pp. 90–93.
18. Robert Rosenthal and Lenore Jacobson. *Pygmalion in the Classroom.* New York: Holt, Rinehart, and Winston, 1968, pp. 5–9.
19. Robert Rosenthal and Donald Rubin. "Interpersonal Expectancy Effects: the First 345 Studies." *The Behavioral and Brain Sciences.* 3, 1976, pp. 377–415.
20. Thomas L. Good. "Teacher Expectations and Student Perceptions: A Decade of Research." *Educational Leadership,* 38, 5, February 1981, pp. 122–128.
21. Thomas Good, p. 123.
22. U.S. Commission on Civil Rights. *Teachers and Students.* Washington, D.C.: U.S. Government Printing Office, 1973.
23. U.S. Commission on Civil Rights. *Teachers and Students,* pp. 17–18.
24. Myra and David Sadker. "Sexism in the Classroom of the '80's." *Psychology Today,* March 1985, pp. 54–57.
25. Myra and David Sadker, p. 56.
26. S. Stainback and W. Stainback. "A Review of Research on Interactions Between Severely Handicapped and Nonhandicapped Students." *The Journal of the Association for the Severely Handicapped.* 6, 1981, pp. 23–29.
27. J. J. Bak, E. M. Cooper, K. M. Doborth and G. N. Siperstein. "Special Class Placement as Labels." *Exceptional Children.* 54, 1987, pp. 151–155.
28. M. E. Van Bourgondien. "Children's Responses to Retarded Peers as a Function of Social Behaviors, Labeling, and Age." *Exceptional Children.* 53, 1987, pp. 432–439.
29. H. Goodman, J. Gottlieb, and R. Harrison. "Social Acceptance of EMRs Integrated into a Nongraded Elementary School." *American Journal of Mental Deficiency.* 76, 1972, pp. 412–417.
30. F. Gibbons and S. M. Kassin. "Behavioral Expectations of Retarded and Nonretarded Children." *Journal of Applied Developmental Psychology.* 3, 1982, pp. 85–104.
31. N. Certo, N. Haring and R. York (eds.). *Public School Integration of Severely Handicapped Students.* Baltimore: Brookes Publishing Co., 1984, pp. 15–24; see also, L. M. Voeltz. "Children's Attitudes Toward Handicapped Peers." *American Journal of Mental Deficiency.* 84, 1980, pp. 455–464.
32. Council on Interracial Books for Children. *Interracial Books for Children Bulletin.* 8(6–7), 1977, p. 1.
33. T. C. Lovitt. "What Should We Call Them?" *Exceptional Teacher.* 1(1), pp. 5–7.
34. Ann Bastian. *Choosing Equality: The Case for Democratic Schooling.* Philadelphia: Temple University Press, 1986, p. 15.
35. Goodlad, *A Place Called School,* p. 131.
36. Jeannie Oaks. *Keeping Track: How Schools Structure Inequality.* New Haven: Yale University Press, 1985.
37. Jean Anyon. "Social Class and the Hidden Curriculum of Work," in Jeanne Ballantine, ed. *School and Society, A Unified Reader.* Mountain View, CA: Mayfield Publishing Co., 1989, pp. 257–279.
38. Anyon, p. 263.
39. S. Bowles and H. Gintis. *Schooling in Capitalist America.* Boston: Routledge and Kegan Paul, 1979.
40. B. Bernstein. *Class, Codes, and Controls.* 2nd Ed. London: Routledge and Kegan Paul, 1977.
41. J. Cummins. "From Multicultural to Anti-racist Education: An Analysis of Programmes and Policies in Ontario." In T. Skutnabb-Kangas and J. Cummins, eds.

Minority Education. Clevedon, England: Multilingual Matters, 1988, pp. 127–160.

42. Tove Skutnabb-Kangas. "Multilingualism and the Education of Minority Children." In Kangas and Cummins, *Minority Education*, pp. 9–44.

43. U.S. Department of Education. *Schools that Work. Educating Disadvantaged Children*. Washington, D.C.: U.S. Government Printing Office, 1987, p. 11.

44. Northwest Regional Educational Laboratory. *Effective Practices in Indian Education*. Portland, Oregon: Research and Development Program for Indian Education, 1985.

PART Two

MODELS AND STRATEGIES

Chapter
6

Overview of Instructional Models and Strategies

Key Terms:

cultural education
empowerment
global education
intergroup education

language education
models
strategies

Individual models and strategies are described in separate chapters, but before describing them, we need to define pertinent instructional terminology and explain the nature and function of instructional models and strategies. The term *model* refers to the overall structure or pattern for teaching particular content; the term *strategy* refers to overall approaches or methods for applying or utilizing certain principles in the classroom. Here the models provide structure for pluralistic teaching; the strategies provide approaches for implementing pluralistic teaching.

A variety of terms exist to describe different types of instruction. Often, the terms overlap in meaning or intent, such as "transcultural education," "intercultural education," and "cross-cultural education." The three terms refer to the same goal, reducing ethnocentrism, but approach the goal in slightly different ways. There is confusion about the meanings of "multicultural education," "multiethnic education," "bilingual education" and other cultural approaches.

MODELS AND STRATEGIES COMPARED

To avoid the pitfalls of terms that come into fashion and then are soon obsolete, the models and strategies described in this text go beyond rhetoric; they operate on four instructional dimensions: (1) cultural education, (2) language education, (3) intergroup education, and (4) human rights education. Cultural education builds cognitive understandings about cultural groups. The scope may range from a study of a single cultural group, e.g., Japanese Americans; dual cultural groups, e.g., bicultural Hispanic and Anglo American groups; to many groups in a nation, e.g., multiethnic; or the world, e.g., global education. Language education builds literacy in a modern foreign language; its focus ranges from literacy in one language through literacy in two languages, bilingual instruction. In the U.S. bilingual instruction is generally used for compensatory purposes while single foreign language studies are used for enrichment. Intergroup education builds positive relations between students who differ by social class, gender, race, handicap, or religion. The intergroup focus is not on cultural or language literacy; the focus is on relationships which emphasize process. Human rights education builds ethical relationships among students, and like the intergroup approach, emphasizes process.

The research basis for each approach is analyzed by chapter. None of the approaches has a particularly strong research base, but a search for a strong research base for most educational approaches is disappointing. Most instructional approaches do not operate from a research basis as does the practice of medicine. Rather, instructional approaches operate on a consensus rationale in which educators collectively agree that certain approaches are "the current, best practices." Research findings, when applicable, are used to form the consensus. Sleeter and Grant,[1] in their study of instructional approaches for dealing with race, class, and gender, identified five approaches: (1) teaching the exceptional and the culturally different, (2) human relations, (3) single-group studies, (4) multicultural education, and (5) multicultural education that is social reconstruction. With the exception of language education, which was not within the focus of their study, their recommendations parallel the recommended approaches discussed here. What they call "single-group," I call "ethnic studies"; what they call "human relations," I call "intergroup relations"; what they call "multicultural education that is social reconstructionist," I call "human rights," which strives toward a society based on justice. The models and strategies are either *product* or *process oriented*. The orientations of the cultural and language education approaches are toward a product, such as knowledge about a specific culture or language; the orientations of the intergroup and human rights approaches are toward a process, such as improved relation between genders or ethical treatment of handicapped students. Table 6.1 summarizes existing instructional approaches.

These models and strategies have emerged as a result of the collective activities of educators, concerned citizens, public school teachers, parents, and hosts of other people who believe that communal living can be vastly improved through education. By now, these activities are recognized as the forces or impulses to democratize public schooling, a force deeply embedded in the democratic cultural praxis of American society. The intellectual basis for democratizing public schooling was established during the early decades of this century by educational scholars such as John Dewey, George Counts, Boyd Bode, C. H. Judd, and others.[2] In our times, emphasis is placed on democratizing schools through empowerment of students, or what I call liberation of the mind from ignorance. Teachers, and the schools they inhabit, are viewed as

Table 6.1   INSTRUCTIONAL APPROACHES, MODELS AND STRATEGIES, AND GOALS

Instructional Approaches	Models-Strategies	Goals
Cultural Education	Ethnic Studies; Bicultural Instruction; Multiethnic Education; Global Education	Cultural and ethnic single, dual or, multiple group literacy; focus on cognitive understanding of other cultures; scope ranges from single group to many groups within nation or world
Language Education	Modern Foreign Languages;	Communicative competence in foreign language
	Bilingual Instruction	American English literacy and possibly maintain first language
Intergroup Education	Human Relations; Nonsexist Instruction; Multicultural Education	Positive relationships among students who differ due to class, culture, gender, handicap, race
Human Rights	Social Justice; Social Contract; Natural Rights	Ethical classroom interaction among students; classroom as community of scholars

liberating forces who empower students to pursue their self-interests within a just human community. Contemporary scholars who stress empowerment are Michael Apple,[3] James Banks,[4] Paulo Freire,[5] Henry Giroux,[6] and Joel Spring.[7]

Democratizing schools is by no means an easy task. Traditionally, public schools and their curricula have not been designed to focus specifically on democratic living. Rather, they have been designed to focus on teaching the fundamentals of academic disciplines. Teachers and other public school professionals have been trained in the pedagogy of the academic disciplines, particularly those who work in the secondary levels, although elementary level teachers have also been taught the methodology of discrete disciplines. Teachers have tended to view their primary function as "history" teachers or "language arts" teachers, that is, as transmitters of the basics of some academic discipline. Those who wish to democratize schooling, teaching, and learning confront a difficult situation: focusing on democratic living is at best a secondary function of teachers. Actually, a focus on democratic living means that students will learn how to use knowledge to pursue their self-interests as well as create a just, human community. Democratic living can be learned within or through the study of traditional subjects taught nontraditionally.

The instructional models and strategies are premised on the notion that teachers need conceptual frameworks to use as a basis for preparing students to live in a democratic, pluralistic society. As such, the models and strategies can be utilized concurrently with other teaching and learning activities. In essence, the models and strategies provide a means by which a teacher can develop a multidimensional focus while teaching, rather than a unidimensional focus. For example, while students are being taught how to read they can also be taught how to share interpretations of what they read. With the ethnic studies model, the literature the students read would reflect multiethnic themes, people, and situations. With the intergroup relations strategy, ethnic minority and ethnic majority students would be encouraged to share interpretations of what they read. By developing a multidimensional focus, teachers can infuse or integrate the multiethnic models and strategies with their goals for other teaching and learning activities.

The models and strategies suffer from the perceptions of some educators that they are coded words for "minority education" or "disadvantaged education"; they are intended to be inclusive rather than exclusive, providing conceptual frameworks applicable to all public school classrooms and all students. While they are discrete, they are by no means mutually exclusive. The models and strategies are generic and therefore can be utilized by any classroom teacher while teaching in any established area of studies. For example, secondary teachers such as physical education teachers, science teachers, industrial arts, and home economics teachers all can utilize the models and strategies within their specialties, just as elementary teachers can utilize them during any of their daily activities in music, art, language arts, science, mathematics, social studies, and physical education. The models and strategies have these characteristics in common:

1. They provide means by which equal educational opportunities can be provided for all students.
2. They spring from a sociocultural basis, particularly from notions about culture and language.
3. They are inclusive of all students from all groups.

GLOBAL EDUCATION AND THE MODELS-STRATEGIES

While the text does not treat global education as it does other areas of pluralistic education, the conclusion should not be made that global awareness is not important for effective pluralistic teachers. Quite the opposite! We live in an interdependent world. We all share the same planet, the same air, and the same water. With the advent of global telecommunications, events that happen across the world can be transmitted instantaneously into one's living room, bringing the world into our homes.

Global education fosters the notions that we live in a human community, a global village so to speak, in which all humans are linked; ethnic and national boundaries are transcended; commonalities rather than differences among the peoples of different nations are sought. Yet, people still live within a nation which in turn must manage the ethnic and cultural desires of its people with broader national needs. Therefore, there is potential conflict between the forces of ethnicity and nationalism within most nations. Knowing the nature of the conflict between the two group phenomena is essential for understanding the pluralism of the global village.

Nationalism and ethnicity are similar group phenomena. Both involve group identity, a sense of peoplehood, and allegiance to some group. The etymology of *ethnic* is the Greek *ethnos* meaning "race." The origin of *nation* is the Latin *natio* meaning "birth." Both are rooted in reference to human groups. While the two are similar group phenomena, they differ in scale. An ethnic group tends to be a cultural organization holding in common core values, customs, language, and ancestry. Nation is a much larger-scale cultural organization consisting of a legal, formal political entity holding in common geographic boundaries and governmental institutions as well as core values, customs, and ancestry, i.e., nationalism is a formalized extension of ethnicity.

Most nations are multiethnic and encompass a number of different ethnic groups within their borders. Connor's survey[8] of 171 countries revealed that only 9 percent contained one ethnic group; 38 percent of the countries contained an ethnic group consisting of three-quarters of their citizens; 24 percent consisted of an ethnic group that comprised a little more than half of their citizens; in 29 percent of the countries the dominant ethnic group consisted of less than half the total population. Although a few countries are ethnically homogeneous (9%), the greater number of countries must confront the possibility that their variegated ethnic groups may conflict with each other, or they may conflict with the ethnic groups who control the national government. Consequently, the national government will strive to reduce or eliminate ethnic group conflict for purposes of fostering national group cohesion.

A common problem among nations is how to build national unity while allowing ethnic group diversity. If ethnic groups are given too much autonomy, then national fragmentation is probable. Ethnic groups may demand too much autonomy and attempt to break away from the nation. If ethnic groups are suppressed too much, then ethnic group dissent manifests itself. In an attempt to gain some autonomy, the suppressed ethnic groups may form separatist movements. Too much or not enough autonomy both threaten national cohesion.

Some countries deal with ethnic group diversity by allowing ethnic groups to maintain their languages and cultures. India, for example, allows ethnic and national loyalty by encouraging bilingualism, i.e., a speaking knowledge of the national language, Hindi, and a speaking knowledge of one's own ethnic group language. Other countries emphasize integration into the national culture. The United States, for example, encourages assimilation into its "melting pot," thereby emphasizing English-only monolingualism. A speaking knowledge of one's ethnic group language, if not English, is not acquired in school. The intent of U.S. bilingual education programs is to facilitate the learning of English rather than to maintain the student's ethnic group language.

Nations face at least two communication imperatives for global survival: how to maintain national cohesion and how to maintain international competitiveness. If a nation is confused by citizens who speak different languages and represent different cultures, national unity and cohesion are not possible. If its citizens do not know the languages in which scientific, technologic, and economic advances are made, then the nation will have little or no access to important knowledge necessary for international trade and commerce. Consequently, most nations require a lingua franca, or a common communication system that all citizens can use to conduct business and political affairs on a national scale. They also need knowledge of other languages to provide access to technologic, scientific, and economic activities on a global scale.

Global education has a two-pronged focus: interdependence and cultural pluralism. According to Hoopes, global education prepares students ". . . to cope with global interdependence and cultural pluralism, which involves relationships, events, and forces that cannot be contained within old national or cultural boundaries."[9] As such, global education has three pervasive goals:

1. Global education provides experiences that reduce provincialism and ethnocentrism; this goal can be addressed through teaching materials and methods that teach about cultural relativism; the Cultural Education, Chapter 7, and the Language Education, Chapter 8, approaches are useful with this goal;

2. Global education provides experiences that prepare students to deal rationally with global pluralism; useful to this goal is the text's discussion about cultural relativism and ethical transcendence; Chapter 9, Intergroup Education Strategies, might be used to teach what happens when people of different cultures (or nations) come into contact for the first time;

3. Global education provides those experiences that teach students to think of themselves as individuals, as citizens of a nation, and as members of an overall human community; this goal expands the cultural reference of self-concept to include the entire world, i.e., global education teaches students to think in terms of a global self-concept, one that considers the views and perspectives of members of the human community; Chapter 10, Classroom Management and Human Rights, might be helpful to this goal since it deals with people as members of human communities who enter into social contracts.

These goals are based on a desire to help students acquire sensitivity and awareness of other cultures within other nations. Emphasis is on acquiring knowledge and data about other people and their cultures rather than merely the political or geographic aspects of other nations. The models and strategies described in the chapters that follow can be used to study the peoples and cultures of other nations. This is especially true with the Cultural Education and Language Education models. Both can be used to study either the cultures or languages existing within other nations. Of course, learning the language of another culture can do much to increase the global awareness of students especially if the cultural base of the language is studied. The Intergroup Education approach can be used to help students understand what happens when a person travels to other countries and faces different folkways and values. Human Rights can be used to help students understand the need for universally agreed upon ethics which can be used by peoples and cultures globally. The concepts of cultural relativity and ethical transcendence can be useful tools for understanding other cultures in the world.

SUMMARY

Each model or strategy has a discrete function. Still, there is no reason why all of them couldn't be utilized in a synthesis approach. In other words, different aspects of each model or strategy could be incorporated into a reconstituted model. A teacher may want to improve interpersonal relations and increase the students' knowledge about certain ethnic groups. By combining the intergroup relations strategy with the ethnic studies model, students could work together on projects which focus on ethnic-group history or culture. Or, a teacher may want to foster the students' right to their home language or dialect using aspects of the bilingual model and human rights strategy combined. Each model or strategy can be utilized discretely, but for greater impact on attitude formation and change, it is advisable that more than one of them be utilized simultaneously. In particular, the bilingual instruction model would yield minimal impact on attitude formation and change if used without the bicultural model, which is a variant of the ethnic studies model. The models and strategies can be used for their combined effect—to build cultural understanding and respect. We are now ready to examine in detail the models and strategies.

STUDY QUESTIONS

(*Note:* These questions may require that students read parts of other chapters.)

1. Explain the "consensus rationale" used by educators when seeking a basis for instruction.
2. Review the research on an instructional approach. Then explain the difficulty with using these types of research findings to support an instructional approach.
3. Explain how the goals of Cultural Education and Intergroup Education may differ. Explain how they may appear to be similar.

4. Explain the difference in the goals of Foreign Language Education and Bilingual Instruction. Explain how they may appear to be similar.

5. Explain the goals of the Human Rights approach. Review in Chapter 1 the idea of ethical transcendence and link it to the Human Rights approach.

NOTES

1. Christine E. Sleeter and Carl A. Grant. *Making Choices for Multicultural Education*. Columbus: Merrill, 1988.
2. John Dewey. *How We Think*. Boston: Heath, 1910; see also, George Counts. *Dare the School Build a New Social Order?* New York: John Day, 1932; Boyd Bode. *Modern Educational Theories*. New York: Macmillan, 1927; C. H. Judd. *Education and Social Progress*. New York: Harcourt Brace Jovanovich, 1934.
3. Michael Apple. *Education and Power*. Boston: Routledge & Kegan Paul, 1982.
4. James Banks. *Multiethnic Education*, 2nd ed. Boston: Allyn & Bacon, 1988.
5. Paulo Freire. *The Politics of Education: Culture, Power and Liberation*. South Hadley, MA.: Bergin & Garvey Publishers, 1985.
6. Henry Giroux. *Theory and Resistance: A Pedagogy for the Opposition*. South Hadley, MA.: Bergin & Garvey Publishers, 1983.
7. Joel Spring. *American Education: An Introduction to Social and Political Aspects*. New York: Longman, 1985.
8. W. Connor. "A Nation is a Nation, is a State, is an Ethnic Group." *Ethnic and Racial Studies*, 1, 1978, pp. 187–194.
9. David S. Hoopes. *Intercultural Education*. Bloomington, Ind.: Phi Delta Kappa Education Foundation, 1980, p. 19.

Chapter
7

Cultural Education:
Concepts and Methods

Key Terms:

cultural lag
cultural literacy
intercultural education

cultural adaptation
language borrowing

Teachers have always taught culture. They teach the scholastic culture of Western civilization when they teach mathematics, history, literature, language, and science. They teach the Greek ideal that a healthy body and a rational mind characterize the educated person when they teach health, physical education, and vocational subjects. The issue is not should culture be taught? The issue is, how can students learn about their specific cultural heritages and the heritages of others?

Of course the general American core culture must be taught. Hirsch, in his *Cultural Literacy*,[1] defined the core culture as having three segments: one is the civil religion, a commitment to civic values such as freedom, equality, liberty, and justice; another segment is the vocabulary of public discourse, American English, which allows for public debate and discussion on any topic; the third segment consists of the legends, technologies, customs, and politics that define the core culture. The content of this segment is defined by commonly held knowledge transmitted by literature and folklore. Hirsch defined the core culture:

> American cultural literacy has a bias toward English literate traditions. . . . It is not a weakness of our literate culture that it has its origins in English traditions. . . .[2]

The concern is that Americans should share a common national culture that is taught in the schools. Hirsch then proposes a cultural vocabulary of literary allusions, historic dates, geographic locations, adages, historic and folkloric persons, and scientific concepts as the basic vocabulary of the "literate" American. Examples are: "1776, *1984* (the novel), 'Abandon all hope, ye who enter here', Asia Minor, DNA, 'Leave no stone unturned', and David Hume."[3] The examples are reflective of the challenge that Hirsch faces—defining the core American culture is an arduous task!

Currently, there is no consensus about what historic or literary events constitute the core American culture. For example, what ethics are central to the American civil religion, Hirsch's first core component mentioned above? In a very unscientific poll of at least fifteen of my graduate courses in the "social foundations of education" consisting of about 300 teachers at all levels, I've asked, "What ethical values are core to the American culture?" And, "which do you teach?" Two ethical systems were reported as core and taught by them:

Natural Rights

All humans are created equal with inalienable rights to life, liberty, own-ership of property, and happiness. No person should be deprived of these rights without due process of law and every person is assured equal protection of the law.

Protestant Work Ethic

Work brings salvation; virtues: (1) neatness and punctuality, (2) honesty, patriotism, and loyalty to God and country; (3) striving for personal achievement-competitiveness; (4) respect for authority; (5) postpone-ment of immediate gratification; (6) obeying rules and regulations; (7) respect for the property of others.

The Ten Commandments

Thou shalt have no other gods before me.

Thou shalt not make any graven images of me.

Thou shalt not take the name of God in vain.

Thou shalt keep the sabbath.

Thou shalt honor thy mother and father.

Thou shalt not kill.

Thou shalt not commit adultery.

Thou shalt not steal.

Thou shalt not bear false witness against thy neighbor.

Thou shalt not covet thy neighbor's property, nor his wife.

These ethical systems represent opposing assumptions about the purpose of life and the moral nature of humans. Which system is dominant? If they are equally dominant, then how can a core operate with opposing beliefs? Are there other ethical systems not identified by my students? Clearly, much work is needed before a consensus regarding the core culture can be reached, and once reached, then approaches and curriculum materials can be developed to teach the core. This chapter does not explain how to teach the core American culture. Instead, the chapter provides an analysis of the Ethnic Studies model which explains how teachers can help students understand their own specific cultural heritage and the cultural heritage of others.

Why teach about cultural differences? Current American society consists of a vast array of cultural differences that have substantially enriched the society. Almost daily one is reminded of the richness of cultural diversity existent in our society which is the product of cultural differences. There is another reason to teach about cultural differences—perhaps the most important reason—social harmony.

We are experiencing a resurgence of racial and ethnic group tensions. Schools and colleges reflect the tensions. High schools in the Pacific Northwest, especially in Idaho, Montana, and Washington, have been inundated with white supremacy literature. In the Idaho Panhandle, the Church of Jesus Christ Christian-Aryans Nations, congregates to plan the formation of a white republic which would exclude non-Christians and non-Whites.[4] Eastern and Midwestern colleges and universities have experienced anti-Jewish and anti-Black student activities.[5] These activities are symptomatic of an age-old problem of prejudice and stereotyping that is based on ignorance of cultural differences.

Fundamentally, people fear the unknown. Much like children who fear the darkened attic because they do not know its content, people fear the cultural stranger because they do not know the content of the stranger's culture. Herein lies the central purpose for teaching cultural difference. By learning about the cultural differences prevailing in the United States and throughout the world, ethnocentrisms and stereotypes about people can be diminished. Diminution of prejudices and stereotypes offers the potential for lowering ethnic group strife. The practice of teaching about ethnic groups in some kind of classroom arrangement is not new. Such teaching existed in the New England colonies, primarily to preserve German Lutheranism and the German language and culture[6]; in the latter decades of the eighteenth century, Japanese and Chinese ethnic group schools were established in Hawaii and in California[7]; almost simultaneously on the East Coast, especially in New York City, Jewish schools were established. The Japanese, Chinese, and Jewish schools were attempts to maintain each group's religion, language, and culture. They were supplemental to the public schools so that students attended them after public school hours, in the evenings, or on weekends. These schools provided more than religious instruction; they taught the group's culture and language along with its religion, with the goal of maintaining the group's language and culture.[8]

ORIGINS OF ETHNIC STUDIES

Teaching about ethnic groups was primarily within the sphere of church-related education until the twentieth century when Julius Drachsler[9] and other scholars proposed intercultural studies for the public schools. The idea of the intercultural studies approach was to teach all students about the cultures of the new

European immigrants and thereby foster better cultural understanding among students. Cultural pluralism was the philosophic base of intercultural education. By teaching about the new immigrant cultures and nurturing respect and understanding for the immigrants' languages, customs, and traditions, intercultural education eased the otherwise harsh melting pot assimilation process experienced by the immigrant students. It also taught nonimmigrant students to understand the cultures of immigrant students. Ethnic-group community social agencies, such as Jane Addams's Hull House in Chicago, used intercultural education with adults and younger immigrants.[10] However, intercultural education emerged as a reaction to existing Americanization programs which emphasized American English and history and deemphasized and frowned upon foreign languages and cultures. Intercultural education was perceived as a buffer program for new immigrants rather than as a means of promoting cultural awareness and understanding among all students.

During the zenith of the xenophobic 1920s a New Jersey classroom teacher by the name of Rachel Davis DuBois developed the idea that ethnic conflict and intergroup strife could be ameliorated by teaching her students about cultural differences.[11] This was an era when some viewed cultural differences as un-American; the ideology of Americanization was pervasive, promising to melt away all ethnic group differences. Public schools were to be the smelters. .

Americanization was not adopted by all school districts. Rather, cultural pluralism was favored because it allowed for "unity within diversity," i.e., that a unified, harmonious community was possible with a recognition and appreciation of cultural differences (see Chapter 2). Some school districts that had large ethnic group populations, such as New York, Chicago, and Toledo, developed school activities, clubs, or curriculum materials that portrayed the ethnic groups of their respective communities.[12] DuBois was in the pluralist camp; her idea was that if students knew about their own ethnic groups, and if they knew about the cultures of other ethnic groups, stereotypes and prejudices between the different ethnic groups would be diminished if not eradicated. She developed a series of school assemblies which celebrated the achievements, history, and contributions of various ethnic groups. These assemblies consisted of drama, oratory, music, art, and guest speakers. Teachers and students were expected to follow the assemblies with classroom studies of the various groups.

During graduate school at Teachers College, DuBois met such education notables as George Counts and Harold Rugg who encouraged her to develop and disseminate her ideas for "intercultural education." Taking their advice, she soon became prominent in New York state, and up and down the Eastern Seaboard, for her ideas about how to teach about cultural differences. In 1936 she was hired by the Progressive Education Association to continue her work in intercultural education. In 1938 she was asked to resign from the PEA; while no one was critical of her work from an academic standpoint, her approach proved to be too liberal for some members of the organization who favored a type of benevolent Americanization. Yet, the U.S. Office of Education contracted with her to develop units about various ethnic groups which were programmed for radio presentations, "Americans All—Immigrants All," and broadcast free of charge throughout the United States.[13]

After World War II, Stanford University educators Stewart Cole, James Quillen, and Mildred Wiese attempted to resurrect intercultural education.[14] They conducted intercultural education summer workshops at Stanford for teachers, administrators, and community leaders using materials by Rachel DuBois, Ruth Benedict, Gordon Allport, and W. Lloyd Warner. The workshops were premised on the idea that knowledge about specific ethnic groups will reduce ethnic group tensions and improve intercultural relations. The workshops focused on activities that could be conducted in any elementary or secondary school. The workshops were not intended for schools with only minority group students.

In the mid-1960s minority groups were compelled to pressure public schools, colleges, and universities to implement ethnic studies courses and programs as a means to desegregate the school and university monocultural programs. At first, these ethnic studies programs and courses were simply a way to give ethnic minority groups instruction in their languages and cultures within the educational system. Later, as the programs and courses developed, their goals expanded to include fostering cultural understanding and respect for these languages and cultures. Rather than experience the fate of intercultural education, the ethnic studies programs and courses made an appeal to all students, thereby eliminating the "buffer" or "desegregation only" conception of ethnic studies and replacing it with the goal of cultural and ethnic understanding as the *raison d'être* of the courses and programs. Now some public schools, colleges, and universities have ethnic studies programs: some programs focus on specific ethnic groups (e.g., Italian American, African American Studies); others include several ethnic groups, using "Ethnic Studies" as an umbrella (e.g., Ethnic Studies: Chicano Studies and Native American Studies).

In the 1970s educators revived DuBois' basic idea, that is, knowledge about cultural differences could lower ethnic and racial conflict and strife, under the rubric of "ethnic studies," "multiethnic education," "multicultural education," or "global education." The new intercultural education was to permeate throughout the curriculum.[15] Teachers in most subject areas were encouraged to develop units about cultural differences that would become a part of their regular classroom lessons. Banks[16] coined the idea as "ethnic literacy," based on the premise that teachers, once understanding key anthropologic and sociologic concepts regarding cultural development, could teach about cultural differences.

ETHNIC STUDIES MODEL

- *Goal:* To foster increased knowledge about ethnic groups.
- *Operational assumption:* Increased knowledge about a group can foster a better understanding about the people in the group.

• *Conceptual structure:* To study an ethnic group, it should be approached as

1. a group that is organic and in the process of changing and growing;
2. a group that is organized by a generic system of values and beliefs;
3. a group that is internally diverse;
4. a group that is similar to and different from other groups.

CRITICAL FACTORS FOR UTILIZATION

Using the ethnic studies model requires knowledge about the difference between teaching an experience and teaching about an experience. When Louis Armstrong was asked, "What is jazz?" he replied, "If you don't know, I can't tell you." The same answer applies when the question is asked, "What's it like to be a Japanese American or a Seminole American (or any other ethnic)?" The answer is not flippant; an ethnic experience per se cannot be taught. Teachers can teach about ethnic experiences, but they cannot teach what it feels like to be a member of an ethnic group. Membership in an ethnic group and participation in any or all of its social, cultural, political, or economic activities is a human experience unique to each person within the group. Teachers can teach only data and generalizations that describe the nature of an ethnic group. These data and generalizations can provide a view of an ethnic group's perspectives, an understanding of how and why the group has evolved, an awareness of its past experiences and present conditions, and sensitivity to its hopes, aspirations, and plights. To understand ethnic-group phenomena, a group must be viewed from within and from outside; or, to understand the nature of an ethnic-group experience, students should study how members perceive them. Key questions here are: How does the group define itself? What means does the group use to define itself? The insider perceptions are provided by the group's self-defined history, music, literature, language, and art forms. The outsider perceptions are provided by other groups who interact, or who have interacted, with the ethnic group under study.

When studying a group's self-perceptions, generalizations provide a frame of reference within which the group experience can be understood. The generalizations should not be considered "truths" or "verities"; rather they provide a benchmark for use in becoming better informed about the group. The generalizations should not be construed as the characteristics of individual group members, lest they promote stereotypes. Consider the generalization that racial minority groups have been oppressed by laws and social customs. There are sufficient data to support the generalization; still, not all racial minority persons have personally experienced oppression; nor do all racial minority persons feel oppressed. An individual's reaction depends upon unique experiences, life situation, and circumstances. An individual reaction at variance with the generalization does not invalidate the generalization; rather, the reaction indicates the multidimensionality of the ethnic experience.

Generalizations about ethnic groups should emphasize the dynamic nature of ethnic-group development. All too often, ethnic groups are portrayed as sleeping dinosaurs who erupt into frenetic activism for short periods of time and then recede into antiquated sleep. The implication is that ethnic groups, like dinosaurs, are unchangeable and unadaptable organisms. In fact, if ethnic groups were like dinosaurs, they too would experience extinction. The dynamics that sustain the organic development of ethnic groups can be described as the human forces of change and conservation. As an ethnic group grows and develops, it must contend with the human impulse to conserve past practices, customs, and folkways and the impulse to change behaviors to adapt to current pressures of the physical and human environment. A balance between the two forces must be maintained continuously; conservation of too much of the past leads to decadence, or cultural lag. Too much or too rapid change causes disorientation, a sense of rootlessness, or what Toffler calls "future shock." To survive and to flourish, ethnic groups confront two forces, conserving and adapting behaviors, beliefs, and folkways in a continuous process of growth and development, a balancing act that produces stress and strives to minimize it. Figure 7.1 illustrates the dynamics of ethnic-group development.

THE MODEL'S OPERATIONAL PRINCIPLES

Teachers should approach teaching and learning about ethnic groups as a legitimate topic worthy of serious thought. Ethnic biases, stereotypes, and racist attitudes are learned in various ways in and out of the classroom. They can be countered by a serious study of ethnic groups, especially if imaginative and creative methods are used. Antiquated approaches such as rote memorization of names of popular ethnic heroes are inappropriate. Rather, multimedia techniques and multiinstructional patterns (peer tutoring, field trips, simulations,

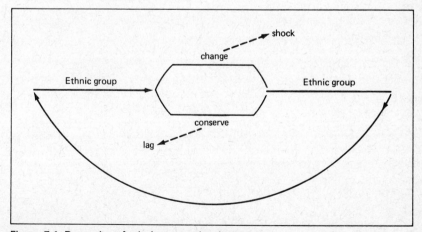

Figure 7.1 Dynamics of ethnic-group development

etc.) are now recognized means by which teaching and learning can be both serious and interesting. A serious study of U.S. ethnic groups would include but not be confined to the four principles which follow.

1. *Ethnic groups have unique experiences within the broader American society.* This principle focuses on the unique experiences ethnic groups have within the broader American society. For example, Native Americans, African Americans, and Irish Americans joined the broader American society under different circumstances. Irish Americans emigrated to the United States, accommodated to the Anglo conformity melting pot, and progressed into the middle and upper classes. Black Americans were forced to migrate to the United States and then were enslaved for almost 175 years. After emancipation, they were segregated for 90 more years, and then progressed from enslaved status to lower-, middle-, and upper-middle-class status. Native Americans migrated to the North American continent long before Europeans arrived. The European colonizers declared them separate nations, making and then breaking treaties with each nation. Native Americans were eventually declared U.S. citizens (1924) but retained separate nation status. Forced from their homelands, they were placed on reservations; some were taken from the reservations, while others were kept there. Social status for North Americans is tribally defined and should not be compared to the black and Irish American notions of social class status. Irish Americans encountered hostility toward their religion, Roman Catholicism. Blacks encountered slavery, and later, racial segregation and discrimination; Native Americans encountered dislocation, relocation, and separate nation status. Each group, in the attempt to participate in American life, encountered different experiences that influenced and formed its unique relationship with the broader society.

Each group should be studied as a unique ethnic group, not as though its early experiences were the same as or similar to those of other groups. The tendency is to lump ethnic groups together, assuming that each has undergone the same assimilation experience. Thus we have the myth that just as the Irish (or any other immigrant group) have been assimilated after starting at the bottom, so will Puerto Ricans (or some other ethnic minority group) be assimilated after starting at the bottom. For these purposes, Puerto Ricans are not foreign immigrants; they are U.S. citizens who merely choose to move from the island of Puerto Rico to the continental United States.

2. *Ethnic groups have definable demographic characteristics.* Ethnic-group peoples tend to live in certain areas, speak certain languages or dialects, and maintain their ancestral ties. Examples are: Japanese Americans tend to reside in the western United States and in Hawaii, although the U.S. government relocated them to various areas of the West and Midwest during World War II; Cuban Americans tend to maintain their Spanish language and culture while blending into the social scene. In particular, Cuban Americans, like other Spanish-speaking groups, have developed a bilingual capability in Spanish and English which is surpassed by few other groups. Greek Americans tend to maintain their ancestral ties with their mother country, Greece, and its traditions.

3. *Ethnic groups have elements of group homogeneity as well as heterogeneity; that is, intragroup differences and similarities exist.* The principle's best example is the Native American group. Native Americans are a tribal group, and in order of intimacy and interdependence, loyalty is first to the family, then to the clan, and then to the tribe. Within tribal groups there are variations. Among the Apaches (tribe) there are at least three distinctly different subtribal groups, each having different customs and traditions. Within each of the three subtribal groups, there are of course many families and clans to which individuals are primarily loyal. Thus, ethnic groups exhibit internal diversity in terms of traditions, customs, languages. For instance, at least 46 distinct languages are known to exist among Native Americans. Still, ethnic groups exhibit common values and beliefs. Generally speaking, Native Americans believe that people are a part of nature and must learn to adapt their ways to nature. An abiding respect for the ecology of the land, sea, and rivers is clearly a value held in common among Native Americans. Again, not every Native American holds these beliefs and values; nevertheless, as a group, Native Americans hold in common these values and beliefs.

4. *Ethnic groups have world views which can be understood through their literature, folklore, music, and other humanistic art forms.* A group's world view can be understood by a study of its humanistic expressions. For example, as I have read the fiction and poetry of black writers, as I have listened to the music and folklore of black musicians and folklorists, I have been struck by the underlying message: a deeply felt assertion and affirmation of life and a genuine belief in the message of Christ that hope and love will prevail in the end. At first, the spirit of the Negro spirituals, the poetry of Langston Hughes, or the fiction of Maya Angelou seem to be cries of despair. But as I listen and read more carefully, a profound sense of hope and compassion for other humans emerges. A group's world view can be understood by its humanistic expressions, but one should read a group's literature and study the group's humanistic tradition broadly and deeply. The adage "a little learning is a dangerous thing" holds true. A superficial study of a group's humanistic tradition can create stereotypes and misconceptions, doing it and the students little justice. In a very real way, the group's humanistic tradition should be approached with sensitivity to prevent reinforcing prevailing stereotypes and biases about the group.

TEACHING METHODS

Since the model is so amenable to the teaching of social studies and language arts, I will suggest methods outside these disciplines. The following are intended as suggestions which may lead to broader and deeper studies about ethnic groups:

Science

Students can research famous scientists, such as black inventors and medical doctors.

Students can study contributions Native Americans have made to pharmaceutical medicines.

Students can research various versions of the creation and evolution of the earth and the universe.

Students can study the similarities and differences of biologically different people. (A rigorous study of the concept of race, I feel, would serve to dispel most myths about racial superiority.)

Math

Students can study various ethnic groups' concepts of time and space.

Students can study how ethnic groups historically have calculated seasons and time of year. (A simple study of different calendars would go far in expanding the students' understanding of how different cultures measure time, e.g., Chinese or Aztec calendars.)

Home Economics

Students can study differing ethnic-group family patterns: nuclear, extended, single-parent families.

Students can study the differing foods, hairstyles, clothing styles (traditional) of various ethnic groups.

Students can study the viability of diverse ethnic group diets.

Physical Education

Students can study and learn the differing organized games of ethnic groups.

Students can study and learn the differing dances of ethnic groups.

Teaching and learning about different ethnic groups is essential if students are to live and work in a society based on pluralism. Clearly, knowledge about different ethnic groups can lead to a better understanding of the groups.

USING THE ETHNIC STUDIES MODEL

The model is a conceptual frame of reference that can be used to teach or study any type of human group. It could be used to teach or study about the role of women in U.S. society, the role of certain cultural groups, such as pioneers, cowboys, trappers or traders, or the role of ethnic groups such as Irish Americans or Chinese Americans. Further, the model can be used on all grade levels and in any sociocultural setting. Clearly, the model has use in urban and rural areas where ethnic minority students are highly concentrated. But it is equally useful in suburban and other culturally homogeneous communities.

DEMONSTRATION LESSON

Rather than end this chapter with discussion questions, a demonstration lesson using the Ethnic Studies Model is provided.

Title: Roots of the American Horseman
Goal: To acquaint students with the historical basis of the American cowboy. Also, to provide information about the impact of Hispanic culture on the American culture.
Objectives: As a consequence of this lesson, students will:

1. know the historical basis of the American cowboy;
2. understand the concept of cultural adaptation;
3. understand the concept of language borrowing;
4. understand the impact of Hispanic culture on the American scene;
5. know and understand various vocabulary items that are rooted in the Spanish language.

What follows is a narrative explaining the content of the lesson plan, "Roots of the American Horseman":

The American cowboy is truly an American invention. Riding tall in the saddle astride his strong and loyal pinto pony, his face to the wind, his sunburned face toward the sunset, the cowboy has ridden in the imaginations of most Americans. Thousands of stories and movies exist about this legendary figure. He is so much a part of the American scene that even cowboy boots and shirts are purchased for men, women, teenagers, and children in most parts of the United States. Automobiles, such as the "Bronco," the "Mustang," and the "Pinto" are named after familiar cowboy horses. To many people, the cowboy represents the American ideals of rugged individualism and self-reliance. Just what are the roots of the cowboy? Why did he develop in the United States?

The cowboy's roots took hold in what is now the United States Southwest, especially Texas, New Mexico, Arizona, and Southern California. Between the years 1500–1845 when the southwestern United States belonged to Spain (1522–1810) and then later Mexico (1821–1845), the Spanish or Mexican colonists and pioneers met their need for meat by either hunting or raising it.

The early Spanish explorers, especially Francisco Vasquéz de Coronado, and the early Spanish colonizer Don Juan Oñate, brought horses, cattle, sheep, goats, and other livestock from Spain to the newfound territory between the years 1540 and 1598. While Don Oñate successfully established a Spanish colony in New Mexico in 1598 (before the eastern Jamestown Colony was founded), both his expedition and the expedition of other explorers lost many of their livestock. The herds were large and many cattle, horses, and sheep strayed. Soon wild herds roamed the territory; anyone who could capture, tame, and brand the livestock could claim ownership of it. Two different occupations sprang up from this situation: (1) the cowboy (*vaquero*) to tend cattle and (2) the shepherd (*pastor*) to tend sheep. These horsemen (Mexican Indian, mostly) developed the American horsemen culture, because they developed the tools, the special language, the code of beliefs, and the customs that English-speaking cowboys adopted. The English-speaking cowboys borrowed the culture from the Spanish and later Mexican horsemen by simply translating the horsemen's culture into the English language. There are some familiar ranching terms that the English-speaking cowboys borrowed, translated, or shortened from the original Spanish-Mexican cowboys. Aside from the many place names, like San Diego, Los

Angeles, California, San Antonio, Palo Duro, Rio Grande, and so on, many words of Spanish origin have been incorporated into the English language either literally, with slight changes in spelling or pronunciation, or otherwise made into a "new" English word. Here is a list of Spanish words of the range along with the corresponding words that they became in English:

lazo	lasso
la reata	lariat
bronco	bronco
mesteño	mustang
cañon	canyon
rancho	ranch
ranchero	rancher
corral	corral
chaparral	chaparral
chaparreras	chaps
rodeo = roundup	rodeo = contest
vaquero	buckaroo
coyote	coyote
patio	patio

Vaqueros—The Tending Horsemen

To settle the vast, arid Southwest territory, the Spanish and Mexican governments gave people land grants consisting of many thousands of acres of open rangeland. Because the dry, arid territory was not very well suited for farming, many of the land grants became *ranchos* (ranches) or "ranges" on which cattle and sheep were raised. The *vacas* (Spanish for cows) were tended by *vaqueros* or "cowboys." Most *vaqueros* were men who were part Indian and part Spanish. The Spanish word for this mixed breed was *mestizo;* however, the *vaqueros* were more Indian than Spanish, and during the Mexican era, the *vaqueros* flourished on the *ranchos.*

Some of the *vaqueros* were Black, especially after the Civil War, when Blacks were emancipated. The Black cowboys rode the cattle drives alongside the White and Mexican cowboys. The *vaqueros* developed a special *silla* (saddle) which had a horn. The *vaquero* used the horn for different purposes, but especially to drape *la reata* (lariat) or to tie his rope in a dolly welter knot (*dale vuelta*) around the horn after throwing the *lazo* (lasso).

The *vaquero's* work outfit was adapted for work and climatic conditions. He wore a large *sombrero* (a hat that provides shade) to protect his face and head from the hot sun. Special high-heeled, pointed-toe boots that would fit snugly into the stirrup were designed. The boot could also slip off easily if the *vaquero's* foot slipped too far into the stirrup. Many times when the *vaquero* would be riding fast to prevent a stampede, or to chase down strays, his foot would slip into the stirrup, causing him to fall from his horse. Rather than being stuck in the stirrup, and possibly being dragged to death by his fast-moving horse, the *vaquero* in this precarious position could simply pull his foot out of the boot and fall safely to the ground. The *vaquero* also wore leather *chaparreras* (chaps) around his legs to protect them from the common, thorny thicket *chaparral* (bushes). The *vaquero*, when he could afford it, also wore a buckskin jacket with silver buttons.

Vaqueros—Ripping and Roaring

There are some false ideas about *vaqueros*. Most did not roar into a town, get drunk, and then commence to rip it up with their guns. In fact, the average *vaquero* did not carry a pistol nor did he indulge in gun duels. Rather, the *vaquero* tested his skill in horsemanship, cattle roping, and branding at annual *rodeos* (roundups) when cattle were rounded up for branding or slaughtering. During the *rodeo*, especially in the early evenings, the *vaqueros* would have *bronco* (wild, untamed horse) riding contests, cattle roping contests, and bull riding contests. Occasionally, a bear would wander into the rodeo area and supposedly the *vaqueros* would attempt to ride it! More likely, the *vaqueros* would rope the bear, and then release it before getting it too angry. The western rodeo of today has its roots in the early *vaquero* roundup contests.

It is true that the *vaquero* would sing and play the guitar in the evenings, especially during the long trail rides when herds were driven to distant markets. The *vaquero* sang for his own entertainment; he also sang to pacify the cattle made nervous by the howls of the coyotes or the smell of nearby bears. The coyotes and bears, hearing the *vaquero*'s voice, would keep away from the herd. The songs were usually *corridos* or running accounts of adventures or stories that happened to the *vaquero*. English-speaking cowboys adopted this custom and created their own *corridos*, such as the ballad of "The Chisholm Trail."

Some *vaqueros* also tended large herds of sheep. The *vaqueros* would guard the sheep in the evenings as they guarded the cattle. Many times the herds were so large that the *vaqueros* would also train dogs to guard the sheep. These dogs were scampy and quick. When a sheep would wander from the herd, the sheepdog would chase the sheep back to the flock by barking and nipping at its heels. To the sheep-tending horseman, there was no dishonor attached to sheepherding. But, later in the history of the American West, when cattle ranchers and sheep ranchers were at odds over the open range and grazing rights issues, cattle ranchers gave sheepherding a negative connotation.

*Corrido de Kansas**

(Corrido *is a running account of the* vaquero's *adventures or misadventures. It follows the ballad form: the first stanza introduces the song, the middle stanzas tell the story, and the last stanza summarizes or concludes the story.*)

Cuando salimos pa' Kansas	When we left for Kansas
Con una grande partida,	With a large party,
Nos decía el caporal:	The foreman said to us:
—No cuento ni con mi vida.—	"I don't count on even my own life."
Qinientos novillos eran	There were fifteen-hundred steers
Pero todos muy livianos,	And they were all very wild,
No los podíamos reparar	We could not keep them herded
Siendo treinta mexicanos.	Being only thirty Mexicans.

---

* *The Corrido de Kansas is a folksong. The above version was taught to me by my uncle.*

Cuando llegamos a Kansas	When we arrived in Kansas
Un torito se peló	A young steer took out (of
Fué a tajarle un mozo joven	the herd),
Y el cavallo se voltió.	A young boy went to cut
	him off
	And his horse fell down.

Cuando llegamos a Kansas
Un torito se peló
Fué a tajarle un mozo joven
Y el cavallo se voltió.

When we arrived in Kansas
A young steer took out (of
     the herd),
A young boy went to cut
     him off
And his horse fell down.

Cuando dimos visto a Kansas
Se vió un fuerte aguacero,
No los podiamos reparar
Ni formar un tiroteo.

When we came in sight of
     Kansas
There was a heavy rain-
     shower,
We could not keep them
     herded
Nor get a shooting started.

Cuando dimos visto a Kansas
Era puritita correr,
Eran los caminos largos,
Y pensaba yo en volver.

When we came in sight of
     Kansas
It was nothing but running,
The roads were long,
And I thought about turning
     back.

La madre de un adventurero
Le pregunta al caporal:
—Oiga, déme razón di my
     hijo,
Que no lo he visto llegar.—

The mother of a driver
Asks the foreman:
"Listen, give me news of my
     son,
As I have not seen him
     arrive."

—Señora, le voy a decir
Pero no se vaya a llorar,
A su hijo le mató un novillo
En la puerta de un corral.

"Lady, I will tell you
But don't go and cry,
A steer killed your son
On the top of a corral.

Trienta pesos alcanzó
Pero todo limitado,
Y trescientos puse yo
Pa' haberlo sepultado.

Thirty pesos were left over
But it was all owed,
And I put in three hundred
To have him buried.

Todos los adventureros
Lo fueron a acompañar,
Con sus sombreros en las
     manos,
A verlo sepultar.—

All the drivers
Went to accompany him,
With their hats in their
     hands,
To see him buried."

Some very good books that provide more details about cowboy roots are listed below:

Dary, David. *Cowboy Culture: A Saga of Five Centuries*. New York: Avon Books, 1981.

Dobie, Frank J. *The Longhorns*. Bromhall House (New York).

Dobie, Frank J. *A Vaquero of the Brush Country*. New York: Little, Brown & Co., 1929.

Fehrenbach, T. R. *Lone Star*. New York: Macmillan, 1968.

Haley, Evetts J. *The X I T Ranch of Texas*. Norman: University of Oklahoma Press, 1954.

McWilliams, Carey. *North from Mexico*. New York: Greenwood Press, 1968.

Roots of the American Horseman is written in very general terms so that it can be used in a number of ways:

1. To teach about the impact of Hispanics on American culture.
2. To teach economic principles regarding the occupation of ranching.
3. To teach anthropological theories about modes of dressing and the development of tools to accomplish tasks.
4. To teach linguistic principles regarding language borrowing, word origins, and cognates.
5. All of the above could be used while teaching the language arts, reading and writing especially. Students could research in detail for information about an array of items in the lesson. Everything from the use of horses on the North American continent to the use of branding irons. After conducting the research, students should prepare both an oral presentation as well as a written report on their projects.
6. Much could be done with the cowboy ballad or the corrido in terms of creative expression. Students could commit to memory old traditional cowboy ballads as well as more contemporary ballads. Music is an end in itself and learning it should be a part of education.
7. Keep in mind that the ethnic studies model can be used concurrently with the teaching of most, if not all, academic subjects (which is desirable).

NOTES

1. E. D. Hirsch. *Cultural Literacy: What Every American Needs to Know*. New York: Vintage Press, 1988, p. 102–103.
2. Hirsch. *Cultural Literacy*, 106.
3. Hirsch. *Cultural Literacy*, 146–216.
4. Associated Press. "Aryans Call for a Republic," *Billings (Montana) Gazette*, October 5, 1986, p. 1.
5. "Racial Incidents Worry Campus Officials," *Chronicle of Higher Education*, March 18, 1987, p. 1.
6. Joshua Fishman. *Language Loyalty in the United States*. The Hague: Mouton, 1966; see also, Garcia. *Learning in Two Languages*. Bloomington, Ind.: Phi Delta Kappa Education Foundation, 1976.
7. John E. Reinecke. *Language and Dialect in Hawaii*. Honolulu: University of Hawaii Press, 1969, pp. 119–132; see also, Arnold Leibowitz. *Educational Policy and Po-*

litical Acceptance. Washington, D.C.: Center for Applied Linguistics, 1971, pp. 6–44.

8. Fishman. *Language Loyalty.*

9. Julius Drachsler. *Democracy and Assimilation.* New York: Macmillan, 1920; see also, William Vickery and Stewart Cole. *Intercultural Education in American Schools.* New York: Harper & Row, 1943.

10. Mark Krug. *The Melting of the Ethnics.* Bloomington, Ind.: Phi Delta Kappa Foundation, 1975, pp. 63–77.

11. Rachel DuBois. *Build Together Americans.* New York: Hinds, Hayden & Eldredge, 1945.

12. Nicholas V. Montalto. "The Intercultural Education Movement, 1924–1941," in B. Weiss, ed. *American Education and the European Immigrant, 1840–1940.* Champaign: University of Illinois Press, 1982, 142–160.

13. "Uncle Sam Schoolmaster," *Radio Guide Weekly,* December 10, 1938, p. 1.

14. Stewart G. Cole, James Quillen, and Mildred Wiese. *Charting Intercultural Education: 1945–1955.* Palo Alto: Stanford University Press, 1946.

15. James Banks, Carlos E. Cortes, Geneva Gay, Ricardo L. Garcia, and Anna S. Ochoa. *Curriculum Guidelines for Multiethnic Education.* Washington, D.C.: National Council for the Social Studies, 1976.

16. James Banks. *Teaching Strategies for Ethnic Studies,* 3rd Ed. Boston: Allyn & Bacon, pp. 53–92; see also, James Banks. *Multiethnic Education: Theory and Practice,* 2nd Ed. Boston: Allyn & Bacon, 1988.

Chapter
8

Language Education: Concepts and Methods

Key Terms:

assimilation
audio-lingual method
bilingualism: additive, dominant,
   subtractive
bilingual method

direct method
grammar-translations
language acquisition
lingua franca

All teachers teach language. Consciously and unconsciously teachers in the United States teach the full range of the language arts of standard American English. The phenomenon is so self-evident that most teachers rarely think of themselves as language teachers. They go about their daily lessons cajoling students to listen, take good notes, and to think before they speak. "Make sure brain is in gear before engaging tongue," goes the adage. Thinking, communicating, knowing are ultimate educational aims and all are taught through the medium of the English language. This is as it should be; the better the students use the English language, the better they think, know, and communicate. These opening words illustrate how much language education is misunderstood. This chapter will analyze language education. It begins with the global dimensions of language education, linking them to conflicting U.S. language legacies: linguistic pluralism versus English-only ethnocentrism. Then first and second acquisition are reviewed as they relate to language education instructional methods. The chapter ends with a summary of research findings and problems about bilingualism in the United States.

GLOBAL DIMENSIONS OF LANGUAGE EDUCATION

Language is central to nationalism and the development of national identity. A nation's official language(s) carries and conveys the nation's symbols: oaths of allegiance, national anthems, and slogans in the national language embody the nation's spirit. The language serves to facilitate communication among the

153

citizenry as well as to act as the national unification agent. Some nations have names and languages which are synonymous; for example, Spain and Spanish, Germany and German. Other nations have no such correspondence between names and their official languages; for example, United States and English, Canada and French and English. All nations have one or more languages recognized as their official language(s). Some countries, such as France, have one official language which is regulated by a language academy. Other countries, such as Canada, have an official bilingual policy which allows for two languages to coexist as the official languages. Some countries, India and the Soviet Union for example, have one official language which is used nationally, but allow regional languages and dialects to be used and taught within their respective regions.

To understand the link between nationalism and a nation's language education programs—a discussion about the linkage between nationalism, ethnicity, and national purposes for schools is presented, followed by an overview of the language education programs of two very different nations, the Republic of the Philippines and the Soviet Union. Are there language education commonalities between these two disparate nations that might teach us something about language education within a global context? Both are described to provide data from which tentative inferences are drawn regarding the basic thesis that *national cohesion and international competition are potent forces that shape a country's language education programs.* These forces influence how people, at the local school and community levels, perceive the importance or unimportance of certain languages, causing them to value or devalue knowledge of those languages.

NATIONALISM, ETHNICITY, AND SCHOOLS

Schools throughout the world serve a nation-building function primarily because the future of all nations resides in their youth, the young people who will someday be citizens influencing government policies and economic activities. The language or languages these future citizens speak, the history they know, and the scientific and technologic tools they use all mesh to form a worldview that can advance or retard a nation's progress.[1] World powers, like the Soviet Union and the United States, recognize the nation-building potency of their schools by compelling parents to enroll their children in school. Violation of compulsory education laws is considered an offense against the state.

The nationalistic goals of most nations are linked to the purposes of their schools. What schools teach, and more specifically, *which language(s) they teach,* can serve to build national cohesion and provide access to critically important knowledge. Or, the language(s) taught can serve to enclose a nation in a verbal cocoon, thereby isolating a nation on a global scale.[2] And, the language(s) taught can serve to protect the economic interests of particular social classes or ethnic groups within a nation.

Language Education in the Philippines

The Republic of the Philippines consists of 51 provinces in which ten regional languages, referred to as *vernaculars*, and three foreign languages, *Arabic, English, Spanish*, are spoken. These vernaculars are indigenous to the Philippines: *Bikol, Cebuano, Hiligaynon, Ilokano, Kapampangan, Maranao-Maguin Dango, Pangasinon, Tausug, Tagalog, Waray*. Arabic was introduced through immigration. Spanish and English were introduced as colonial languages by Spain (1565–1898) and the United States (1898–1946). During the colonial regimes, the languages of the respective colonizers were used by many of the upper and middle classes. Still, many of the indigenous people maintained loyalty to their ethnic group languages and cultures. Access to educational and governmental resources, during the colonial regimes, required knowledge of Spanish and English, respectively.[3]

Before gaining independence from the United States, the Philippine people sought to build a new nation representative of their indigenous cultures and languages. A constitutional government, patterned after the U.S. Constitution, was established with the addition of a clause stipulating bilingualism as the nation's policy:

> The Congress shall take steps toward the development and adoption of a common national language based on one of the existing native languages. Until otherwise provided by law, English and Spanish shall continue as official languages (Philippine Constitution, 1935).

In 1935 the Institute of National Languages was formed to select a new national language, a lingua franca.

After an extensive study of all the vernaculars, *Tagalog* was recommended as the most appropriate vernacular and was adopted as the national language. The new language, as the nation's lingua franca, went into effect when the U.S. granted independence to the Philippines on July 4, 1946. The term *Pilipino* was adopted in 1987 as the official name of the new language. The instituted bilingual education policy required that students learn Pilipino and English; students could be taught in their native vernaculars in grades 1 and 2, or as needed. A subsequent curricular pattern evolved.[4]

> Grades 1–2: Native language as medium of instruction may be used for nonlanguage arts subjects, as needed; Pilipino and English introduced either as first or second language, depending upon the student's first language;

> Grades 3–10: Pilipino as medium of instruction for social studies, and health and physical education; English as medium of instruction for all sciences and mathematics; the language arts of both Pilipino and English are taught.

In 1985 the Linguistic Society of the Philippines conducted an evaluation of the bilingual education policy. Specifically, the evaluation examined (1) the English and Pilipino language proficiency and academic achievement of students in grades 4, 6, 10 in five subjects—Pilipino and English language arts, Social Studies, Sciences, and Mathematics—concurrently, the teachers' proficiencies in Pilipino and English were assessed; (2) the level of awareness and attitudes of governmental and nongovernmental officials regarding the bilingual education policy; and (3) the status of the bilingual education policy at the tertiary level—community colleges, vocational schools, colleges—through a survey of faculty, administrators, and students.[5]

The study's results, in summary form, indicated that about 98 percent of the schools had implemented the bilingual education policy but, the students' academic achievement reflected a pattern of progressive regression, that is, as the students progressed in grade levels, they regressed in proficiency in the subject matter taught. Also, more than 75 percent of the teachers scored poorly on the subject matter tests. Further, most of the teachers were not fluent in Pilipino, and some did not teach the language because of their lack of fluency. At the organizational level, more than 75 percent of the respondents indicated that they had never heard of the bilingual education policy. They also reported that English proficiency was an important consideration for employment. Knowledge of Pilipino was considered less important when compared to English proficiency. At the tertiary level, more than 50 percent of those surveyed indicated that English was superior to Pilipino as a medium of instruction and as a language tool for scholarly research. Of the tertiary institutions surveyed, only 35 percent reported that the bilingual education policy had been implemented.

Language Education in the Soviet Union

The Soviet Union is a multilingual federation consisting of 35 formerly independent republics and at least 70 sizable territorial ethnic groups.[6] Each republic and each ethnic group once operated as independent entities having their own governments, languages, and cultures. Through conquest and colonialism the Russian republic evolved as the Soviet Union's central republic although its centralizing efforts were perennially frustrated. The non-Russian republics, and the independent ethnic groups simply did not want to be Russian. They preferred their own cultures and languages.[7] Current events in the Soviet Union indicate that the problem persists. Estonia, one of the Soviet Union's republics forcibly acquired in 1940 along with Lithuania and Latvia, recently declared its native language its official language to be used in all public affairs.

The last attempts to Russianize the Soviet Union prior to the 1918 Bolshevik revolution met with only moderate success at extremely great cost in terms of warfare and human lives.[8] These last attempts provided the Bolshevik revolutionaries with support for their cause. Lenin promised the non-Russian people cultural and educational independence if they would support his cause. After the revolution a pluralistic compromise was struck, making Soviet unification possible: all republics and all ethnic groups were assured they could maintain their respective languages and cultures in the public schools so long as the groups would also learn the Russian language as the nation's lingua franca.[9]

Due to catastrophic events after the 1918 revolution, namely an economic depression and World War II, along with Stalin's repressive regime, the pluralistic compromise was hardly implemented. With the demise of Stalin, and the push of the 1950s to lead the world in science and technology, a more concerted effort was made to implement the pluralistic compromise, effectuating the language education policy that in the Soviet Union (1) all students can be taught in their home language, (2) all students are taught Russian, and (3) all students are taught a foreign language, usually English, German, or French. The broad pattern of language education curricula for the Soviet education system is:

Grades 1–2: The native language can serve as the medium of instruction.

Grades 3–10: The native language can serve as the medium of instruction in certain subjects. Russian is taught as a second language, or, Russian is used as the medium of instruction.

Grades 4–10: Study of a foreign language is required.

The Soviet policy of linguistic pluralism and its language education practices differ substantially.[10] Five kinds of schools exist in the Soviet Union: four have curricula instructed almost entirely in Russian, and one remaining kind of school has a bilingually instructed curriculum.[11] The first kind uses Russian as the medium of instruction for Russian students in the Russian republic; the second kind is a Russian-medium school in the Russian republic for indigenous, non-Russian-speaking minorities, for example, Bashkirs and Yakuts; the third kind is a Russian medium school for non-Russian speakers who have emigrated to the Russian republic; the fourth kind is a Russian medium school for Russian students who have emigrated to other Soviet republics. The fifth kind, the bilingual school, consists of a curriculum taught in two or more non-Russian languages for two or more non-Russian-speaking ethnic groups. The study of a foreign language is mandatory in all five kinds of schools.[12]

What inferences and conclusions are allowable given the brief overviews of the language education programs of these two nations? At best, any inferences or conclusions are speculative given the general overviews; both nations are linguistically complex. Currently, both are undergoing internal strife. However, there exist striking similarities and differences between the language education programs of the Philippines and the Soviets:

- Both allow use of the native language as a medium of instruction during the early grades. The approach allows some primary students a smooth transition from home to school as the students are allowed to learn in the language spoken at home. But, this practice is clearly temporary because by the third grade students receive instruction in the nation's lingua franca regardless of the language spoken at home; nonetheless, the approach does allow a modicum of language maintenance for local ethnic groups which may serve to lower ethnic group alienation and discontent within the community.

Both require full literacy in a standardized national language. Here the similarity is outweighed by the differences in the two nations; Pilipino as a lingua franca is in direct competition with English, a former colonial language. English appears to be leading the race primarily because it is perceived as a language of opportunity and upward mobility. Note that both organizational personnel and post-secondary school faculty and administration valued English over Pilipino as reflected in their attitude and awareness of the bilingual education policy study conducted by the Linguistic Society of the Philippines; while, the "progressive regression" of the students studied can be attributed somewhat to their teachers' lack of fluency in Pilipino, in a larger sense, the fact that English is valued more highly than Pilipino by organizational and postsecondary personnel could account for the students' academic regression; the students' reasoning may run, "Why learn in a less valued language?" Or, "If you want to make it in the real world, it's better to learn English. After all, even many of our teachers are not proficient in Pilipino." Also, by resisting the official lingua franca, the English-speaking citizens are promoting English as a replacement, a de facto lingua franca.

In contrast, the Soviet Union has a pluralistic policy regarding local languages and cultures but in practice the Russian-medium schools consist of four-fifths of the Soviets' public school system; while the Soviets are permissive, allowing bilingual schools to exist, the overwhelming majority of schools tend to operate with Russian as the medium of instruction. The Soviets' lingua franca is well established in the schools in contrast to Pilipino which is not well established in the greater community. In the Soviet Union, the lingua franca is apparently perceived as a language of opportunity while Pilipino is not thusly perceived by English-speaking Philippine citizens. Like the Philippines, the language of the dominant classes prevails. In the Soviet Union, knowledge of Russian is needed for upward mobility within government and education circles which is also the Philippine situation.

Both the Philippine and the Soviet curricula require a foreign language. In both nations students are required to learn a language that will access technologic, scientific, and economic knowledge beyond the confines of their national boundaries.

Language education programs and curricula are inextricably linked to a nation's political goals and communication imperatives. Citizens within a nation will respond to political goals such as consolidating national cohesion by learning the lingua franca when knowledge of the language also provides economic or academic opportunities as reflected in the Soviet Union with knowledge of Russian; citizens will be less responsive to a lingua franca when knowledge of the language is not perceived as conferring advantages as reflected in the Philippines with knowledge of Pilipino. Also, citizens will respond favorably to foreign language programs when they perceive that the foreign language confers advantages, thereby enhancing a nation's access to critical scientific, technologic, and economic knowledge as reflected in the Philippines and the Soviet Union.

These conclusions require modification of my thesis, to wit: National cohesion and international competition are potent forces that shape a country's language education programs; these forces influence how people, at local school and community levels, perceive the importance or unimportance of certain languages causing them to value or devalue knowledge of certain languages. *Self-interests, especially when knowledge of a particular language confers economic or academic advantages, serve to monitor a government's language education policies.*

Perhaps people are motivated to learn languages for factors that override economic self-interests? When a national government and ethnic groups conflict regarding adoption and implementation of a lingua franca, which side prevails? Would the ethnic groups maintain language loyalties and abjure economic gain? Would a national government be able to coerce ethnic groups to speak its lingua franca if the groups simply refused to speak it?

LANGUAGE LEGACIES IN CONFLICT

In the United States, language education reflects the ambivalence of a nation attempting to develop a national identity and culture and yet respect the cultural and religious rights of different ethnic groups. At times, learning a second language has been favored; at other times, speaking a second language has been considered un-American. We have vacillated between an informal policy of English-only ethnocentrism and one of permissive linguistic pluralism—two language legacies in conflict.

Currently, more than 25 European languages are spoken in the United States, such as French, German, Hungarian, Italian, Norwegian, Polish, Russian, Spanish, Swedish, and Yiddish (an international language). Add to these, Asian (Cambodian, Chinese, Hmong, Japanese, Laotian, Vietnamese), Middle Eastern, and the languages spoken by Native Americans, and a portrait of linguistic pluralism appears.[13] Yet, currently seven states have voted to make English their official language: California, Georgia, Illinois, Indiana, Kentucky, Nebraska, and Virginia. In the U.S. Congress, a joint resolution has been proposed, SJ #20, proposing that the U.S. Constitution be amended to read:

1. The English language shall be the official language of the United States.
2. The Congress shall have the power to enforce this article by appropriate legislation.[14]

Proponents of the legislation argue that multilingualism is inimical to national solidarity and that it fosters English illiteracy among those for whom English is a second language. Opponents argue that multilingualism, especially when used in educational programs (bilingual education) and with emergency services and ballots, assists non-English speakers as they make the transition from their first language to English. Both opponents and proponents laud adults who speak two or more languages so long as one of them is English.

Clearly, American English is the nation's lingua franca, the nation's de facto national language. American English is the nation's language of business, commerce, education, government, and most religions. Anyone who wishes to assimilate into the mainstream must be literate in American English. Still, the U.S. Constitution provides religious freedom which serves to spawn religious pluralism and the ideology of *e pluribus unum*, that is, "in many, one." In the past as immigrants settled throughout the United States, they gravitated toward communities and neighborhoods where others spoke the same language and shared the same cultural heritage. By maintaining one's language, one could maintain one's religion and culture, thereby easing the shock of assimilation into the English-speaking mainstream culture.[15]

Contemporary language education programs reflect the conflicting legacies. Various forms of assimilation, internationalization, pluralization, and vernacularization are found in U.S. public schools operating under these rubrics: "transitional bilingual education," "foreign language education," "maintenance bilingual education," and "restoration bilingual education." These programs mirror a history of second language instruction in U.S. public and private schools. For discussion purposes, I have organized a chronology of second language instruction into four time periods. (Much of the material in this section was originally reported in my booklet, *Learning in Two Languages*)[16]:

1550–1815: Language instruction for religious reasons;

1816–1914: Language instruction for maintenance of native or non-English languages;

1915–1958: Emergence of English-only ethnocentrism;
Waning of language instruction for religious and language maintenance;

1959–1989: Resurgence of foreign language education for global political, scientific, and economic purposes;
Emergence of bilingual instruction for compensatory or remedial purposes.

During the first period, 1550 to 1815, bilingual instruction was first used in what is now the southwestern United States. In the later 1550s Jesuit and Franciscan missionaries utilized the tribal dialects to teach Christianity to southwestern Native Americans. In what is now New England, bilingual instruction was used by Protestant missionaries in Native American schools; indigenous dialects were used to introduce Native Americans to the "habits and art of civilization." Knowledge of the English language, Christian beliefs, and Anglo culture were considered "civilized." The Native American dialects were tolerated rather than respected. No attempt was made to develop literacy in the dialects. Also, in New England, bilingual instruction was utilized by the German Lutherans to teach the High German dialect. The Lutherans formed bilingual seminaries to teach in both German and English languages. By 1880, more than 140 Lutheran bilingual schools were established. In 1815, a conference of the Evangelical Lutheran Teachers in Virginia issued a resolution calling for bilingual (German/English) instruction for Lutheran students. The resolution suggested that if teachers could not teach bilingually, then the local congregations were to procure a bilingual minister who would teach bilingually for three months each year in the Lutheran schools.

Before the second period, bilingual instruction was used for religious instruction in church-related schools, including the schools for Native Americans. Although the private schools continued to operate, the second period, 1816 to 1914, saw the rise of free public schools that used bilingual instruction. In 1834, a free school law passed in Pennsylvania allowed instruction in both German and English for students who did not speak English as a primary language. In 1839 the state of Ohio required German and English bilingual instruction for German American students in elementary schools. During the second period, eleven states and one territory enacted laws that allowed bilingual instruction in schools. These were: Pennsylvania (1834), Ohio (1839), Territory of New Mexico (now Arizona and New Mexico) (1850), Wisconsin (1855), Illinois (1857), Iowa (1861), Kentucky and Minnesota (1867), Indiana (1869), Oregon (1872), Colorado (1887), and Nebraska (1913). Throughout most of the second period, city school districts such as Cincinnati, Dayton, Indianapolis, and Baltimore maintained bilingual public schools. In the Territory of New Mexico, provisions were made for bilingual (Spanish and English) instruction; these provisions were rarely implemented in the few public schools established during the early years of the territory. Bilingual instruction waned for Native Americans after a congressional commission established boarding schools and assimilation policies for Native Americans; the bilingual schools were a threat to the government's expansionistic plans. The purpose of boarding schools was to remove Native American children from their homelands and to eradicate their languages and cultures, replacing them with English and Anglo culture in hopes that the children would not return to their homelands. Then, after several generations, land abandoned by the assimilating Native Americans would be available for Anglo pioneers. By 1871, the government took complete control of the schools, imposed an English-only rule, and eliminated the missionary bilingual schools. Even the schools operated by Native Americans—such as the Cherokee system of 21 schools and two academies—were eliminated by government takeover. The policy precipitated the decline of Native American literacy.

In the third period, 1915–1958, both religious and public bilingual instruction decreased. Yet this period saw the largest influx of non-English-speaking immigrants. Between 1887 and 1920, more than twenty distinguishable European languages (other than English) were spoken by U.S. citizens. During this period numerous Asian languages were brought into the country. In addition, the tribes of Native Americans spoke many distinguishable dialects. During this period of tremendous population growth, language legislation and laws were most restrictive. English-only statutes and policies were enforced in most states. These statutes prohibited the use of any language (except English) as a medium of instruction in the public schools. In some states, the statutes provided for revocation of a teacher's certification, if caught in the "criminal act" of using any language other than English to teach. Students who violated the English-only rules of their schools were subjected to physical punishment or paying small fines or detention in a study hall. As recently as the 1950s I knew teachers who "dared" to teach in Spanish in New Mexico. Given circumstances of geographic isolation, these teachers did not lose certification—but there was always that risk!

The diminution of bilingual instruction and the sprouting of English-only statutes or laws can be attributed to the strong nationalistic sentiments that pervaded the United States. During the period between 1880 and 1958, the country was engaged in two world wars, two police actions—Spanish-American War and Korean War—in addition to other military incursions. The use of any language other than English was viewed as un-American or unpatriotic. Non-English speakers were viewed with suspicion. Non-English speakers tended to discontinue speaking their primary language and to discourage their children from learning it. Still, by 1958 more than 25 European languages were spoken by U.S. citizens. Some bilingual schools were established during the third period, notably those for Chinese, French, Greek, Jewish, and Japanese American students. The Chinese and Japanese American schools were criticized strongly prior to World War II. Most of the schools were disbanded during the war, and only a few survived after the war.

The fourth period, 1959–1989, experienced a resurgence of bilingual instruction. In 1966, Dade County schools felt the impact of more than 20,000 Cuban Spanish-speaking refugee students. Two model bilingual programs were established to accommodate the Spanish-speaking students. The Coral Way elementary school was set up as a completely bilingual school. Other schools in Dade County provided Spanish language arts instruction at all grades for Spanish-speaking students. The projects used federal and local funds to finance the two model programs, and in a sense, the Dade County experiment was the first time the federal government was involved in the implementation of bilingual public schools.

In 1968, Public Law 90-247, the Bilingual Education Act, was enacted. The Bilingual Education Act, the seventh amendment to the Elementary and Secondary Education Act of 1965 (Title VII), declared that it was "to be the policy of the United States to provide financial assistance to local education agencies to develop and carry out new and imaginative elementary and secondary school programs designed to meet the special education needs . . . [of] children who come from environments where the dominant language is other than English." The act stipulated that it would be the policy of the U.S. government to assist financially in the development and implementation of bilingual education programs in the public schools in the United States and its trust territories.

In 1973, the act was changed to the Comprehensive Bilingual Education Amendment Act of 1973. The act was amended to extend, improve, and expand assistance for the training of bilingual teachers and bilingual teacher trainers.

The act's policy recognized that (1) large numbers of children have limited English-speaking ability, (2) many of these children have a cultural heritage which differs from that of English-speaking people, and (3) a primary means by which a child learns is through using his or her language and cultural heritage. The act provided financial assistance for extending and improving existing bilingual-bicultural programs in the public schools, for improving resource and dissemination centers, and for developing and publishing bilingual-bicultural curriculum materials.

A major catalyst for bilingual instruction was the 1974 Supreme Court ruling in *Lau* v. *Nichols* that provisions for the same teachers, programs, and textbooks in the same language for all students in the San Francisco school district did not provide equal educational opportunity when the native language of a sizable portion of the student body was not English. In this case, the students were Chinese Americans, who showed low academic achievement and high attrition. Their primary language was Chinese. While the ruling did not mandate bilingual instruction for non-English-speaking or limited English-speaking students, it did stipulate that special educational programs were necessary if schools were to provide equal educational opportunity for such students. The *Lau* decision may have as much impact for linguistic minorities as did *Brown* v. *Topeka Board of Education* for Black Americans. While *Lau* did not establish a bilingual policy for the United States, it made bilingual instruction lawful in the public schools. Moreover, linguistic minorities no longer leave their native language(s) at the schoolyard gates.

The fourth period, 1959–1989, also experienced a resurgence of foreign language education for global political, scientific, and economic purposes. Primarily because of the Soviet Union's scientific advances in the late 1950s, especially in space technology and the launching of the first space satellite *Sputnik*, foreign language programs were introduced into the elementary grades and expanded at the secondary grades along with mathematics and science education. By the 1959–1960 school year approximately 8,000 elementary schools offered FLES (Foreign Languages for Elementary Students) programs.[17] The FLES programs relied heavily on federal funds provided by the National Defense Education Act (NDEA). When federal funding ended, the public schools tried to continue the FLES programs, but without these funds, the schools could not maintain their initial objectives with FLES and by slow degrees they were discontinued. Between 1968 and 1978 the political climate favored bilingual instruction for remedial purposes for students for whom English was their second language. As the political climate turned against remedial bilingual education in the late 1970s, the FLES movement resurfaced in response to geopolitical forces. The need to communicate with other countries, and the need to understand the cultures of other countries, became clear, precipitating "global education" programs and the study of foreign languages. During 1984–1985 at least 16 cities—among them, Culver City (California), San Diego, Fort Worth, Baton Rouge, Tulsa, Milwaukee, Washington, D.C., Eugene (Oregon), and Holliston (Massachusetts)— offered foreign language programs at the elementary grades.[18]

In the late 1970s and early 1980s, a national debate regarding the efficacy of bilingual education was aired. The American Institute for Research (AIR),[19] conducted a study of federally funded bilingual education programs. The study's scope included 38 locations, 150 schools, with 384 classrooms and with 11,073 students. The study's findings were inconclusive; the bilingual programs neither advanced nor retarded the academic achievement of its Hispanic students. Critics reasoned that since bilingual education produced inconclusive effects that the money spent for it could be spent more prudently with other programs. By the mid-1980s the federal bilingual education policy was under scrutiny by Congress; at the time of this writing the 1973 bilingual act was under review with the possibility that it may emerge as an "English-as-a-Second-Language Act (English only)," or the new law may stipulate all federally funded bilingual programs to be transitional.

In retrospect, three American ethnic groups have fought gallantly for bilingual-bicultural instruction: Native Americans, German Americans, and Mexican Americans. Native Americans have confronted a history of concerted efforts by the U.S. government and its agents, the Bureau of Indian Affairs and Christian missionaries, to obliterate their languages and cultures.[20] In spite of those concerted efforts which began before the Declaration of Independence was signed, Native Americans have used the bilingual-bicultural method to build for themselves educational systems far superior to those developed by non-Native Americans. The best example is the educational system built by the Cherokee tribe. When the Oklahoma Cherokee Nation built an education system, they built it with a common school system, a normal school system, and a higher education system. By 1852, according to Weinberg,[21] the Oklahoma Cherokees had a better school system than either of the neighboring states of Arkansas or Missouri. The Cherokee system was a bilingual system; Cherokee language and culture were taught on the basis of the language syllabary developed by the Cherokee scholar, Sequoyah.

German Americans confronted American anti-Germanic attitudes which go back to before World War I. Fishman, in his analysis of language loyalty in the United States,[22] reported that German Americans were the most literate bilingual ethnic group in the United States. They produced bilingual literature, radio programs and school curricula; yet, German Americans were not allowed to maintain their languages and cultures through the public schools. Some important exceptions to this generalization assisted the growth of bilingual-bicultural education, in particular the development of bilingual public schools in Ohio and Indiana.[23] In fact, German Americans fought vigorously for bilingual-bicultural instruction, but because the German nation has twice in this century been the political enemy of the U.S. government, the German American struggle for bilingual-bicultural instruction succumbed.

Mexican Americans have struggled for bilingual instruction for a long time. For example, the original constitution of the state of New Mexico stipulated that Spanish-speaking teachers were to be trained so as to teach the

Spanish-speaking natives of New Mexico. The bilingual teaching stipulation was largely ignored in New Mexico. Further, in violation of the state constitution, the Spanish language was prohibited in all public institutions, including the public schools, in New Mexico. Other southwestern states also prohibited the use of any language other than English in their public schools. Yet, in remote areas of the Southwest, a few teachers utilized the bilingual-bicultural method. While Mexican American culture developed in the Southwest, its development was not supported by the educational system.

FIRST AND SECOND LANGUAGE ACQUISITION

Most humans follow the same pattern when they acquire their first language. Language acquisition is a metacognitive process; language is the linguistic schemata between cognition and actual speech.[24] The schemata is an inherent competence, i.e., people have the innate ability to learn the sounds, rules, and patterns of any human language. Through personal interaction, infants experiment with speech, attempting to communicate. Their babble may be serious attempts to communicate but until they commence the stage of telegraphic speech, "me hungry," they do not communicate meaningfully with adults. Eventually, infants discover simple sentences, "I am hungry," more complex sentences, and finally full discourse. Adults provide a rich learning environment and rarely correct grammar or pronunciation. Instead they help infants find the right words to communicate their intent. Incrementally, infants creatively reconstruct the language spoken by adults and eventually communicate with it.[25]

Second language acquisition follows a similar, basic pattern as first language acquisition. Dulay and Burt[26] recorded the English speech patterns of 145 children, ages 5 and 8, whose first language was Spanish and who were learning English as a second language. Dulay and Burt analyzed the speech samples for developmental and interference errors. "Developmental errors" are mistakes that most infants make when they are learning English as a first language. "Interference errors" are mistakes or habits that bilingual persons transfer from their first language to utterances in the second, such as the "foreign syntax" of some bilinguals. Eighty-five percent of the errors were developmental; 10 percent were interference; the remainder were attributed to individual differences. The children were acquiring English much like children who acquire English as a first language.

The fundamental goal of language acquisition is communicative competence.[27] Communicative competence refers to the ability for people to speak meaningfully so that native speakers of the language can understand the messages being sent and respond with a meaningful message, that is, a person has communicative competence when he or she speaks and can be understood by native speakers of the language. Competence refers to understanding and speaking a language; daily, thousands of people fill their basic needs without reading or writing because they accomplish their business affairs through speaking. Yet, some tasks require reading and writing abilities. The ideal goal of language acquisition is literacy which refers to the ability to use the full range of the language arts, listening comprehension, speaking, reading, and writing. Similarly, we refer to people who speak two languages in terms of their bilingual speaking competency or their bilingual literacy. For example, a primary school youngster living on the Northern Cheyenne Indian Reservation may speak Cheyenne and English but read and write only in English; or, a Ph.D. candidate may be fully literate in English but may only read and write French well enough to pass a paper-and-pencil test in French. The Cheyenne youngster is communicatively competent in two languages but is literate only in English; the Ph.D. candidate is literate in English, somewhat literate in French but is communicatively competent only in English because the candidate does not speak French well enough to communicate meaningfully with other French speakers.

With bilingual students, the competency/literacy distinction is critically important. A bilingual's level of competence can have one of three effects on academic achievement: (1) additive bilingualism enhances academic achievement; (2) dominant bilingualism neither enhances nor retards academic achievement; or (3) subtractive bilingualism retards achievement.[28] Additive bilinguals are equally competent and literate in two languages. They benefit from the linguistic and semantic flexibility that the two languages provide.[29] Dominant bilinguals are fully literate in their first language and are somewhat competent or literate in their second language and are not affected in a positive or negative direction regarding academic achievement in their first language. Subtractive bilinguals lack competence in either language; they are not able to communicate meaningfully (when speaking) in either language and cannot achieve optimally in academic areas that require competence in a standard language. Consequently, subtractive bilinguals should develop full communicative competence and rudimentary literacy in their first language before they are formally introduced to their second language.

LANGUAGE EDUCATION INSTRUCTIONAL APPROACHES

Acquiring a second language is different from learning a second language. To acquire a second language implies to "catch" the language in the process of trying to communicate with it, a type of internalization of t..e language. Language learning implies "to ingest" the language in the process of trying to understand it. My "catch-ingest" distinction reflects two opposing theoretical views regarding second language instruction, the behavioral and developmental views. The behavioral view is that language is learned through a process of habit formation in which: (1) the learner imitates the sounds and patterns of the target language used by the teacher; (2) the teacher reinforces the learner's attempt by correcting or praising the learner; (3) the learner tries again to use the sounds and patterns of the teacher; (4) again, the teacher reinforces the learner's attempts by correcting errors and praising correct utterances; and (5) with this stimulus-response-reinforce procedure, the learner's language habits are conditioned to be the same as the teacher's. Thus, language is ingested.[30]

The developmental view is that language is an innate capacity. Language develops through a process of creative construction in which (1) the learner attempts to communicate with the target language; (2) the teacher provides experiences that require the learner to communicate with the target language; (3) through trial and error, the learner intuits, or "catches on," the target language's sounds and patterns; (4) once intuiting the rules of the language, the learner monitors or self-corrects errors; (5) through trial and error experimentation, the learner creatively reconstructs the language. Thereby, language is internalized.[31]

Instructional approaches for second language teaching tend to operate from behavioral or developmental bases. Following is a summary of second language teaching methods:

- Grammar-Translation: Learners are taught the grammatical rules and phonetics sounds of the target language. Instruction is in the learners' first language. Paradigms, declensions, conjugations are memorized. Latin grammar is considered to be the "all-purpose" tool for analyzing the target language. Behaviorally based.
- Direct-Natural: Learners are immersed in the second language; instruction is in the target language through monologues in which the teacher, through gestures and pantomime, attempts to engage learners in the use of target language. Grammar and phonetics are deferred or not taught at all. Developmentally based.
- Audio-Lingual: Learners are engaged in structured dialogues in the target language. Dialogues based on conversational syntactic patterns; learners are drilled in the patterns and the phonetics of the target language. Grammar, if taught, is taught concurrently with the structured patterns. Quasibehaviorally-quasidevelopmentally based.
- Bilingual: Actually this is not a second-language instructional method, but the bilingual "method" is an instructional strategy for teaching traditional subjects to learners while they are learning a second language. In the U.S., two differing bilingual strategies are used: *Transistional*-learners are taught traditional subjects in their first language; English is concurrently taught as a second language. When learners can receive instruction in English, use of the first language for traditional subjects is dropped. *Maintenance*-learners are taught traditional subjects in their first language; they also study the language arts of the first language; English is eventually taught as a second language. When learners can receive instruction in English, use of the first language is shared with use of the second language (English) for teaching traditional subjects. As strategies, the transitional approach uses the first language as a bridge to the second; the maintenance approach uses the first language as a "hold-

ing pattern" until the second language is learned. Then instruction is maintained in both the first and second languages.

While there is no single method that works best in all classrooms, language educators currently favor methodology that facilitates speaking and communicating in the target language.[32] Past language methodologies were criticized because they did not always teach students to speak and communicate in the target language, leading to the emergence of pragmatic, developmental approaches variously called such names as "Total Physical Response," "The Natural Approach," or "Immersion." The innovations have in common the pragmatic goal of communicative competence, that is, teaching the students to use the target language for immediate, communication purposes without use of the students' first language.[33]

Keep in mind that many people throughout the world learn to use a second language without the benefit of formal instruction, meaning that there are factors other than teaching methods which enhance second language learning. Key among these are the learners' motivation for and attitude toward learning the second language. Motivation is linked to the purposes for learning a second language.

People who profit from speaking a second language are highly motivated to learn. Schools, such as Berlitz or the Alliance Française, that teach business people in second languages are quite successful primarily because their students are highly motivated to learn the second language so that they can conduct business affairs in the target language. People also learn a second language for academic purposes, which is the reason why Ph.D. candidates are required to know a second language. Purportedly, the candidate will use the second language to conduct research in that language. For those candidates for whom the second language will be used for research purposes, there is high motivation to learn the second language. Also, linguistic minority and immigrant youngsters who do not speak English have an academic purpose for learning English, the primary purpose of bilingual education in the United States. For the latter group, second language instruction is viewed as remedial while in the instances of the business people and Ph.D. candidates, second language instruction is seen as enrichment.

Learning to speak a second language can have potent implications for the individual.[34] Language and self-identity are intimately linked. While language does not control one's self-identity, the language one speaks can have an influence on how one is perceived by others (see looking-glass self, Chapter 2). In turn, how one is perceived influences how one perceives one self. Also, how one speaks a language influences how much the person can assimilate into the target language's culture. As a consequence, how well one learns a second language is related to how much the person wants to be like the people who speak the target language. Learning a second language for assimilation is not a new idea. Millions of European immigrants learned to speak American English to hasten their assimilation into American society. In the Soviet Union, the individual is given the opportunity to attend school that uses the person's first language as the medium of instruction. But, if the individual wishes to be assimilated into the educational, scientific, or political mainstream, the person must learn Russian (see global language policy, this chapter, pp. 153–159).

To the individual, learning a second language has the potential for being a sociopolitical act. For businessmen, or college professors, learning a second language may be purely utilitarian. Yet, if either wishes to communicate effectively in their second languages, then they will be required to assimilate to some extent into the cultures of the languages they speak. In our pluralistic society, English is the de facto national language. The better one speaks American English, the better one can be assimilated into the mainstream culture. Herein is the rub for minorities for whom English is a second language.

Motivation of linguistic minorities for learning English is linked to how much they wish to be assimilated into the mainstream culture. Because the mainstream culture is closely related to the White, Anglo-Saxon, Protestant ethnic group, assimilation into the mainstream largely implies assimilation into the WASP ethnic group, Or, speaking English like a mainstream American implies that the person is "like" members of the WASP group, even if the WASP group will not assimilate the person into the group. In the United States, most English-as-a-second-language learners are members of minority groups, Asians (Southeast Asian groups, et al.), Hispanics, and Native Americans. Though many of them may be willing to assimilate, they may be prevented from assimilation due to racist or social class biases in their communities.[35] Or, they may be pressured by peers to stay within their ethnic group by refusing to learn to talk "White." Yet, the more the learner wishes to speak like the target language speakers, the more readily will the learner acquire communicative competence in the second language, i.e., English.[36] The rationale for maintenance bilingual education (see above) is to allow the linguistic minority student to maintain the first language and its culture while at the same time learning English and its culture. The transitional bilingual strategy uses the first language (and perhaps culture) only until the learner is ready to receive instruction in English only, thereby triggering the sociopolitical rub: "Forget my first language and culture. It is of little consequence. Learn English and its culture. Risk, being assimilated into the Anglo group; risk alienation from parents, relatives, and peers."

Learning a second language is contingent upon two important factors: (1) the quality of instruction in the second language, and (2) the quantity of the second language that the learner is willing to learn. In the case of middle-class, English-speaking students, factor one is a function of having good teachers; factor two is a factor of utility—how the second language will be used is the primary incentive. In the case of lower-class, linguistic minority students, the first factor is a function of how good teachers use the student's language and cultural backgrounds as media of instruction. The second factor is a function with sociopolitical dimensions: "What will happen to me if I learn English as a second language?" The issue here is not whether linguistic minorities should learn English; they should be fully literate in American English. The issue is: What is the most humane way to achieve full English literacy for linguistic minorities?

BASIC ISSUES IN BILINGUAL INSTRUCTION

There are basic issues pertaining to bilingual instruction. These issues are raised here in question and answer form.

What is bilingualism? The greatest degree of bilingualism is full literacy in two languages. "Full literacy" means that a bilingual person can speak, read, and write in two languages with the same proficiency as native speakers of the two languages. Of course, this is achieved by few bilinguals; most bilinguals can best be described in terms of degrees of literacy in two languages. Some bilinguals may be fully literate in one language, but may only understand a second language. Or, some bilinguals may speak two languages but may be fully literate only in one language. Some bilinguals may be fully literate in one language but may only read in a second language. Some bilinguals may be fully literate in two languages, but may only speak one language with the control of a native speaker. Figure 8.1 illustrates the varying degrees of bilingual literacy.

Does bilingualism enhance the reading and language achievement of the bilingual student? In studies of bilinguals who were instructed in their second language, which was weaker, adverse effects were shown in school progress and results. Macnamara's studies[37] in Ireland of bilinguals instructed in Gaelic instead of English showed a deterioration in school achievement. In the majority of Macnamara's studies on mathematics achievement, it was reported that bilinguals were slower than monolinguals in problem arithmetic (verbal reasoning) but not in mechanical arithmetic (computation). Macnamara attributed the differences in the findings to the differences in tasks. In

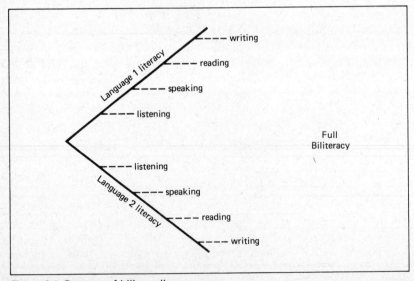

Figure 8.1 Degrees of bilingualism

tasks of mechanical arithmetic the subjects were required to carry out an operation with arithmetical symbols, but in tasks of problematic arithmetic the subjects were required to read and interpret prose statements. In a study on the effects of bilingualism on reading, Macnamara[38] found that articulation and oral communication in the weaker language were slower for the bilingual and that encoding of ideas and organizing of syntactic patterns possibly occurred with less rapidity in the weaker language. The general finding that, for the bilingual, reading in a weaker language takes longer than reading in the stronger was reported by studies in 1959 and 1960. Earlier studies reported like results. Welsh bilinguals instructed in their weaker language demonstrated progressive retardation in all areas of school achievement.[39] Such a retardation was also reported to occur over two years of primary teaching in the vernacular in Manila.[40]

Complete reliance upon the above findings would lend support to the assumption that bilingualism, per se, is detrimental to language development. Yet in studies where the bilingual's second language was not the weaker language, and where the bilingual could develop both languages fully, the bilingual's language development was not impaired. Having two languages seemed to have a positive effect on school achievement. Apparently, being bilingual facilitated the awareness that there are varying ways to say the same thing. Peal and Lambert[41] explored the effects of bilingualism on intellectual functioning and reported that when socioenvironmental variables are controlled bilinguals perform better than monolinguals on verbal and non-verbal intelligence tests. The investigators reported that the bilingual subjects had several advantages over their monolingual peers: (1) a language asset, (2) greater cognitive flexibility, and (3) a greater ability in concept formation than the monolingual. The investigators concluded that the bilinguals appeared to have a more diversified set of mental abilities than the monolinguals.

Lambert, Just, and Segalowitz[42] conducted a longitudinal study of middle-class English-speaking children who were taught French, which was also used as the medium of instruction. After two years of instruction in their weaker language, general improvement was experienced by the bilingual children. Even though the children were instructed in French, their weaker language, they demonstrated an optimum level of skills in both the productive and reproductive aspects of French, and a generally excellent control of their home language, English. The investigators reported that socioenvironmental variables were accounted for in the study, and that if conflict occurred between the children's two languages, its negative effect was minimal.

In another study conducted in Sweden, bilingual children were organized into two groups.[43] The experimental group of bilingual elementary-school children received an initial ten weeks of reading instruction in Pitean, the local dialect, after which they were advanced to classes conducted in literary Swedish. The control group of bilinguals, who were also Pitean-Swedish speakers, received all reading instruction in literary Swedish. At the end of the first ten weeks the Pitean-taught group had progressed further in reading than the Swedish-taught group. At the end of the school year, the experimental group performed significantly better than the control group on word recognition, speed, fluency, and accuracy of reading in literary Swedish. Beginning reading instruction in the stronger language and then switching to the school dialect had positive effects in this study.

Like results were reported in similar studies conducted in Mexico.[44] The test data in these studies indicated that the bilinguals, who were initially taught in the vernacular, read with greater comprehension than those initially taught in the Spanish of the school. These studies also reported that bilinguals initially instructed in the vernacular achieved literacy in both languages within two years. Studies in the United States on bilingualism reported that Spanish-English bilingualism does not negatively affect the Mexican American's syntactic language development. Peña[45] conducted a study to ascertain whether Mexican American first graders could control basic syntactic patterns of Spanish and English. Peña reported that the bilingual first graders could utilize basic Spanish and English syntactic patterns, and that the bilinguals had little or no difficulty generating transformations in Spanish and English. Garcia[46] conducted a study to identify and compare the oral English syntactic sentence patterns of bilingual adolescent lower-class and middle-class Mexican Americans. The results of the study indicated that the bilinguals used all of the patterns basic to standard English, and that they expressed a style consistent with their socioeconomic status. The Mexican Americans were found to be native English speakers in the syntactic sense because they used syntactic patterns much like monolingual English speakers. Kessler's study[47] on the syntactic acquisitions of Italian English 6- to 8-year-old bilingual children indicates that syntactic structures shared by the two languages develop in the same sequential pattern at approximately the same rate. Kessler's study, while thoroughly developed and executed, requires replication with a larger sample, but it points to the positive cognitive effects of bilingualism.

A cautious caveat: the jury is still out regarding the effects of bilingualism on cognitive development. In well-controlled studies with middle-class subjects (see the Canadian and Swedish studies cited above), bilingualism appears to positively affect cognitive development. Two studies do not a theory make. Much still must be empirically verified regarding cognitive development with middle-class monolinguals as well as with the language development of middle-class bilinguals. Also, we do not know enough about the impact of bilingual instruction on the academic achievement of linguistic minorities primarily because of ambiguities when evaluating public school bilingual programs. Methodologically, it is extremely difficult to control important variables when evaluating public school bilingual programs. Such variables as the quality of instruction, the students' degree or types of bilingualism (see p. 166, this chapter for explanation) the socioeconomic status of the students and the home language are variables that cannot be experimentally controlled as is the nature of most research with continuing public school programs of any kind. As with many debates about which method is superior to accomplish an educational goal, what is missing are critical questions regarding the effectiveness of the teachers and the quality of their instruction as well as questions regarding the amount of administrative support and the resources actually provided.

Last, we are still learning much about cognitive development and language acquisition. Piaget's seminal research on cognitive development posited that cognitive development precedes language development; in opposition, the Whorf-Sapir hypothesis assumes that language development precedes much of cognitive development. Current thinking is that the "chicken and egg" come together, or that language and cognitive development are interactive.[48]

Are elementary school students, say in grades K–3, really very bilingual? Much depends on the student's home environment. Most elementary K–3 students are not fully literate in any language; the same holds true with bilingual students. Yet some K–3 students can speak two languages equally well. Others can speak a non-English language such as Vietnamese, but barely speak English. Some students can understand and speak a second language minimally, but speak English as well as any other K–3 student. Generally, K–3 bilingual students will control one of their two languages better. The bilingual instruction premise is that students should first develop literacy in their stronger language, and then develop literacy in their weaker language.

What about African American students who speak Black English? Are they bilingual? If Black English were recognized in our society as a valid language, then African American students literate in Black English and school English would be bilingual. Linguists recognize Black English as a valid dialect of American English, so African American students literate in two English dialects would be "bidialectal." There probably is no essential difference between a bilingual and a bidialectal, except, of course, that they speak different languages or dialects.

Should African American students receive bidialectal instruction? As with bilingual instruction, much depends on the wishes of the students' parents. There is no valid educational objection to African American students developing full literacy in Black English and school English. Yet, racism is still so strong in our society that many African American parents feel that their youngsters will be discriminated against if they speak Black English. Therefore, these parents stress learning school English for social uses and allow Black English only for informal occasions. Other parents feel that Black English should be taught along with school English. In my opinion, Black English is a valid American English dialect; some of it should be taught to all students. Elementary and secondary language arts curricula stress that there are three American English dialects: Eastern, Southern, and General American. The triad is no longer accurate; it should be abandoned and replaced with a paradigm that focuses on the dialectal diversity of American English.

STUDY QUESTIONS

1. Compare and contrast the four language policies of assimilation, pluralization, internationalization, vernacularization.
2. Describe the process by which people acquire their first language.
3. Describe how second language acquisition is similar to first language acquisition; then explain how the two differ.
4. Define bilingualism; then explain the differences between additive, dominant, and subtractive bilingualism.
5. Explain the basic difference between foreign language instruction and bilingual instruction.
6. What is meant by "bilingual literacy"? What must the student be able to do to be considered "bilingually literate"?
7. What might be the underlying reasons why bilingual education has been such a volatile issue in the United States? How has the issue been addressed in our time?

DEMONSTRATION LESSON

Title: A Modified Immersion Approach
Goal: To "draw out" the English language from the minds of students for whom English is a second language;
Rationale: The immersion approach is based on the assumption that language must be elicited—to "draw out" from the person a language unfamiliar to that person. Teachers are the elicitors; they provide a language environment and language experiences that allow the student to experiment with the language. The environment must consist of students who are highly motivated to learn the language; teachers must create a climate that allows for much trial and error so that students can struggle with the language without threat to their self-esteem.
Assumptions: What students think, they can talk about; what they can talk about can be expressed in writing or some other medium; talking and other expressive media must be shared with others; through interaction, students will learn to communicate with each other in the unfamiliar language.

Objectives: As a result of this lesson, students will (in English) be able to:

1. describe neighborhood scenes in photographs,
2. describe the storyline or content of a song,
3. describe the smell of foods,
4. describe the tastes of foods,
5. describe the feel of objects.

Methods for implementing objectives:

1. Provide students with cameras; instruct them to take photographs of common scenes; the teacher may have to show students how to use the cameras and what kinds of pictures to take; have the film developed and made into slides. THEN, ask the student to narrate a slide show using the photographs taken; student must use his or her own photographs and must explain the content of the

photographs in English; other students should be encouraged to add comments or ask questions about the scenes.

2. Play recordings of popular songs to students; have students explain the storyline or events in the song; teacher may have to identify key words in the songs; this is a listening exercise, and because song lyrics are highly idiomatic, this exercise may prove difficult at first.

3. Objectives 3 and 4 can be combined; prepare simple foods, or use crackers, cookies, candies; have students describe the smell and taste of the foodstuff; teacher may have to provide adjectives, such as "salty," "hot"; this exercise may prove to be the easiest since some tastes and smells are no doubt universal; saltine crackers in any culture are still "salty".

4. Objective 5 requires students to describe how objects feel; use sandpaper, a lead pipe, a Coca-Cola bottle, or any other commonplace object; have the students shut their eyes; then direct them to touch the object and describe it in English; like objective 3 above, this may prove to be an easy exercise since textures, roughness, smoothness, and so forth, are also universal.

Note: At first, there will be some awkwardness since the students may have no idea of what the teacher is about; the teacher should identify a student who could be coached ahead of time who could model the expected behavior—talking in English using whatever English words seem appropriate; teacher may suggest appropriate adjectives, nouns.

NOTES

1. B. Bullivant. Power and control in the multiethnic school. *Ethnic and Racial Studies*, 5, 53–70, 1982.
2. T. Griffen. Nationalism and the emergence of a new standard Welsh. *Language Problems and Language Planning*, 4, 187–194, 1980.
3. C. Luzares. Language in education in the Philippines. In R. B. Kaplan (ed.). *Annual Review of Applied Linguistics 1981*. Rowley, MA: Newbury House, 1982.
4. A. Gonzalez. Language policy and language-in-education in the Philippines. In R. B. Kaplan (ed.), *Annual Review of Applied Linguistics 1981*. Rowley, MA: Newbury House, 1982.
5. Linguistic Society of the Philippines. *Eleven Years of Bilingual Schooling in the Philippines—1974–1985*. Washington, D.C.: Center for Applied Linguistics, 1986.
6. Central Statistical Board of the USSR. *Peoples of the USSR, 1922–82*. Moscow: Novosti, 1982.
7. W. Shimoniak. Education of minorities in the U.S.S.R. *School & Society*, 1, 58–65, 1972.
8. V. Kumanev. Universal literacy of the formerly backward peoples of the Soviet Union. In W. McCormack and S. Wurm (eds.), *Languages and Society*. The Hague: Mouton, 1979.
9. J. Zajda. *Education in the U.S.S.R.* Oxford: Pergamon Press, 1980.
10. M. Shorish. Planning by decree: The Soviet language policy in central Asia. *Language Problems and Language Planning*, 8, 35–49, 1984.
11. G. Lewis. *Bilingual and Bilingual Education: A Comparative Study*. Alburquerque: University of New Mexico Press, 1980.

12. B. Comrie. *The Languages of the Soviet Union*. Cambridge: Cambridge University Press, 1981.
13. Charles Ferguson and Shirley Heath. *Languages in the USA*. Cambridge: Cambridge University Press, 1981.
14. *Congressional Record* (Senate). Washington, D.C.: U.S. Government Printing Office, January 22, 1985, p. S468.
15. Oscar Handlin. *Immigration as a Factor in American History*. Englewood Cliffs, N.J.: Prentice-Hall, 1959, p. 16.
16. Ricardo Garcia. *Learning in Two Languages*. Fastback no. 84. Bloomington, Ind.: Phi Delta Kappa Education Foundation, 1976.
17. Edwin Zeydel. *Report of Surveys and Studies in the Teaching of Modern Foreign Languages*. New York: Modern Language Association, 1964.
18. "Foreign Language in the Elementary School." *Education Letter*. Cambridge, Mass.: Harvard University Press, November 1985, p. 4; see also, Nancy Rhodes and A. R. Schreibstein. *Foreign Languages in the Elementary School*. Washington, D.C.: Center for Applied Linguistics, 1983, ERIC ED 209 940.
19. American Institute for Research. *Evaluation of the Impact of ESEA Title VII Spanish/English Education Program*. Los Angeles, 1977.
20. Meyer Weinberg. *A Chance to Learn*. New York: Cambridge University Press, 1977, pp. 178–229.
21. Weinberg, pp. 184–185.
22. Joshua Fishman. *Language Loyalty in the United States*. The Hague: Mouton, 1966, pp. 380–385.
23. Fishman. *Language Loyalty*, pp. 392–417.
24. W. T. Littlewood. *Communicative Language Teaching*. London: Cambridge University Press, 1981; see also, Noam Chomsky. *Syntactic Structures*. The Hague: Mouton, 1957.
25. John Macnamara. "Cognitive Basis of Language Learning in Infants," *Psychological Review*, 1972, 79:1–14.
26. H. C. Dulay and M. K. Burt. "A New Perspective on Creative Construction Processes in Child Second Language Acquisition," *Language Learning*, 1974, 24:253–278.
27. Dell Hymes. "Models in the Interaction of Language and Social Life," in J. Gumperz and D. Hymes, eds., *Directions in sociolinguistics*. New York: Holt, Rinehart & Winston, 1972.
28. J. Cummins. "Linguistic Interdependence and the Educational Development of Bilingual Children," *Review of Educational Research*, 1979, 49:222–251.
29. Elizabeth Peal and Wallace Lambert. *The Relation of Bilingualism and Intelligence*. Washington, D.C.: American Psychological Association, 1962, p. 27.
30. B. F. Skinner. *Verbal Behavior*. New York: Appleton-Century-Crofts, 1957; see also, L. Bloomfield. *Language*. London: Allen & Unwin, 1935.
31. Evelyn Hatch. *Psycholinguistics: A Second Language Perspective*. Rowley, Mass.: Newbury House, 1983, pp. 152–187; see also, Chomsky, *Syntactic Structures*, 1957.
32. Raymond J. Rodriguez and Robert White. "From Role Play to the Real World," in J. Ollers and P. Richard-Amato, eds., *Methods That Work: A Smorgasbord of Ideas for Language Teachers*. Rowley, Mass.: Newbury House, 1983, pp. 226–238.
33. Stephen D. Krashen and Tracy Terrell. *The Natural Approach*. Hayward, CA.: Alemany Press, 1983, pp. 7–21.
34. Lerita Coleman. "Language and the Evolution of Identity and Self-Concept," in

Frank Kessel, ed., *The Development of Language and Language Researchers*. London: Lawrence Erlbaum Association, 1988, pp. 319–338.

35. Barry McLaughlin. *Second-Language Acquisition in Childhood*. London: Lawrence Erlbaum Association, 1984, pp. 2–4.

36. Kenji Hakuta. "Why Bilinguals?" in Kessel, *Development of Language*, pp. 299–314.

37. John Macnamara. *Bilingualism in Primary Education*. Edinburgh: University of Edinburgh Press, 1966, Ch. 6.

38. John Macnamara, "Reading in a Second Language," *Improving Reading Throughout the World*. Newark, N.J.: International Reading Association, 1968, Ch. 5.

39. D. J. Saer. "The Effects of Bilingualism on Intelligence," *British Journal of Psychology*, (April 1923): 25–38.

40. Manila Department of Education. *The Relative Effectiveness of the Vernacular and of English as Media of Instruction*. Manila: Bureau of Public Schools, 1953, Ch. 14.

41. Elizabeth Peal and Wallace Lambert. *The Relation of Bilingualism and Intelligence*. Washington, D.C.: American Psychological Association, 1962, p. 27.

42. Wallace Lambert, J. Just, and N. Segalowitz, "Some Cognitive Consequences of Following the Curricula of the Early School Grades in a Foreign Language." *Monograph Series on Language and Literature*. James Alatis, ed., Washington, D.C.: Georgetown University Press, 1970, p. 259.

43. Tana Osterberg,. *Bilingualism and the First School Language*. Umea: Vasterbottens TrychKeri AB, 1961, 85–103.

44. A. Barrera-Vasquez. *The Tarascan Project in Mexico: Use of Vernacular Languages in Education*. Paris: UNESCO, 1953, pp. 77–86.

45. Albar Peña. *A Comparative Study of Selected Syntactical Structures of the Oral Language Status in Spanish and English of Disadvantaged First-Grade Spanish Speaking Children*. Austin: University of Texas Press, 1967.

46. Ricardo Garcia. *Identification and Comparison of Oral English Syntactic Patterns of Spanish-English Speaking Hispanos*. Unpublished dissertation, University of Denver, 1973.

47. C. Kessler. *Acquisition of Syntax in Bilingual Children*. Washington, D.C.: Georgetown University Press, 1971.

48. Eugene E. Garcia. *Early Childhood Bilingualism*. Alburquerque: University of New Mexico Press, 1983, p. 163.

Chapter
9

Intergroup Relations
Strategies

Key Terms:

    contact thesis
    cooperative learning
    equal status

    equalitarian norms
    interpersonal relations
    trust relationship

The intergroup relations approach will be described as a strategy that can be used to foster cross-group understandings in most classrooms. The approach can be used to improve communi. ˙tions and relationships between groups of students who perceive that they ˎ significantly different—in the social sense—from other groups within or wiˑˑout the classroom. Group differences here refer to differences due to culture, handicapping conditions, gender-role expectations, religious, racial and social class affiliations. Many of the differences perceived by the students are merely superficial impressions based on little real knowledge about the substance of the differences; some of the perceived differences are rooted in prevailing stereotypes and biases. All the perceptions are real, as perceptions, and should be dealt with rather than avoided. The intergroup relations approach springs from the study of human relations and is based on the contact thesis validated by Gordon Allport and Kenneth Clark in the 1950s watershed research conducted on racial prejudice. Their classic texts are *The Nature of Prejudice* (Allport) and *Prejudice and Your Child* (Clark).

The contact thesis posits that people who work as equals on a common task over a sustained period of time can develop positive attitudes and trust relationships with each other. The intergroup relations strategy will be described as a means to improve relationships between students as well as to improve the academic achievement of all students. The strategy's contact thesis will be coupled with current research findings pertaining to cooperative learning activities. Cooperative learning activities, when coupled with the intergroup strategy, promises to enhance the self-esteem and improve the academic achievement of all students involved.

THE PURPOSE OF INTERGROUP RELATIONS

The following poem is dedicated to one of my many students.

> He comes to my room,
> rather,
> he puffs to my room
> gasping and exhaling the air
> of a cigarette hastily wasted.
>
> So he puffs to my room
> slouched shouldered.
>
> caged
>
> and bound to learn.

What always struck me when teaching in New Mexico, Wisconsin, Colorado, Kansas, Oklahoma, Utah, and Montana, is that students were strangers to each other. They came to class and fell into a role as student and often developed only a few real friends. Otherwise they were strangers. Also, the very role of being a student somehow precluded any chance of developing genuine relationships in the classroom, unless the teacher somehow intervened. The intergroup relations approach attempts to make friends out of strangers.

The intergroup relations approach has its origin in a nationwide project conducted by the American Council of Education (ACE).[1] In an attempt to alleviate the intense anti-Jewish and antiracial minority feelings that existed after World War II, ACE infused the intergroup relations notion in teacher training programs and secondary and elementary schools in the United States. Throughout the country, teacher training programs[2] were chosen to implement an intergroup relations program for prospective teachers. At the public school level, classroom teachers and administrators were trained to use intergroup relations strategies. Special curriculum materials were developed by teachers which fit their respective intergroup relations needs.[3] The project officially started in 1945 and ended sometime in 1952. Its purpose was to reduce, if not remove, the level of conflict that existed between Christians, Jews, Whites, and racial minorities. Much stress was placed on the similarities held in common by the various groups, although religious and cultural differences were also recognized as positive factors which needed understanding. The essence of the project was in the attempt to build religious and cultural understanding. The motives for the movement were honest. Based on the desire to increase communication between diverse groups, its ultimate goals were to reduce conflict and to foster harmonious intergroup relations.

In our time, concerns about intergroup relations expand from improving relations among racial and religious groups to include relations between the genders, between handicapped and nonhandicapped, and between middle-class and lower-class students. Traditional role relationships between men and women are currently undergoing changes. What was considered appropriate male and female behavior in past decades is now often considered sexist. Much ambiguity exists regarding gender behaviors and roles so that male and female students are often uncertain as to what is appropriate (see Chapter 2, for gender factors). Also, what is considered appropriate gender-roles and behaviors in the classroom may be at variance in the students' homes and communities. In this case, the teacher may be promoting gender equality but attitudes in the home and community may be more conservative. Students need help managing gender relationships, and the conflicting views thereof, both within the classroom and within the broader community. Also new to intergroup relations is the challenge posed by PL 94–142 Education for all Handicapped Children mandating mainstreaming of handicapped students. The initial experience with mainstreaming has proved to be problematic due to stereotypes held by non-handicapped students. A pervasive stereotype is that all handicapped kids are "airheads," that is, they're all "mentally retarded." The stereotype is based on ignorance. The range of handicapping conditions extends from the solely physiological to the solely intellectual. Industrial giants Henry Ford and Nelson Rockefeller suffered from dyslexia, a motor-perceptual brain disorder that impedes reading, and Winston Churchill and Albert Einstein were thought to be below normal students by some of their teachers.

The essence of the intergroup relations approach is empathy.[4] The approach provides a means by which students learn about the views, feelings, and perceptions of other students who may differ. Emphasis is upon building positive relationships between students who would otherwise know little about each other. Even in desegregated classrooms, White and non-White students many times are not encouraged to intermingle, sharing their views, feelings, or perceptions.[5] In fact, experience shows that many White and non-White students in desegregated classrooms rarely talk with each other, much less develop long-lasting personal relationships.

In classes where handicapped students are mainstreamed, the normal students often resent their presence and shun them during free-time activities, such as during interest center groups and recess play in elementary schools. The Native American saying that a person should walk in the moccasins of another for many days before judging that person best exemplifies the essence of the intergroup relations approach. As with the Native American adage, a person must get into the shoes of another and view the world from that person's point of view in order to genuinely understand the other's actions and beliefs. The hope is that building empathy through planned and sustained interpersonal contact among differing students will lead to improved intergroup relations in the classroom and in society. What follows is a conceptual overview of the intergroup relations approach.

CONCEPTUAL OVERVIEW OF INTERGROUP RELATIONS

- *Goal:* To foster favorable attitudes among students through interpersonal experiences.

- *Philosophic bases:* Speaking generally, communication and understanding between student groups have been limited, restricted, or nonexistent. Students need to develop positive, genuine interpersonal relationships with group members outside their groups through planned interpersonal relations. Because this strategy can be used to ameliorate relationships between groups of students who differ for any number of reasons, including cultures, handicaps, races, religions, social classes, and nontraditional gender-role attitudes, I use the following "coded" language to convey the generic scope of the intergroup relations strategy:
  1. *Regular* students are normal, middle class, traditionally oriented majority group students;
  2. *Different* students are students whose physical or intellectual traits, nontraditional gender-role orientations, racial, cultural, or social class attributes vary from the *regular* students.

- *Rationale:* Positive attitudes among students can be formed through interpersonal experiences if
  1. different students and regular students have equal status;
  2. different students and regular students work on common tasks together;
  3. different students and regular students contact is sustained and ongoing;
  4. different students and regular students contact is directed by teacher stressing equalitarian norms.

Interpersonal contact and communication among students is essential. The approach is based on the contact thesis[6] of interpersonal contact which posits that sustained, controlled contact between people on the same status working at a task they hold in common can foster better understanding among the people, even though they differ racially, ethnically, or culturally. The key notion is that teachers can provide sustained, controlled contact among students so long as effort is made to provide equal status to all the students, something that is not always done in the *realpolitik* of the classroom. Mere contact alone, without conscious efforts to insure equal status among students, will not necessarily foster positive intergroup relations, as has been the experience of newly desegregated classrooms. Leadership on the teachers' part to control and sustain the interpersonal contact is therefore essential.

CRITICAL FACTORS

Teachers can foster genuine relationships by planning ongoing interpersonal learning tasks. Most critical is the teacher's leadership to insure that the interpersonal relationships, and the contact therein, are meaningful—that is, the relationships should foster better understanding of and empathy for students' feelings and beliefs. The contact must not be haphazard, contrived (fake), or arbitrary. Students as equals should be engaged in meaningful, common learning tasks which foster interdependence and cooperation. Also, the contact should lead to positive long-range behavioral changes which are assumed to be antecedents to cognitive and attitude changes. Once students begin to understand each other, form friendships, and in other ways relate to each other, their attitudes toward each other and toward their respective groups should improve.

INQUIRY GENERALIZATION FOR THE STUDY OF INTERGROUP RELATIONS

Each person needs to belong or have a sense of belonging to a group.

Separated or segregated people develop myths, prejudices, and stereotypes about each other.

There is one biological race—the human race—but some characteristics make a social difference.

These are generalizations about intergroup relations processes that students should be taught. All too often, students are not taught about group processes because much more effort is made to teach students their individual uniqueness. While individuality is important for students to know and practice, they should know that people live and function both as individuals and as members of groups.

STRATEGIES FOR FAVORABLE INTERGROUP RELATIONS

A study of family life patterns. This strategy requires that students study each other's families. The study, if handled maturely, should provide insight into the backgrounds and experiences of students from nontraditional families, extended families and single-parent families. the study should include, but would not be limited to, an analysis of family roles, family livelihood, family problems and concerns, and family recreation patterns.

A study of minority and majority group communities. This strategy includes a study of minority and majority group communities. The study would include, but not be limited to, an analysis of organizing generalizations:

1. Communities have similarities and differences.
2. Communities require interlocking relationships, i.e., human interdependence.
3. Community conditions are results of current forces as well as the community's history.

A study of intergroup experiences. This strategy gets at the crux of the intergroup relations approach because all students are taught to analyze objectively the intergroup relations process. The strategy answers this question: What happens when a minority group and a majority group come into contact?

1. Students study in-group/out-group processes, stereotyping, ethnocentrism, elitism, racism, sexism, discrimination.
2. Students study attitudes, values, beliefs of peers through surveys, personal interviews, and panel discussions.
3. Students study their own attitudes, values, beliefs as well as their ancestral ties through genealogies, historical lifelines, and "roots" family study.

A study of sexism, gender-role stereotyping, and gender bias. This strategy emphasizes the idea that each person can develop a unique self concept and that gender-role attitudes are learned rather than innate characteristics.

1. Students study the sociocultural concepts of self-concept, social roles, gender roles, and gender-role stereotyping;
2. Students study how different societies teach their conception of gender roles through toys, games, and play activities;
3. Students study the autobiographies/biographies of men and women who have defied the gender-role stereotypes of their generation, e.g., Marie Curie, scientist, or Robert Frost, poet;
4. For more mature students, the study of existing biological differences between men and women and how they are interpreted differently in different societies. (Here I refer to the nurture/nature issue regarding sex differences; students would need to be able to read and evaluate studies conducted by adults for other adults.)

A study of social stratification in industrial and nonindustrial societies. This strategy emphasizes the universal nature of social stratification and the division of labor. By comparing stratification systems in industrial, hunting and gathering, and agricultural societies, students can gain insight into the economic and political reasons for social classes and social roles.

1. Students should study how families "make a living" in a hunting-gathering society, in an agricultural society, and in an industrial society;
2. Students should study the specific characteristics of the stratification systems of industrial societies;
3. Students should study how social classes are like ethnic groups which have distinct values, beliefs, behavioral patterns (customs, traditions, folkways), and dialects;
4. Students should study how social class membership is initially a matter of luck but that in dynamic societies some upward mobility is possible.

A study of handicapping conditions. This strategy requires accurate, timely information at the factual as well as the emotional levels regarding handicapping conditions. The strategy requires a candid examination of handicapping conditions and the social difficulties faced by handicapped individuals.

1. By reading and discussing biographies or autobiographies of handicapped individuals, e.g., Helen Keller or Louis Braille, students can learn about the social and personal impact of handicapping conditions;

2. By researching and group reporting, students can get accurate information about specific handicapping conditions, e.g., Down syndrome, dyslexia, hearing impaired;
3. By role playing and assuming a handicapping condition, students can gain an awareness of the condition's impact on the individual, e.g., ear plugs for hearing impaired or blindfold for visually impaired;
4. By practicing signing, students can learn how specific handicapping conditions require overcompensatory use of other senses to overcome the specific handicap.

A study of racism, prejudice, stereotyping in ethnically and racially homogeneous classrooms. This strategy is intended for classrooms where no visible ethnic or racial mixture of students exists.

1. Students experience in-group/out-group processes vicariously through open-ended stories, role playing, simulations.
2. Students visit and study ethnic minority community action agencies.
3. Students visit and study schools with high concentrations of ethnic minority students.
4. Resource speakers from ethnic minority groups are incorporated into courses of study.

A study of intergroup relations with emphasis on the nature of racism between in- and out-groups. Such a study requires a serious study of the following characteristics of racist and prejudiced thinking.

Emotional racism. This kind of racism ranges from slight distaste to extreme hate of ethnically and racially different out-groups.

Cognitive racism. This kind of racism focuses on perceptions of meanings and understandings of what out-group people are like. Whatever the facts may be about the out-group people, the racist person has his or her stereotypes as "facts" about out-group peoples.

Action racism. This kind of racism is observable; avoidance, discourtesy, exclusion, exploitation, and violence against out-group peoples are evident behaviors of this kind of racism. This is what is considered racial and ethnic discrimination.

Value racism. This kind of racism focuses on the values a racist person wishes to maintain or preserve. Preservation of racist values insures material gain; it becomes necessary to maintain racist values to insure material gain and economic security.

The intergroup relations approach can be used to develop positive relationships between students who differ because of social class and religious affiliations. Remember, the model's essence is to build empathy. Its limits are defined by the specific circumstances of one's classroom. For example, current stereotypes about sexual attractiveness—the very thin, svelte figure—may cause anxiety among teenage girls, provoking anorectic eating disorders. A teacher could use the Intergroup Education Model to counter the specific stereotype.

Ultimately, the model can be used to improve communications between any groups of students. *Caveat: The model is used to change behaviors, and in the process, can potentially change attitudes.* Responsible use of the model can activate positive behaviors and attitudes; irresponsible use can reinforce negative behaviors and attitudes. Through careful planning and thorough research regarding any of the topics confronted, teachers should be able to use the model effectively. Teachers should not play with the behaviors and attitudes of students. Therefore the model should not be used flippantly.

COOPERATIVE LEARNING AND INTERGROUP RELATIONS

An important outgrowth of intergroup education is the research conducted by Robert Slavin and his colleagues at the Center for Social Organization of Schools at Johns Hopkins University on what they call "cooperative learning." The idea of cooperative learning was garnered from Slavin's earlier research on the contact thesis. The cooperative learning thesis raised the question: Will sustained contact working toward a common goal improve learning as well as interpersonal relations? After conducting well-designed quantitative studies as well as well-conceived ethnographic studies, Slavin and his co-workers concluded that "for academic achievement, cooperative learning techniques are no worse than traditional techniques, and in most cases they are significantly better."[7]

In Johnson, Johnson, and Holubec's book, *Circles of Learning: Cooperation in the Classroom,*[8] learning to cooperate is defined as a basic academic and social skill; basic elements of cooperative learning applicable to elementary or secondary classrooms are identified as:

1. Positive interdependence and individual accountability: students as team members are individually accountable for learning the assigned lessons. Each student is evaluated by the teacher as occurs in a competitive classroom setting. Yet, students are encouraged to rely upon each other, sharing their knowledge so that all team members learn the assigned lessons;

2. Positive interdependence and shared leadership: all the students on a team are equals and are encouraged by the teacher (and teammates) to share their knowledge and skills for achievement of the assigned lessons; every team member gains from the participation (positive interdependence). There is no need for a formal leader because each team member, from time to time, will assume the role of the "formal" leader depending upon the task at hand. The problem with having a formal leader is that often the formal leader is expected to do all of the work; the leader learns much but the remaining team members learn little; for

interdependence to be effective, all team members must be both "team players" and "team leaders" from time to time;

3. Heterogeneous mixing and learning social interaction skills: By mixing the students into heterogeneous teams—mixing students who differ by academic abilities, cultures, genders, physical abilities, races, religions, ad infinitum—students develop social interaction skills while they are learning specific academic skills or knowledge, the contact thesis in action. Positive attitudes toward individuals from differing groups are "caught" indirectly rather than "taught" directly. Students learn the importance of understanding individual differences and seeking common grounds from which they may operate to achieve the assigned lessons;

4. Teacher facilitates group activities, students evaluate group progress: teacher's role is twofold, (1) teacher evaluates individual progress of each team member, and (2) teacher provides team feedback regarding their activities and problems that the team may be experiencing, providing possible solutions as options; students evaluate their team's progress, based on the teacher's feedback and their own observations. Then students reach consensus regarding a course of action so that the team can operate effectively to achieve the assigned tasks.

Cooperative learning is an active learning strategy; the classroom is viewed as a learning machine in which students, through their learning activities, are the fuel that drives the machine. Students are placed by the teachers into four to five-member teams; the students are heterogeneous in ability (includes handicapped) and gender; they are mixed across social class, race, ethnic, and religious group lines. The student team is given the educational goal: everyone on the team is to learn what the teacher has prescribed as the goal. Then the teacher presents the lesson; students in their teams attempt to learn the lesson by coaching and otherwise assisting each other. All students on a team must master the lesson; it is the team's responsibility to insure that each member individually has mastered the lesson. A team is rewarded through social recognition when all of its members have learned the lesson. To insure individual accountability, each student is assessed individually.

Under experimental conditions, the cooperative elements described above increase the academic achievement of all the students, and in particular, the approach increases the academic achievement of lower-class students. Slavin[9] attributed the cooperative learning link with improved academic achievement to the following factors:

1. Students are highly motivated to learn from their fellow team members;
2. Students learn by teaching, i.e., they learn the lesson by having to explain it to other team members;
3. Students are challenged to make the lesson relevant to their schemata and experiences by translating the teacher's language to their own language, i.e., putting the lesson in their own words;
4. Students are in a "safe" learning environment in that they are free to

admit ignorance or make a mistake among their team members without social humiliation;

5. Students are individually accountable to their team members to learn.

The promise of the cooperative learning strategy is that it fosters increased academic achievement as well as positive intergroup relations among students, including minorities, so-called low ability students, lower-class students, and mainstreamed handicapped students.

Not all cooperative learning activities work. Students, as team members, must be committed to achieving the team's goals; this means that a team's success is directly related to each individual's motivation to learn as well as the individual's actual achievement of the prescribed lessons. Also, teams need time, at least five to six weeks, to develop as viable, functioning teams. During the formative stages of these weeks, academic achievement and individual motivation will fluctuate. Time is needed for the team members to develop trust relationships with each other. Short-lived teams, say two to three weeks in duration, do not allow for trust to mature among team members. Therefore, teachers should design cooperative learning activities that progress from simple tasks to more complicated tasks. Successful achievement of the simple tasks will motivate students to try a more complicated task. With incremental steps, students will be allowed to grow as individuals as well as team members. Cooperative learning as a strategy to improve interpersonal relations as well as to improve academic achievement of all students involved promises much. The research on the approach indicates that the approach keeps its promise. Yet, as with all instructional approaches, teachers should not assume that the approach will work with all students or under any type of conditions. Rather, teachers should experiment with the approach keeping in mind that there is no "one best way" for all students to learn.

Teachers as leaders are central to effective intergroup and cooperative learning activities. As leaders, teachers should keep communications channels open with their students (leadership and teaching are described in Chapter 10). Teachers need to observe and listen to their students very carefully. For example, note these very probable classroom scenes:

STUDENT: But, Mr. Antonucci, I couldn't do the math problems 'cause I didn't have no paper to do them.
ANTONUCCI: Aw, come on! Who are you trying to kid? That's the same old story! You'll never pass this class with those excuses.

Or:

STUDENT: I couldn't do the math questions 'cause I didn't have no paper to do them.
ANTONUCCI: Let's see now, you're telling me you couldn't do the math problems because you didn't have any paper, right?

With the first situation, teacher Antonucci assumed that this student was lying; the teacher, operating on the assumption that this student couldn't be trusted, closed communications with the student by judging his response as a ploy to avoid doing the assignment. Yet the student may have been telling the truth. There are students who don't have paper readily at hand. And there are students who would rather spend their free time doing something other than math problems! Antonucci, in the second situation, attempted to maintain communications by trying to understand the student's perspective. He did this by recapitulating the response. Once understanding the student's perspective, Antonucci was in a position to evaluate whether or not his student's answer was a cover-up for not wanting to do the math problems. In the second situation, the teacher maintained open communications with the student by attempting to understand the student's perspective and thus may eventually be able to discover why the student didn't do the homework.

Teachers should listen to their students without immediately judging the students' responses or behaviors. In the pluralistic teaching-learning setting, it becomes important for teachers to consider when their students are genuinely acting from orientations that may differ from their own. There are no easy answers to the question of when the student is "jiving" and when the student is really acting from an orientation that differs from the teacher's.

Students should not be allowed to use their differences as a cover-up for refusing to learn fundamental skills. They are compelled to live in a highly technological society and fundamental literacy skills in math, science, and language are essential. All students should be expected to master literacy skills in math, science, and language without using the potential cop-out of ethnicity, gender, handicap, or social class as a means to avoid the discipline these academic areas impose. Because cultural, gender, handicap, and social class differences are real, it is necessary that teachers maintain communications with their students so as to determine when a student is acting from valid differences or personal irresponsibility.

SUMMARY

The intergroup relations approach is a strategy teachers can use to foster cross-group understandings in most classrooms. While misunderstandings occur between students, the misunderstandings may be superficial and transitory; at other times, misunderstandings among students may be rooted in family or community biases or stereotypes about people from a particular group.

The essence of the intergroup relations approach is empathy building among students, that is, helping students to appreciate the experience that members of other groups have as a result of group stigmatizing or stereotyping. Victims of stigmatizing can be almost any individual whose group within a given social context is an out-group. Empathy building is achieved in various ways. The most direct way to build empathy is through contact between individuals from groups that are at odds with each other. The contact thesis posits that empathy can be achieved when students work together on a common task as equals over a sustained period of time. In other words, the students must work together on a common task with enough time to develop trust and interdependence.

A promising approach, cooperative learning, is based on research utilizing the contact thesis. Basically, cooperative learning teaches students to work on specific projects in which they (the team members) as individuals are responsible to all the other members for learning. They help each other master the knowledge or skill posed to them by the teacher. The research on cooperative learning is thus far positive in that students participating in cooperative learning activities have reported gains in academic achievement as well as gains in motivation to learn traditional school subjects.

Teachers need to develop a trust relationship with their students which is possible if teachers work diligently at maintaining communications with their students. Basically, teachers must keep their end of the communication line open; they must also genuinely listen to what their students have to say without faking interest. At times, due to a teacher's biases or experiences, the teacher will impute certain attitudes (based on the biases or experiences) in students, when in fact, the imputations are merely biases of the teacher rather than real attitudes of the students. The students will sense the biases of the teacher and possibly shut out communications with the teacher. Under these circumstances, a trust relationship does not exist and the teacher's ability to teach is impaired.

STUDY QUESTIONS

1. Define the key characteristics of the contact thesis.
2. Explain the operational assumption of the intergroup relations strategy.
3. Explain the basic goal of the intergroup relations strategy.
4. The intergroup relations strategy has a four-part rationale. Describe each part of the rationale and explain the importance of each.
5. Describe how the intergroup relations strategy might be used to reduce sexist attitudes among students. Then explain how the strategy might be used to improve the mainstreaming experience for handicapped students.
6. What are the key characteristics of cooperative learning? Why do researchers believe that cooperative learning works?
7. What is the difference between "intergroup relations" and "interpersonal relations" as teaching strategies?

DEMONSTRATION LESSON

Title: Did you Hear About? or Tell Me a Story!
Goal: To build empathy in students by teaching them the art of telling a story which requires an understanding of the cultural basis of the story.
Rationale: By telling a story taken from a culture other than the student's, the student will develop the ability to look at things from a different point of view, that is, the point of view of the original storyteller. Somewhat like Method Acting, the student

will have to be the original storyteller; by "walking in the storyteller's shoes," the student puts himself or herself in the place of the storyteller, gaining an insight to the perspectives of the original storyteller. However, learning to tell the story must be accomplished within a team. Teams should be formed which are as mixed as possible regarding such variables as differences in ability, ethnicity, gender, handicap, race, religion, or social class. Each team member is to help the other team members learn to tell a specific story; team members should be given an array of stories from many different cultural sources and allowed to select the stories. But, a student must select a story from a culture different from her or his own culture.

Objectives: As a consequence of this lesson, students will:

1. know a specific story from a culture different from their own;
2. tell a story from a culture different from their own;
3. demonstrate an appreciation for the cultural perspective of the story by the way they tell the story;
4. convey the cultural perspective of the story while they tell the story;
5. explain in some detail the cultural perspective of the story when asked by students or teacher;
6. work cooperatively with team members to help them learn and tell their individual stories.

Grade Levels: K–12 with adaptations depending on the maturity of the students; the lesson can be used as part of a literature-based elementary language arts curriculum; it can also be used at the middle and high school levels in English, drama, speech and social studies classes.

Procedures:

A. Teacher collects stories from different cultures. A children's library will have ample stories which are useful for most grades including the high school level; one excellent source is: N. Livo and S. Rietz. *Storytelling* (Littleton, Co: Libraries Unlimited, 1986).
B. Teacher assigns students to teams insuring group heterogeneity; teams given selections from which individuals select a story to tell; during the selection process, each student should freely discuss story preferences, stories already known; once selection is made, the teacher should have students check the story content for any stereotypes or biases; with younger students, the teacher may have to determine the story's appropriateness.
C. Teacher distributes and explains the criteria (listed below) for telling a good story; then students are to practice telling the story with each other using the criteria as a way of coaching each other; team helps each member to develop the best possible presentation of the story; initially, the student will have to read and practice telling the story at home or in a secluded part of the school.
D. The event: intersperse the actual telling of the stories to the class; otherwise, students will soon grow jaded if all the stories are told in sequence. Teacher and students as a whole can evaluate the telling of the story using the criteria.

Criteria for Good Storytelling:

Remember the lesson's goal, to build empathy by understanding a cultural perspective different from the student's; also, remember that some students will be better actors than others, but that all of the students can gain from team coaching in both terms of self-esteem as well as in actual storytelling performance. The following questions can serve as a basic criteria for the storytelling:

1. Did the opening narrative establish the time, place, and character(s) in the story?
2. Did the opening narrative directly state, or imply, the point or theme of the story?
3. Was the storyline told compellingly, that is, were the events presented so that each sequence naturally flowed into the next sequence? (Students may simply string sequences together, as in "then this happened," "and then," "and," "then" and so on.)
4. What about word choice? Did the student use words that created imagery? Students may have to be taught about figures of speech, for example, onomatopoeia or words that imitate sounds: "The thunder bounced from mountain to mountain top, broooom, brooom, brooom. . . ." Or, a metaphor or word or words that compare: *The ox plowed through the marketplace, pushing aside carts and display stands, knocking people aside as it drove a furrow through the crowd.* (Ox running through market compared to farmer plowing a field.)
5. Were nonverbal means, gestures, pauses, body movements, used effectively? A little "ham" acting should be allowed but emphasis should be kept on knowing and telling the story so that others will know it.
6. What was the point of the story? Was the point clear by the content of the story? Was the story told in such a way that the point was clear?

A Warming-Up Exercise:

Distribute copies of the following summary of a Maricopa (Arizona) Indian story. Have the students in teams read and analyze the story using the guidelines following the story and that end this demonstration lesson.

> The Almighty Creator made all the animals of the world. The Almighty expected them to live in harmony. But, the rabbits found that they enjoyed using snakes as whips; they would whip each other, in jest, with the snakes. The snakes did not like being whips; it was painful. The snakes complained to the rabbits; the rabbits laughed at them. The snakes went to the Almighty. The Almighty gave them teeth and rattles. The teeth were poisonous. When any other animal tried to use them as whips, the snakes were to use their rattles as a warning to keep away. If the animals did not respect the snake's warning and commenced to use the snake as a whip, then the snake could bite the animal. Soon the other animals, including the rabbits, learned to respect the rights of snakes who did not desire to be used as whips.

1. Students should identify: the main characters, setting, and plot of the story; the basic conflict and theme (what it's about).
2. Students should practice retelling the story as is, or, tell it within contemporary times using other characters; this can be done within the teams using the criteria for a well-told story.
3. Students should be challenged to think in terms of a different viewpoint: are rattlesnakes enemies to humans or to other animals? Do rattlesnakes, like other animals, have an important part in nature? Or, are they to be used only as playthings?
4. Students may be challenged to discuss why some people would consider rattlesnakes as "bad" guys? Or, they may discuss the circumstances that make animals "bad" guys or "good" guys. The idea here is to begin the process of learning to perceive the same phenomenon from different points of view.

NOTES

1. Hilda Taba, Elizabeth Brady, and John T. Robinson. *Intergroup Education in Public Schools.* Washington, D.C.: American Council on Education, 1952.
2. Lloyd Allen Cook. *Intergroup Relations in Teacher Education.* Washington, D.C.: American Council on Education, 1951.
3. ————. *Elementary Curriculum in Intergroup Relations.* Washington, D.C.: American Council on Education, 1950.
4. Jean D. Grambs, *Understanding Intergroup Relations.* Washington, D.C.: National Education Association, 1973, Stock no. 387–11840.
5. ————. *Intergroup Education: Methods and Materials.* Englewood Cliffs, N.J.: Prentice-Hall, 1968.
6. F. James Davis. *Minority-Dominant Relations.* Arlington Heights, Ill.: AHM Publishing, 1978, pp.56–57.
7. R. Slavin. "Cooperative Learning." *Review of Educational Research.* Summer 1980, 50, #2, pp. 315–342; see also, R. Slavin. "A Case Study of Psychological Research Affecting Classroom Practice: Student Team Learning." *Elementary School Journal.* 82, 1, 1981, pp. 5–17.
8. David Johnson, Robert Johnson, and Ellen Holubec. *Circles of Learning: Cooperation in the Classroom.* Edina, Minn.: Interaction Book Co., 1986.
9. R. Slavin. "When Does Cooperative Learning Increase Student Achievement?" *Psychological Bulletin.* 94, 1983, pp. 429–445. See also, R. Slavin. *Cooperative Learning.* New York: Longman, 1983.

Chapter
10

Classroom Management and Human Rights Strategies

Key Terms:

> civil rights
> cultural rights
> civil disobedience
> correlative responsibilities
> ethical transcendence

> human rights
> *in loco parentis*
> leadership styles
> natural law
> social contract

The notion of cultural relativity and how teachers should develop the ability to perceive other cultures from the viewpoint of the respective cultures was discussed in Chapter 1. Cultural relativism as an analytical teaching tool can provide teachers with a means by which they can understand cultural differences within their classrooms. But cultural relativism cannot provide means by which teachers can manage cultural differences in their classrooms while providing all students with equal opportunities to learn. To ensure equal learning opportunities, Chapter 1 also discussed the notion of ethical transcendence, that is, a system of ethics that would transcend all cultural differences within the classroom. The human rights strategy provides a means by which teachers can ethically transcend the differences that are manifested in their classroom.

Chapter 2 discussed how the American Creed provides a basic belief that hard work in the pursuit of self-interests insures individual prosperity. Also discussed were a variety of communal living ideologies and social forces that can impede or enhance one's prosperity. Central to the entire chapter is the idea that Americans operate within a culture of democracy; its parameters are set by what is known as the *social contract*.

Eighteenth century philosophers John Locke and Jean-Jacques Rousseau formulated the notion of the "social contact." In the natural world, they asked, who should govern humans? Kings, churches, generals, dictators, mobs had all proved to be tyrannical; anarchy, or the absence of rulers, proved to be the tyrannosaurus rex of them all! Humans need rulers. They concluded that the least despotic rulers might be the people themselves if they were to form a community and agree upon the rules that would govern the community. Rousseau's definition of the social contract is:

> a form of association which will defend and protect with the whole common force the person and goods of each associate, and in which each, while uniting himself with all, may still obey himself alone, and remain free as before.[1]

Under the social contract, each individual formulates a social contract with the community; the contract would be an agreement that the community would protect the rights of the individual; in turn, the individual would be compelled to respect the rights of others. The rights of all would be codified in the community's laws, which could be changed, if the community members agreed to the changes. The social contract notion was the basis of both the Declaration of Independence and the Constitution.

The Human Rights Classroom Management strategy applies the social contract notion to the classroom. The classroom is construed as a "community of scholars" all engaged in the pursuit of learning, a basic self-interest. The teacher is the leader of the community who must teach the students how to pursue their self-interests—learning—within the guidelines established for the community of scholars. Each student, as an individual member of the community, makes a social contract with the community: "I will enter the community to pursue my self-interest of learning; the community will insure my basic right to learn; I must respect the right of everyone else to learn." The human rights strategy also provides ethical transcendence, that is, a means by which teachers can transcend—in a morally appropriate manner—the many human differences that are manifest among students in classrooms.

BASIS FOR CLASSROOM MANAGEMENT

Teachers are responsible for maintaining a safe learning environment for their students. To manage a classroom effectively a teacher must understand how students are affected by the classroom's physical and human environments and by the teacher's choice of teaching styles. The three key factors, physical environment, human environment, and teaching style, are felt by the students in their totality: students enter a classroom; scan the bulletin boards and the seating arrangements; notice whether or not other students are visiting, studying, sitting casually or stiffly, and listen to their teacher. They soon sense the tone or catch the classroom climate. A drab room with empty bulletin boards, where desks are bolted to the floor, where students are compelled to sit without leaving for long periods of time, has the trappings of an oppressive learning environment. Yet, the teacher's choice of teaching styles in this room could greatly change the human environment so that these dismal trappings would have a smaller impact.

A classroom must be physically safe for students. Teachers should know all emergency procedures—what to do and where to go when fires, tornadoes, and other natural hazards occur. Teachers should be wary of all potentially danger-ous school equipment or tools, and students should be coached in their proper usage. A sharp lead pencil, thrown across an aisle, could strike another student in the eye and cause serious harm. Adequate lighting, ventilation, heating, and cooling should be maintained whenever possible. Unnecessarily stuffy rooms, poorly lighted and overly hot or cold, affect the learning environment nega-tively. Further, the classroom's physical environment should reflect the nature of what is taught and what is learned in the classroom. Students' products, artwork, papers, posters should be displayed along with teacher-made materi-als and visual aids.

The teaching style can overcome the drabbest physical environment. In the reverse, the most tantalizing physical environment will not necessarily overcome overly oppressive or overly lax teaching styles. A teaching style can be thought of as the manner in which a teacher facilitates learning. A teacher's style reflects his or her personality and judgment about how best to facilitate classroom learning. Teachers develop styles compatible with their proclivities, toleration and frustration limitations, preferences, and idiosyncrasies. In other words, a teaching style is the manifestation of one's desire to teach something of value to oneself and to the student.

Teaching styles are usually categorized by the kind of leadership or gov-ernance techniques a teacher uses. The extent to which the teacher allows students to share in the decision-making process in the classroom identifies the type of teaching style utilized. The style can be located on a decision-sharing continuum as an autocratic, democratic, or laissez-faire teaching style, as shown in Figure 10.1. Speaking in absolute terms, an autocratic style will not share the decisionmaking process. What is taught and how concepts are learned are determined by the teacher alone. The style is entirely directive, leaving little room for student involvement or input. The democratic style shares a good portion of the decision-making. While the teacher may reserve the responsibility to choose what will be taught (many times school boards or curriculum directors and committees make this decision for the teacher), the decision-making about how concepts are to be learned is shared with the stu-dents. The style is both directive and nondirective. The laissez-faire style

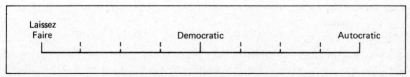

Figure 10.1 Decision-sharing teaching-styles continuum

delegates most, if not all, of the decision-making to the students, so that at any given time they may select what to study and how to study it. In absolute terms, the style is nondirective. These are types of teaching styles, and by necessity they appear rigid and inflexible. They describe the degree in which teachers share the teaching and learning decision-making process. Therefore, an autocratic style is not necessarily an oppressive, overbearing, inhumane teaching style. Neither is a laissez-faire style anarchical, unstructured, or disorganized, or the democratic style kind, understanding, and humane. In fact, many teachers use the three styles interchangeably. A maxim for a good teaching style is flexibility—the ability to choose and use a particular style to bring about desired learning outcomes. The decision as to which teaching style to use may be made on the basis of the degree the teacher feels students should be involved in decision-making. Emphasis here is on the teacher's judgment of the degree of decision-making that is necessary or appropriate. If a classroom is on fire, the teacher had best use an autocratic style to get students out of the room safely. To get students to think creatively, a teacher may want to allow periods of time for free association and other divergent-thinking activities—activities in which students make most of the decisions on how and what to learn.

Teachers are instructional leaders appointed by a school board to achieve the school district's educational goals. Teachers may delegate their authority; they may decide when and how students will share authority; teachers cannot surrender their authority to students. The classroom is not a democracy. Students do not elect their leader. Teachers do not choose their students. By law, teachers are *in loco parentis*, which means that teachers act in place of the parents while students are in class. Acting as reasonable parents, teachers have the basic responsibilities of teaching academic skills and knowledge and socializing students to live in a pluralistic society. As instructional leaders, teachers can guide their behavior on the basis of the body of research on leadership.

Research studies on leadership behavior report that leaders operate within two broad dimensions: task orientation and people orientation. To lead requires both an orientation toward task achievement and good interpersonal relations. Hoy and Miskel define leadership as a

> set of functions, or behaviors, carried out by individuals . . . to assure that tasks, group climate and individual satisfaction relate to the organization's objectives. [Teacher] effectiveness . . . is student achievement in cognitive, affective, and psychomotor areas of development.[2]

The ideal teacher exhibits a high concern for task achievement and a high concern for the students. But under certain conditions, high task orientation may be more effective; under other conditions, high concern for students may be more effective. In other words, an effective leadership style depends upon the situation. Fiedler calls this approach "contingency" leadership.[3] His research on leadership styles shows that matching a leadership style with the situation influences a group's performance. If the leadership style and group's situation are appropriately matched, then high group performance can be anticipated. The opposite is also true; poor matching of leadership style with a group's situation can cause low group performance.

The laissez-faire style shows high concern for students; the autocratic style shows high concern for task achievement; the democratic style shows high concern for students and task achievement. Which style is most effective depends on the classroom situation and on the dispositions of the students and teacher. Operating on a contingency basis, teachers need to match their teaching style with the group's situation. Successfully making the match is the challenge inherent in the art of classroom management.

CLASSROOM MANAGEMENT AND HUMAN RIGHTS

How does effective classroom management relate to human rights? In matters of human rights in the classroom, it is extremely critical that a climate of fair play be maintained if the human rights of everyone in the classroom are to be protected. There are times when the teacher may believe the majority of the class to be wrong (tyranny of the majority) in some matters pertaining to human rights. The teacher is then compelled to assume an autocratic style, directing rather than sharing decisions.

Consider the case of a student who is accused of cheating because answers to the test are written on his desk. Upon inspection, the teacher remembers seeing the writing on the desk during the previous period and also does not recognize the handwriting as that of the accused student. More than likely, the student is innocent of wrongdoing, especially since there is much reason to doubt his culpability. Should the teacher allow the class to decide his innocence or guilt? If he is unpopular or not well-known in the classroom, what chance does he have for fair play? The student may be wrongly accused. Other times the teacher may want to share the decision-making. Consider the case in which a Jewish fourth-grade girl slapped a fourth-grade boy for calling her a "kike" during recess on the playground. The boy complains to his teacher that she "beat him up" without reason and has three of his friends as witnesses. Should the teacher autocratically decide for or against either the boy or the girl? Should the teacher let the incident pass, allowing the students to decide for themselves the locus of wrongdoing? In my view, this case presents an ideal situation to teach all the students some lessons on human rights, such as due process and the rights of the accused, or free speech as a relative right and responsibility. To what degree does anyone have the right to insult someone else? What degree of rights does the insulted person have? Can one decide that the boy was irresponsible in the use of free speech, and thereby negated his right to free speech? In other words, that he deserved the slap because he insulted the girl? What about the girl's use of force to resolve a problem? Should violence be sanctioned or tolerated as a method to solve human problems? The list of ethical questions is endless. What is important is that this case presents a natural—and very real—situation in which human rights are threatened, and a good opportunity to teach how a community of people can share in the protection of rights, the social contract in action!

NONVERBAL MODES IN A PLURALISTIC CLASSROOM

Some general considerations for management of a pluralistic classroom are factors such as the verbal and nonverbal messages conveyed by teachers and the message conveyed by the physical and human space relations within the class. The research on verbal and nonverbal communications[4] in classrooms reports that teachers talk more than they probably should, that they are unaware of the various verbal and nonverbal messages they convey, and that teachers verbally and nonverbally convey preferences for middle-class students.

Key to understanding verbal and nonverbal classroom communications is the answer to the question: How consonant is my denotative message with my connotative message? Or, is what I say, what I convey? I remember a teacher who would say "how interesting" every time we showed her something we had done. After a while, it occurred to us that she didn't mean what she said. Instead by that comment she meant to reject or ignore what we offered without appearing to reject or ignore. She apparently felt it less damaging to appear interested than to simply say, "I can't look now, I'm busy," or "I don't want to look now." To us, she was not an authentic person; she tried to convey the appearance of being interested in her students, but the dissonance between her verbal and nonverbal messages was high enough to cast doubt on her authenticity.

Nonverbal communications often convey unconscious cultural biases. Anthropologist Edward Hall[5] devised a structural approach to understanding nonverbal communications between people of different cultural groups. He categorizes nonverbal communications into kinesics, proxemics, and haptics. These three nonverbal phenomena are popularly known as "body language" or "body talk." They do not include other aspects of nonverbal communications, such as paralanguage (intonational-connotational-tonal nonverbal messages) and olfaction (emission and reception of nonverbal odor messages). Because the complexity of a discussion on all aspects of nonverbal classroom communications would be book length, I will focus on the three aspects Hall identified and researched on a cross-cultural matrix as a way of sensitizing teachers to the nonverbal, cross-cultural dimension of classroom management.

Kinesics deals with the messages conveyed within and without different cultures by body movements. For example, now that female teachers are allowed to wear pantsuits or slacks in the classroom, many female teachers think it perfectly proper to sit on a table or on a desk in front of their classes. In Latino cultures, including the cultures of Puerto Ricans, Cubans, Mexican Americans, and other Central and South American cultures, women who sit on tables in public places are viewed as crude. Women teachers who sit on tables may convey by their kinesics a message of crudeness to their Latino and Latina students, and thereby embarrass the students. In other words, teachers should be aware that their kinesics are culturally conditioned, and that what may seem like perfectly natural body movement in one culture may be viewed differently in another culture. In Indian reservation schools, teachers have noticed that many Native American students don't gaze directly into the eyes of their teachers. Rather, when the teachers speak, the students turn their gaze downward, lowering their eye contact toward the floor. The teachers often interpret these kinesics as messages of "disrespect" and "shiftiness" because, in the teachers' cultures, indirect eye contact conveys distrust and disrespect. But, in the students' cultures, the opposite is true: direct eye contact with elders and adults in authoritative positions is viewed as "disrespectful." Thus, teachers misread their students' kinesics.

Proxemics deal with how people manage their life space, in particular how people interpret body space relationships. How close is too close when a stranger is standing near you? How far is too far when you are talking to a loved one? In a classroom, how do teachers manage the space relations between themselves and their students? How do they manage the body space between students? For example, in a desegregated classroom, do teachers manage classroom experiences so that minority and white students work together on projects? Or, do teachers manage the experiences so that these students rarely work together? Teachers may convey biases through their proxemics. For example, a teacher may hover over a student many times touching the student's shoulder while explaining a math problem. Explaining the same problem to a handicapped student, the teacher may stand erect, avoid physical contact, and explain the problem's operations from a distance. Provided, of course, that both students like to be touched, this kind of proxemic behavior, if it recurs enough to reveal a pattern, conveys preference for the nonhandicapped student and nonpreference, perhaps rejection, of the handicapped student.

Haptics deals with the quality of touch, especially stressing how people interpret touch. An apt illustration of haptics is how people interpret an embrace between adult men. In French, Spanish, Italian, and in other Latino cultures, an embrace is considered natural between adult males; this is not the case among Anglo-American males. In classrooms, how do students interpret the touches of their teachers? Teachers, especially elementary school teachers, are encouraged by their students to touch and to embrace them when students are happy, sad, or need reinforcement. But at the secondary levels, teachers are confronted by various interpretations regarding touch. Because haptics are culturally bound, how secondary students interpret their teachers' touch depends largely on their cultural perspective. Conversely, some teachers don't like to touch their students. Even a light tap of approval on the shoulder is avoided by some teachers. Again, remember that students interpret nontouch or avoidance of touch according to their cultural perspectives.

Teachers may reveal ethnic, gender, or social class biases by the way they manage the space relations in their classrooms. In other words, they may move around their classrooms, approaching closely students of the group they feel most comfortable with and avoiding students from groups they are less comfortable with. Or, teachers may arrange the seating so that preferred students sit close to them and the nonpreferred sit farther away. These are not far-fetched instances. In my experience with classroom spatial arrangements, I have seen classrooms in which all the minority students sat in the back of the class and the White students near the front. Another classroom had African American students sitting at desks bolted to the floor and facing the walls, while the White students all sat at round tables in the center of the room. In each situation, the teachers were managing segregated spatial arrangements in their classes, and in my view, revealing their biases.

RIGHTS AS ETHICAL CONSTRUCTS

Rights are social in character. They occur within social interactions and exist as relationships between humans:

> rights are . . . those conditions that must be fulfilled if human action is to be possible either at all or with general chances of success in achieving the purposes for which humans act.[6]

Rights operate within the context of groups or communities and prescribe the behavioral parameters allowed individuals within their group or community. Consequently, rights define the nature and extent of freedom individuals are allowed in their communities.

Rights, as social interaction entitlements, allow individuals to act as free agents within respective groups or communities; individuals are only constrained by the rights of others. Rights, in other words, are correlative. For every right granted, there is a concurrent responsibility that individuals owe all the members of the community—respect for the rights of others. One only has the rights one respects in others. Or, one cannot have rights without allowing others to have the same rights within the community.

In jurisprudence, a distinction is made between rights granted to individuals by their governments, *civil rights*, their ethnic group, *cultural rights*, and their membership as humans in our global community, *human rights*.

Cultural rights refer to prerogatives of group membership. Some prerogatives: (1) intimacy—individual members provide warmth and emotional support, and much as with the love of parents, intimacy is a birthright one does not have to earn; (2) connectedness—individuals are linked by common beliefs, customs, and histories; they share common ideals and hopes for the future; a sense of self, or self-identity, is forged within the group; (3) community—group members share norms binding them as members of a community. The group collectively construes certain behaviors as appropriate or inappropriate for the group's perpetuation. While group members allow minimal deviations from the norms, extreme deviations are enforced through some kind of punishment, such as imprisonment, banishment, or fines. The group's source of coercive power is conformity. If individuals want to remain in the group, partaking of its prerogatives, the individuals must conform to the group's norms.

Cultural rights are focused on a group's desire to maintain conformity and order in the group. Thus, cultural rights protect the group from arbitrary behaviors of individuals. Civil rights protect the individual from the arbitrary behavior of rulers. Civil rights are rooted in the parliamentary history of England. The twelfth century charter of Henry I and the thirteenth century charter of King John, the *Magna Carta,* were contracts between kings and their barons. The charters explicated the rights of the king and barons, limiting the power of the king. By limiting the power of kings, the charters protected the rights of the barons. Should a king desire to retain the loyalty of his barons, he was practically bound to respect their rights. From these charters came the principle that laws should limit the power of government and protect the individual. In the nineteenth century, a *Bill of Rights* was added to the U.S. Constitution to enumerate the specific rights vested in citizens, protecting them from the arbitrary behaviors of those in power. A nation's civil rights are only as good as the lawmakers who enforce them. Civil rights rely on the goodwill of lawmakers. If they have the will to enforce civil rights, then individuals have little need for concern. The opposite is also true. While honest lawmakers will honor the civil rights of individuals, dishonest lawmakers will not. Once civil rights are promised to a group, the group can apply public pressure on officials to honor the civil rights promised.

Cultural and civil rights are provincial; they exist within the context of a given province, namely a nation or an ethnic group. Enforcement and protection of individual civil rights vary. Some nations enforce civil rights when wronged individuals are able to rally impressive support behind them. Other nations enforce the civil rights of individuals who can afford to pay for the cost of litigating their rights.

Human rights strive to be universal in focus; they attempt to include all ethnic groups, nations, and humans. They transcend the provinciality of cultural and civil rights. But they do not exist in the norms or folkways of established ethnic groups, nor do they exist in the constitutions or civil laws of governments. They have neither the coercive power of cultural rights nor the public pressure of civil rights. Human rights exist as constructs of perfect justice which emphasize what people hold in common—rather than how people differ—as citizens of the global community.

GENESIS OF HUMAN RIGHTS

Human rights emerged from natural law doctrines. The ethical basis of the natural law doctrines is that there exists a universally correct or right way for humans to treat each other. Natural law doctrines presume that ethics must concurrently deal with the good of the whole group as well as the good of the individual within the group, striking a balance between the rights of the group as a whole and the rights of individuals within the whole group.

Ancient Greek notions of the natural law were couched in the world view that the universe was organized in a harmonious order of which humans were an integral part. The universe is governed by its own laws, the natural law, and people as part of the universe are also governed by the natural law. The Roman orator and statesman, Cicero, described the universe as a rational system in which people were governed by rational laws held in common by all.[7] They were compelled to live in kinship with each other and with nature. The natural law bound them together as citizens of a community. Therefore, the highest virtue in this system of natural law was to live according to the natural law.

The emphasis of the Greek natural laws was upon people as members of a human or a political community. People were viewed as social or political animals who could form groups to pursue the greater good of the group. During the latter parts of the Middle Ages in Europe there was a gradual shift in emphasis from viewing people as social beings to viewing them as individuals. Rather than stressing the social or corporate nature of humans, European scholars such as Machiavelli, Adam Smith, and later Thomas Hobbes and John Locke, stressed their individualist nature. Adam Smith's assumption about economics was that people, allowed to pursue their own self-interests within the constraints of the natural law, would attain well-being. The stress on individualism and self-determination also pointed to the need for protection from kings and rulers who would use their powers to abridge individuality and self-determination. The natural law, hindered by capricious kings and rulers, was dysfunctional; however, if people banded together and ruled themselves, then individual initiative and self-determination were possible and the natural law could work. Consequently, people were members of two societies or communities, a human society and a civil society. The human society was governed by natural laws, but since no mechanism existed to enact and enforce the natural laws, a civil society had to enact and enforce civil laws reflecting the natural laws as well as laws to protect individuals from the capriciousness of civil laws. Human rights were given birth by the union of the Greek world view of humans as social beings with the later European world view of humans as individual beings. Human rights, like the natural law, were presumed to exist in the nature of human relations. Within political or social bodies, these natural rights—for example freedom, liberty, individual ownership of property—were inalienable. To insure these rights, government were formed and civil laws enacted, such as the first ten amendments to the U.S. Constitution which guarantee the protection of individual rights.[8]

Consider that we live in two communities, a human community and a civil community. In the human community everyone holds the right to life, liberty, and happiness. The greatest virtue is to use reason and justice to insure everyone the human rights to life, liberty, and happiness. The purpose of the civil community is to enact and maintain laws that preserve these rights for the human community. The rights in a human community are superordinate to the laws of the civil community. When the laws of the civil community violate, prohibit, or attempt to abrogate a human right, people are duty-bound to change, resist, or abolish the unjust civil law, that is, civil disobedience. Our fundamental duty is to reconcile the laws of the civil community with the rights of the human community. As Thomas Jefferson said, "Eternal vigilance is the price of freedom."

The human rights strategy operates in a classroom on basic democratic principles which teachers and students should understand. The first principle is *rule by law* rather than by fiat or totalitarian ruler. The rules of a society are made by the people in the society or human community rather than by some elite group or individual who then imposes the rules on the society. The authority to make, change, or alter rules lies within the society. Rule by law is essentially democratic rule, or a rule by ideal democracy—that is, *demo* meaning "people" and -*cracy* meaning "rule" or "govern." The closest facsimile of ideal or pure democracy in the United States was the town hall meetings which were held in small New England communities in the late eighteenth and early nineteenth centuries. These meetings were called together whenever the community had a problem, faced a crisis, or needed to make a communitywide decision. In the meetings, everyone had an equal status because everyone was an equal member of the community. (African American slaves, Native Americans, and, no doubt, women were excluded from the meetings, or if allowed to attend, had no voting privileges. Note my earlier reference to the town hall meeting as a "facsimile" of ideal democracy.)

The group leader, usually the man who called the meeting, discussed the problem and sought consensus from the group on a solution. Because the problem at hand affected the entire community, individuals were compelled to consider both their individual interests and the collective interests of the community; any decision based upon a consensus was considered the collective will or decision which applied to the whole community. All differences of opinion were yielded when a consensus was reached regarding the solution. A consensus was not simply a 51 percent vote or a majority vote of the group; rather, a consensus was a general climate of opinion held by the plurality of the group, at least two-thirds of the group, that a particular course of action or solution should be followed by individuals in the community. Hence, rule by law is not rule by the majority (51 percent) or rule by fiat or a totalitarian ruler (1 percent); rather, it is rule by the plurality (75–100 percent) or the collective will of members of the community. In a town hall meeting it is apparent that not everyone gets his way; some individuals in the group will not be satisfied with the consensus of opinion. Consequently, through persuasion and appeals to reason, dissatisfied group members can attempt to change the climate of opinion; they can choose to accept the group consensus on a tentative basis, hoping that if the solution or consensus reached proves unworkable, their opinions will appear more reasonable. The town hall meetings call for community involvement, mutual respect, and mature, unselfish cooperation. The fate of the community is also the fate of the individual, as each individual is an integral part of the whole community.

Under a *rule by law* governing system *everyone has inalienable rights and responsibilities*. These rights and responsibilities cannot be earned, given, or taken from anyone. Simply because everyone is a human who consequently lives in the human community, everyone has inherent rights and responsibilities. No one, for example, has to earn the right to be free. Therefore, no one can buy, sell, or give anyone freedom. One presumably is born with the right to be free. Thus, human slavery of any kind is nonexistent when everyone has inalienable rights and responsibilities as a member of the human community.

There are two kinds of rights, substantive and procedural rights. *Substantive rights* are presumed modes of behavior individuals are allowed to use within the human community. For example, individuals have a right to practice a religion of their choice, and a right not to practice any religion at all. *Procedural rights* are presumed modes of behavior by which individuals are treated within the human community. Sometimes procedural rights are conceived of as the due process everyone is entitled to when accused or suspected of a crime. For example, if one is accused of committing a crime, one is presumed to be innocent until found guilty by a jury of peers. The jury must weigh and consider all the incidents and circumstances pertaining to the alleged crime so as to insure fair treatment of the accused individual.

Substantive and procedural rights are relative rather than absolute; that is, individuals do not practice rights in a social vacuum; they must practice their rights relative to the rights of other individuals and the rights of the total human community. Therefore, with every right there exists a concurrent responsibility. Or, everyone must practice rights responsibly, which means that everyone in the human community is required to consider the rights of others as well as the rights of oneself, if the individual and the human community expect to survive. The classic example of a relative, substantive right is freedom of speech: Do I have the right to shout "Fire!" in a crowded theater, when, in fact, no fire exists? Should my freedom of speech be abridged? If I do commit the act, should I be punished in any way? What is my responsibility to the people in the theater? Shouting "Fire!" would no doubt cause pandemonium and chaos. People would desperately try to get out of the crowded theater, jamming the exists and trampling each other; inevitably, many would be injured, perhaps killed. It's clear that my freedom of speech should be abridged; then everyone in the human community should be equally abridged or restrained.

Enacting specific laws to restrain freedom of speech in matters affecting public safety would not be possible. To prohibit yelling "Fire!" in a crowded theater does not prohibit yelling "Fire!" in a crowded terminal, church, or other building. Such laws could be cumbersome and in their final effect unjust in some way to someone. Instead, people are expected to use their rights responsibly, taking into consideration the rights of others. If individuals practice their rights responsibly, they can expect others to do the same. When they violate the rights of others by irresponsible action, they also violate their own rights, because, in the human community, the fates of all members are intertwined. For example, to prohibit protestors from freedom of assembly because their speech may incite a riot also prohibits other protesters on different issues from freedom of assembly. At the same time, protesters allowed freedom of assembly must act responsibly to prevent a riot and protect the public safety. If they do not act responsibly, people may be harmed, property damaged, and ultimately, their views may not be heard. If their goals are to harm others and damage property, they are clearly acting outside the better interests of the human community and outside the parameter of rule by law. In short, they are "outlaws."

What happens when the majority of the human community acts irresponsibly toward an individual or individuals? Unjust laws have been enacted by a majority of the community. The laws were unjust because they violated a categorical imperative or a universal ethic. The majority of a community can be unjust and thereby tyrannous to the human community. To prevent tyranny by the majority, the human community must allow individuals the *right to conscientious objection* or *civil disobedience*.[9] People must be allowed to attempt to change or disobey a law which they consider a violation of a universal ethic. But, the right to civil disobedience has a concurrent responsibility to the human community. If the law is unjust, then people have the responsibility to change the law through the established or agreed upon governmental means or to passively resist the law and thereby possibly effect its change.

The consequences of passive resistance, conscientious objection, and civil disobedience may be harsh. Imprisonment, fines, and social alienation are expensive prices to pay for one's minority opinions. For example, the conscientious objectors of the Vietnam War were of three types: those who fled to Canada and other countries, those who refused to be drafted and were jailed, and those who were drafted into noncombat roles in the armed forces. Under *the ethical code of civil disobedience*, those who fled to other countries were considered to be irresponsible to the human community. They practiced their right to civil disobedience but did not act responsibly to the human community by suffering the consequences of their disobedience. Had all those who fled the United States cluttered the jails and prisons along with others who in fact were imprisoned for their conscientious objection, public outcries and protests against the useless human costs of the war—both people in the prisons and the people in Vietnam—might have ended U.S. military involvement much sooner. Those conscientious objectors drafted into noncombat roles also acted irresponsibly, because while they did not wage war directly on other humans, they indirectly assisted others in their war against humans, and thereby tacitly supported the war effort. If they believed that the war effort violated a universal ethic, and that the draft law was therefore unjust, they must have also believed that any support of the war effort was a violation of the universal ethic. By tacitly supporting the war effort, they violated their conscience and belief that the war was unjust. Also, their tacit support served to lengthen the war; withdrawal of their support might possibly have shortened it.

To prevent tyranny by the majority, everyone in the human community must practice at one time or another the rights and responsibilities of conscientious objection, passive resistance, and civil disobedience. By acting responsibly, by suffering the consequences of civil disobedience, individuals may change the climate of public opinion and thereby neutralize the laws of a tyrannous majority. Civil disobedience is not easy or popular, but it is necessary in a human community. The right to dissent, to challenge the majority, to attempt to change or disobey an unjust law (and suffer the consequences) are essential if a just, human community is desired. Civil disobedience is a categorical imperative.

Human rights evolved as a result of the synthesis between the ancient Greek notion of the natural order of all things and the European worldview that individuals are entitled to freedom of action within the natural order. As such, human rights are predicted on the following *a priori* assumptions:

- *All persons are members of the same race, the human race,* that is, all people share a fundamental humanity that is the same everywhere.
- *All persons exist as ends in themselves,* that is, persons are not born to serve any master unless they choose to serve a master other than themselves.
- *All persons are ethically equal,* that is, all persons are entitled to equal treatment; human rights do not recognize the notions that "some people are more equal than others," and that "some people are more human than others."

Now we are ready to examine the application of human rights in the classroom.

CLASSROOM APPLICATIONS OF HUMAN RIGHTS

Under the human rights strategy, the public school classroom is an involuntary civil community. Students are compelled to attend school. They by and large do not choose what they will be taught nor do they choose who will teach them. They may choose what they will learn by their attention or inattention. Teachers by and large cannot choose whom they will teach. They must teach anyone assigned to their classrooms, regardless of class, race, religion, sex, or physique. In the *realpolitik* of the classroom, teachers can and do show preference for nonminority students. This has been shown in studies conducted by the U.S. Commission on Civil Rights, such as the *Teachers and Students* study cited in Chapter 5, and other studies which reported that minority students receive a disproportionately greater share of suspensions and other in-class punishment. In fact, teachers often expressed a preference for nonminority students.[10] The human rights strategy provides a nonpreferential method for classroom management, in which the public school classroom is a human community governed by the principle of *rule by law*.

In the human community classroom, everyone is a citizen with inalienable rights and responsibilties. All behavior, of both students and teachers, must be guided by the self-interests of the individual balanced by the interests of the group. Rules and regulations in the classroom must be devised to protect the rights of all students and teachers. Consideration must be given to the fact that as an involuntary community, the classroom will be constrained by imposed rules. State laws, city ordinances, and school policies may be imposed on the classroom. For example, some states prohibit bare feet in all public buildings; others prohibit smoking in all public buildings; in some classrooms students can't be barefoot; in some teacher lounges, teachers can't smoke. Teachers are ultimately responsible for providing a safe learning environment. If many of the imposed rules do impinge upon human rights in the classroom, then teachers and students have the responsibility to attempt to change the rules.

Within the classroom community, all citizens are governed by these natural law doctrines:

1. All humans have inalienable rights and responsibilities.
2. All humans live in communities governed by the natural law and the civil law.
3. The civil law is subordinate to the natural law.
4. Disobedience of civil laws that violate the natural law is both a right and a responsibility.

Following are some operational principles for the practice of natural law doctrines.

The principle of inalienable and correlative human rights and responsibilities. The principle presumes that all humans, regardless of race, creed, or national or religious affiliations, have basic rights and responsibilities that cannot be taken away by other humans or by a government. The rights and responsibilities cannot be given away or abandoned. An example is the right to life. All people have the right to live and the responsibility to maintain healthy bodies. No person can arbitrarily kill another person (e.g., the commandment, "Thou shalt not kill"); no person can arbitrarily abandon the right of life (i.e., people have the responsibility of caring for the nourishment and health of their bodies). This is because we all live in a human community and are interdependent. In this example, maintaining healthy bodies allows people to practice their right to life and allows others to benefit from the skills, talents, and contributions healthy people can make to the community. Therefore, rights are correlative. If you have a right to privacy, you also have a responsibility to insist upon your privacy. In turn, I have the responsibility to honor your right to privacy but you must also respect my right to privacy.

The principle that all people live in communities governed by the natural law and the civil law. The assumption here is that all people are citizens of two societies, a natural or human society and a civil society. The human natural society consists of all living things in general and of all human beings in particular. People and the physical environment intertwine to form the basis of the society. The human society is the society referred to as the brotherhood and sisterhood of all people; it has no national boundaries, nor does it have governments. The natural society is governed by the universal ethics of human interaction. Within the classroom community, everyone is interdependent. It serves the greater good to pursue one's interests while also pursuing the interests of the classroom community.

The principle that the civil law is subordinate to the natural law. The assumption here is that students and teachers are capable of knowing the natural law and able to operate under its guidance. Teachers and students cannot operate on natural or civil law if they don't know the laws. They must be taught the natural and civil laws and they must be taught to practice them.

What follows is a summary of this principle's assumptions and its civil laws which serve to protect human rights in the classroom community:

Human rights are basic to a democratic society.

Students must know what their rights are before they can practice them.

Human rights must be valued in a democratic society.

Majority rules should not quash individual students' rights.

Students have the right to be different.

Students have the right to a positive self-concept.

Students can learn to use their rights responsibly.

Phi Delta Kappa's Teacher Education Project on Human Rights is an exemplary human rights program. The preamble to the program follows:

THE HUMAN RIGHTS CREED IN EDUCATION
Preamble

As an educator in a democratic society, concerned with the human rights of people everywhere, I will exemplify in my behavior a commitment to these rights. Educators and the educative process must have a more significant impact in ensuring these rights for all people. Thus, I will translate my belief in basic human rights into daily practice. I believe in the right and its concomitant responsibility:

1. To Equal Opportunity for All in:
   Education
   Housing
   Employment
   The Exercise of the Franchise and Representation in Government
2. Of Due Process and Equal Protection Under the Law
3. Of Freedom of Speech and of the Press
4. To Dissent
5. To Freedom of or from Religion
6. To Privacy
7. To be Different
8. Of Freedom from Self-Incrimination
9. To a Trial by a Jury of Actual Peers
10. To Security of Person and Property
11. To Petition and Redress of Grievances
12. To Freedom of Assembly[11]

The principle of civil disobedience as a right and a responsibility. As with the other principles, teachers and students must know what the principle entails before they can use it. Civil disobedience is not to be taken lightly; rather, as with the other principles, it requires mature judgment as to the greater good of the classroom community and dictates of the conscience. Civil disobedience requires that teachers and students first attempt to change an unjust rule or law within the established governmental system. Second, if the governmental system persists in maintaining the unjust rule, then teachers and students are obligated to resist or disobey the rule and suffer the consequences within the established civil community. Third, if steps 1 and 2 do not achieve a change in the unjust rule, the objectors should take their plea to the public and attempt to sway the climate of opinion in the objectors' favor. If the public is unresponsive, then the objectors must continue dissension and passive resistance until the time the public acts on their pleas for justice. It is critical that teachers and students understand the value of civil disobedience; that is, civil disobedience serves as a check on tyrannous rule by the majority. Without civil disobedience, protection of rights of minorities (any type of minority) is not possible.

An organizational scheme for the human rights approach follows:

Philosophic bases

Natural rights doctrines: All humans have rights to life, liberty, and happiness, *ipso facto*.

Teacher needs

Values students as humans and their right to be human.

Knows when and how to apply differing teaching styles—authoritarian, democratic, laissez faire—to enhance student rights.

Knows when and how to apply civil disobedience.

Understand the complexities of rule by majority and protection of minority rights.

Student needs

All students need to know their human and civil rights with their concurrent responsibilities.

All students need to know how to use their human rights responsibly.

Content

Natural rights doctrines, for example: Magna Carta; Declaration of Independence; Bill of Rights; United Nations' Declaration of Universal Rights; Martin Luther King's "I Have a Dream"; Henry David Thoreau's "Civil Disobedience."

Method

Cycle 1. Formal approach to rights
  A. Teach students their rights.
  B. Teach students to understand principle of rule by majority and protection of minority rights.
  C. Teach students the balance principle, i.e., for every right exists a concurrent responsibility.
  D. Principle of civil disobedience.

Cycle 2. Informal approach
   A. Allow students to practice their rights.
   B. Hold students responsible for practicing or violating rights.
   C. Allow civil disobedience but follow through on its consequences.

Cycle 3. Loop to Cycle 1
   A. Review natural rights doctrines.
   B. Discuss issues raised by students.
   C. Analyze and evaluate with students their use of rights and respon-
      sibilities.
   D. Design (with students) mechanism to continue informal human rights
      practices as an ongoing process, e. g., grievance panel, human rights
      committee, "town hall meetings."

Evaluation

Determine the nature and degree to which students (and teacher) responsibly utilized their human rights.

Determine whether the classroom climate is conducive to the responsible
   utilization of human rights.

The challenge of the human rights approach is to balance the civil rights
of the group (e.g., senior class, homeroom) with the human rights of the
student. The teacher must balance "law" with "order." The human right to
be oneself may conflict with the group's civil rights to an equal educational
opportunity if one student insists on trumpet practice during study sessions,
for example. The teacher determines which rights are to prevail at a given
time. The teacher may want to involve the whole class in making the decision. What's important about the human rights approach is how the teacher
handles conflicts of rights, because it is more difficult to practice respect for
human rights than it is to merely espouse them. For example, in the case of
a fire in a classroom, the teacher should take complete control of the group,
insist on total conformity, and abrogate anyone's right to be different so that
the group can be led out of the room to safety. But in the case of a student
who is accused by the class of stealing the teacher's grade book, the teacher
is challenged to handle the potential violation of rights of the class with discretion in order to foster respect for the rights of the accused—that is, the
right to be considered innocent until proven guilty, or the right to face one's
accuser. The teacher's approach has to be situational, assessing the incident
carefully and then deciding upon an approach that would protect the rights
of the students. Overall, the teacher is challenged to balance the group's and
individual's rights in such a manner that a climate of respect for the rights of
everyone predominates in the classroom.

The following are guidelines which suggest ways and means a teacher can
govern a class with the human rights strategy. The guidelines are general, and
while they may not specifically outline details for a class, they are sufficiently
broad to be applicable to most public school classrooms:

1.0 The right to be different
    1.1 Teacher   courages students to assert their individuality.
    1.2 Teacher adapts lessons and instruction according to student cognitive learning styles.
    1.3 Teacher doesn't use large group instruction all of the time.
    1.4 Teacher enforces dress codes and hair style rules that allow for individual and group differences.
    1.5 Teacher doesn't ignore students who differ with respect to ethnicity, race, national origin, or linguistic background, gender, handicap, social class.
    1.6 Teacher fosters understanding of divergent dialects and speech.
2.0 The right to fair, equal treatment
    2.1 Teacher doesn't have preferred students or "pets."
    2.2 Teacher doesn't show preferential treatment toward students of one ethnic/racial group, gender group, handicap, social class, or religious group.
    2.3 Teacher doesn't discipline more, or discipline more severely, students of out-group affiliations.
3.0 The right to a safe learning environment
    3.1 Teacher doesn't allow students to physically harm each other.
    3.2 The classroom is well ventilated, well lighted, well cooled and heated for comfort of students.
    3.3 Classroom furniture is safe and nonhazardous.
4.0 The right to privacy
    4.1 Teacher does not reveal notes, term papers, or other confidential documents or expressions to the whole class without prior permission of the author.
    4.2 Teacher does not reveal grades on term papers or class projects, remarks on term papers, grades for a project or for a semester without prior permission of the respective students.
    4.3 Teacher does not directly search students, indirectly expect students to report deviant behavior—the tattletale—or unnecessarily embarrass students in the classroom.
5.0 The right to dissent
    5.1 Students are encouraged to agree or disagree with their teacher and their peers.
    5.2 The teacher fosters respect for student dissension as a means for rational understanding of opinions.
    5.3 Teacher allows discussion and dissension pertaining to class and school rules and regulations.
    5.4 Teacher fosters understanding of civil disobedience as a right and a responsibility.
6.0 The right to a safe emotional learning environment
    6.1 Teacher doesn't ridicule, tease, or publicly demean students.
    6.2 Teacher doesn't seat students in segregated arrangements based solely on race, gender, social class, or handicap.

6.3 Teacher doesn't foster unkind labelling or stereotypic slurs or expressions in the classroom.

6.4 Teacher fosters a classroom climate that encourages respect between individual students.

SUMMARY

Teachers are the academic leaders of their classrooms. They may select teaching styles that best fit their personalities as well as the conditions within their respective classrooms. Their selected teaching styles are based on ethical principles that should allow them to reasonably manage their classrooms as well as transcend whatever cultural differences manifest themselves. The Human Rights strategy provides a set of ethical principles based on natural law doctrines. While the ancient Greeks placed emphasis on the group's preponderance over the individual, eighteenth century philosophers placed emphasis on the individual over the group. In our time, societies that operate on natural law doctrines and social contracts strive to balance the rights of individuals and the rights of the group.

Once understanding the ethical basis of the natural rights doctrines, teachers can develop an ethical system for use in the management of their classrooms. The ethical system should transcend whatever cultural differences become manifest in the classroom while at the same time providing all students with an equal opportunity to learn. In a classroom based on natural law doctrines and human rights, students are entitled to the right (1) to be different; (2) to fair, equal treatment; (3) to a physically safe learning environment; (4) to privacy; (5) to dissent; and (6) to a safe emotional learning environment.

STUDY QUESTIONS

1. What is the link between cultural relativism and ethical transcendence? How can the two notions be used jointly to manage an ethically fair classroom?

2. What is meant by tyranny of the majority? How might the notion apply to the classroom?

3. How did the ancient Greeks and the eighteenth century philosophers disagree with their definitions of the natural law? Be specific.

4. According to natural law philosophers, which is superordinate: natural law or civil law? As you answer, consider the notions of cultural relativism and ethical transcendence.

5. Describe what is meant by substantive and procedural rights. Then discuss these rights as they apply to classroom management.

6. Explain the principle of correlative rights and responsibilities. How does the principle apply to the classroom?

7. Read the following incidents and then discuss the questions that follow each.

Incident

Just as a fourth-grade class was leaving the classroom, a student accused Marie of stealing his lunch. Her desk was searched by the teacher, who found his lunch in it. The teacher asked the classmates (all in a hurry to eat their lunches) how to punish Marie. The majority felt she should be punished by classroom confinement for a week rather than eating lunch in the lunchroom with her classmates.

Questions

1. What human rights are threatened in this incident?
2. What about the dangers of rule by majority?
3. As the teacher, how would you handle the incident?

Incident

The word "nigger" is commonly used in the local all-White community to connote any tricky or "foxy" person. A Black youngster moves into the community. During a soccer game, a White friend of the Black child calls him a nigger for executing a tricky play. The Black student, angered by the remark, beats up the White student.

Questions

1. What human rights are involved?
2. Was the Black student's anger understandable?
3. Was the White student's *faux pas* understandable?
4. What intergroup relations strategies might be used to prevent such incidents?

Incident

A Native American student is told to wash off the brown grease smeared on his arms. He does. The next day his sister dies. According to this Native American's religious belief, oil mixed with brown soil should be smeared on the arms of all the family members when a family member is ill. Removal of the "grease" can do harm to the ill person. The parents pull the student out of school.

Questions

1. What human rights are involved?
2. Should the teacher have known better? Was the teacher acting out attitudes about hygiene and cleanliness? Was the teacher acting out an attitude against "silly" superstitions?
3. How much should a teacher know about a student's culture?
4. How might a study of the school's community prevent similar incidents?

Incident

A Jewish American organization feels that Jewish students should be allowed vacations during certain Jewish holidays; arguing that Christians are allowed Christmas and Easter vacations, so should Jewish students be allowed, without penalty, time off for their holidays. A bandwagon is begun: other ethnic groups join the Jewish movement—Puerto Rican, Polish, and Islamic—insisting on free time for religious holiday other than Christmas and Easter.

Questions

1. What human rights are involved?
2. In a pluralistic society, are school able to accommodate all ethnic group holidays? Or should schools become more secular and less Christian?
3. How might "cultural rights" be involved in this incident?

NOTES

1. Jean-Jacques Rousseau. "The Social Contract," in R. Hutchins, *Great Books of the Western World.* Chicago: Encyclopaedia Britannica, 1952, p. 381.
2. Wayne K. Hoy and Cecil G. Miskel. *Educational Administration: Theory, Research, and Practice.* New York: Random House, 1982, p. 181.
3. Fred E. Fiedler. *A Theory of Leadership Effectiveness.* New York: McGraw-Hill, 1967, pp. 36–50.
4. Ned Flanders. *Analyzing Teacher Behavior.* Reading, Mass.: Addison-Wesley, 1970, pp. 14–38.
5. Edward T. Hall. *The Hidden Dimension.* Garden City, N.Y.: Doubleday (Anchor Books), pp. 3–48, 1966; see also, Hall's *Beyond Culture.* New York: Doubleday, 1977.
6. A. Gerwirth. *Human Rights: Essays on Justification and Application.* Chicago: Chicago University Press, 1982, p. 3.
7. Cicero. *De Legibus.* Cambridge, Mass.: Harvard University Press, 1943; see also, Cicero. *De Republica.* Cambridge: Harvard University Press, 1943.
8. For an in-depth history of natural law and human rights, see Melvin Rader. *Ethics and the Human Community.* New York: Holt, Rinehart and Winston, 1964, pp. 15–52; see also, Kenneth Strike and Jonas Soltis. *The Ethics of Teaching.* New York: Teachers College Press, 1985.
9. Henry David Thoreau. "On the Duty of Civil Disobedience," in *Walden.* New York: New American Library (Signet), 1963, pp. 222–240.
10. Betsy Levin. "Recent Developments in the Law of Equal Educational Opportunity." *Journal of Law and Education,* July 1975, p. 418; see also, David L. Kirp. "Student Classification, Public Policy, and the Courts." *Harvard Educational Review* (February 1974): 7–52.
11. Glenn R. Snider, Phi Delta Kappa Commission on Education and Human Rights. "The Human Rights Creed in Education," in *A Guide for Improving Public School Practices in Human Rights.* Bloomington, Inc.: Phi Delta Kappa Educational Foundation, 1975, p. iv. Reprinted with permission of Glenn R. Snider.

Chapter
11

A Synthesis of Pluralistic Teaching

Key Terms:

common schools
intercultural education
Mr. Fix-It

Plato's gadfly
progressive education
social reconstruction

We have come full circle. This book's basic intent is to help teachers become liberating forces in the lives of their students—to make a difference. More than a histrionic platitude full of sound and fury signifying nothing, making a difference is a commitment to educate all students regardless of their ethnicity, gender, handicap, race, religion, or social class. Making a difference includes high expectations and excellence for all students and precludes negative expectations and mediocrity. Teachers are faced with a simple choice but this choice has profound ramifications: they may act as functionaries of the status quo or as gadflies, that is, agents of change. Teachers in the former category—status quo functionaries—are inimical to a pluralistic, democratic society. Teachers in the latter category—gadflies—are indispensable for a pluralistic, democratic society. Teachers as gadflies is an old idea elucidated by Plato:

> I [the teacher] . . . am a sort of gadfly, given to the state by God; and the state is a great and noble steed who is tardy in his motions owing to his very size, and requires to be stirred into life. . . . I am that gadfly . . . attached to the state, and all day long in all places am always fastening upon you [the state], arousing and persuading and reproaching you. You will not easily find another like me.[1]

A gadfly is an irritating, pesky "critter"; one fly can make a horse move, which is no mean achievement when you consider that the horse weighs 500 times more than the fly. The trick is in the fly's persistence; dozens of bites and the horse is forced to react.

Teachers as gadflies are challenged to persistently and tenaciously bite into the ignorance prevalent in our pluralistic society. But, teachers should not think in terms of changing the whole society; the society is much too amorphous. Rather, teachers should think in terms of changing the school in which they teach by the effects they can have on the individual students in their classes. Consequently, teachers as gadflies change students who will in turn change the society they form as adults. The gadfly's bite—the teacher's impact—rescues society from its own inertia and mediocrity, forcing the society to change and to grow. The teacher's efforts must be with individual students in specific schools; social changes begin in the classroom with individual teachers and students engaged in learning.

Teachers can hardly make a difference in the classroom with individual students if their schools prevent them from educating their students. A cursory review of the history of education reveals that schools have often been called upon to make sweeping changes in our pluralistic society and the schools have too readily assumed this responsibility in the rhetoric of meeting the needs of society, thus impeding the educational process and hindering the teachers' efforts to educate their students. I call this quixotic behavior the legacy of Mr. Fix-It.

THE MR. FIX-IT LEGACY

While schools are basically community affairs, political and economic conflict at the state and national levels have led politicians and advocacy groups to use the schools as Mr. Fix-It[2] tools to accomplish broad-based political or economic agendas. As problems erupted or crises climaxed, schools were called upon to fix them, or at least, to bandage them temporarily until people tired of dealing with the problems or until people forgot what the crisis was in the first place! Consequently, the schools have tried to be all things to all people, casting the schools adrift and preventing teachers from educating their students. Let us examine the Mr. Fix-It legacy within the historical context of the common school movement.

The groundswell "common man" era that occurred between the early 1800s and the Civil War gave birth to the common schools. This was the era of Jacksonian democracy, the era when nobility was a political liability; self-reliance and rugged individualism were economic assets. If the common man were to play a role in the emerging democratic society, then the common man must be educated. Much faith was placed in the belief that schools attended in common by members of all social classes could forge a democratic society by assimilating the children of the common man into a national culture based on the Protestant work ethic and Christianity.

The best-known common school leader was Horace Mann. He worked as a state legislator in Massachusetts to establish a board of education to regulate the state's incipient public school system. Once established, he resigned from the state legislature to become the board's first superintendent of public education (1837–1848). As superintendent he aggressively promoted the ideology that schools were the "great equalizers" in a society that was experiencing the emerging problems of industrialization. Through education the poor would be elevated and many of the existing social problems would be solved. The ideology of equalization originated in the legacy of the common school, in which the public schools came to be regarded as "Mr Fix-Its" or fixers of social problems beyond academics.

Mann also believed that religion should not be expunged entirely from schools given the strong link between the family and church. To win widespread support for the common schools, especially from reluctant religious leaders, Mann proposed a compromise dubbed the "Protestant Consensus." Readings from the King James version of the Bible along with Protestant hymns and prayers were to permeate the common school. Schools were not to adopt a specific denominational orthodoxy but they were to be friendly to Protestant Christianity. The Protestant Consensus established the common schools as one of the social agencies, along with the family and church, which would socialize young Americans. When Roman Catholics objected to the Protestant practices in the common schools, they were often ignored. Conflict between Catholics and Protestants erupted in Philadelphia in 1844 over the issue; rioting led to the burning of two Catholic churches, numerous buildings, the death of at least a dozen individuals and the injury of many more.[3] The Consensus and eventual Protestant domination of the common schools forced the development of Catholic schools. Protestant domination of the schools lasted until 1962 when the U.S. Supreme Court ruled in *Murray* v. *Curlett* that schools could not show preference toward a single form of religious expression. In 1963, the Court ruled in *Abington Township* v. *Schempp* that Bible readings, school prayers, and religious observations and services (graduation baccalaureate services) were religious activities that violated the Constitution's First Amendment religious establishment clause.

During the Common Man era the schools focused largely on Protestant, White students. However, White Catholics and Jews were not barred from school attendance. After the Nat Turner rebellion, most of the Southern states made it illegal to teach African Americans to read. The fear existed that educated African Americans would rebel against slavery. In the Northeast, African Americans were allowed to attend common schools. In Boston, where a small concentration of free African Americans resided, the common schools were segregated. In *Roberts* v. *City of Boston* (1849), the Supreme Court ruled that separate but equal schools satisfied the Constitutional test of equal protection of the law. At times in both the North and South, African Americans as well as Native Americans were taught to read by Christian missionaries However, the greatest proportion of Native Americans and African Americans were not included in the embroynic assimilative thrust of the common school movement.

After the Civil War the common school ethos faced its greatest challenge: forging a common culture in an industrializing economy in which the workforce consisted of a growing array of immigrant groups. The schools were challenged to change from an agricultural, rural emphasis to an industrial, urban emphasis. Between the Civil War and World War I, the common school experienced phenomenal growth. Immediately after the Civil War only small numbers of children attended elementary schools. High schools existed only in some affluent, urban areas. In 1874 the Michigan Supreme Court ruled in *Stuart* v. *Kalamazoo* that high schools supported by taxation could be instituted. Similar decisions were rendered in Illinois, Kansas, Missouri, and Wisconsin. By World War I, high schools were considered a regular part of the common school system. During this time, elementary and high school attendance increased threefold to include approximately 22.5 million students. In southern states, racially segregated school systems, including some colleges and universities, operated separately so that Blacks (and Mexican Americans in Texas) and Whites were kept apart.

The expansion of the common schools reflected the society's transformation to an industrialized economy. Two basic changes were concurrently taking place: how people were making a living and where people were living. For a time the common schools resisted changes in curriculum or purposes. The common school operated on a faculty psychology premise in which the main purpose of schooling was to train the mind, as stated in the 1893 National Education Association's "Report of the Committee of Ten on Secondary Schools."[4] The principal purpose of high schools was to prepare students for the duties of life with effective mental training through the study of academic subjects. Elementary schools were to make everyone a reader as preparation for high school.

The faculty psychology approach, with its study of classical literature, Latin, and geometry, was appropriate for training the "Renaissance Man," that is, a person schooled in the seven liberal art disciplines necessary for the life of an educated mind: grammar, logic, rhetoric, arithmetic, astronomy, music, geometry. The common schools had progressed from the repressiveness of the Puritan schools to a nobler conception of the student as a scholar in the classical sense. Rather than learning to read for salvation the student learned to read for the pursuit of the life of the mind. But, the viselike grip of industrialization and the simultaneous influx of non-Protestant, non-English-speaking immigrants pressed the common schools to address the concerns of urban, industrialized areas. The Renaissance man was a noble creature, but he would not work well in a factory operating a machine, paying taxes, and insuring that his children would be educated enough to take their place in society rather than become public charges. (For an historical critique of the common school movement and equalization, see Michael B. Katz, *The Irony of Early School Reform*.[5])

The new approach fit nativist perceptions of the Southern and Eastern European immigrants. Rather than educating them in the classical mode of the Renassiance Man it appeared more appropriate to to train them as workers in an industrial society. The common schools were challenged

> to assimilate . . . these people as a part of our American race, and to implant in their children . . . the Anglo-Saxon conception of righteousness, law and order, and popular government, and to awaken in them a reverence for our democratic institutions and for those things in our national life which we as a people hold to be of abiding worth.[6]

The strongest movement to assimilate the "new" immigrants through the common schools was an Americanization policy. Born in the pre-World War I xenophobic climate, the fear was that the newcomers from Southern and Eastern Europe would not become loyal Americans. Evening classes were scheduled to teach the adults English and American history. During the school day, the newcomers' children were taught American ways of cooking, dressing, and speaking English. The goal was to create 100 percent total Americans.

Before Americanization there existed settlement houses, such as Hull House in Chicago, established to ease the transition of assimilation. The houses served as clearinghouses for jobs, seminars for learning English, and lodges where immigrants from similar groups could meet. Here the immigrants found temporary sanctuary but the settlement houses did not move fast enough for nativists who believed in a kind of pressure cooker assimilation rather than the low heat assimilation practices of the settlement houses. Consequently, the common schools were used to pressure cook the newcomers and create a new cadre of industrial workers. The school's response to industrialization came in the form of the Progressive Education Movement, chronicled in Lawrence Cremin's *The Transformation of the Schools.*[7] The movement was subsumed in a combination of social reform forces at play during the last decade of the nineteenth century and the first two decades of the twentieth century. The schools were called upon to expand their scope beyond training minds; the schools were asked to serve as social agents, preparing their students for all aspects of life. Schools were to educate the whole child. In 1918 the U.S. Bureau of Education (now the Department of Education) endorsed a National Education Association's report on "The Reorganization of Secondary Education," which repudiated its 1893 Committee of Ten report. The main purpose of secondary schools was not to be the training of the mind. Instead, secondary schools were to prepare the whole child for living and working. The "Seven Cardinal Principles of Education"[8] were to be the guideposts of the new holistic purpose: (1) citizenship, (2) command of fundamental processes (the three Rs), (3) ethical character, (4) health, (5) vocation, (6) worthy use of leisure time, and (7) worthy home membership. Now the schools were to educate the body, the mind, and the soul, once the province of religion.

The cardinal principles were not drawn from a vacuum. The basic conception of how children learn was undergoing change. Faculty psychology was undergoing scrutiny; the notion that children learn holistically was revived. In 1894, John Dewey published, "The Child and the Curriculum," which explained his holistic approach used at the University of Chicago's "Laboratory School."[9] Dewey explained how the child's interests and curiosities were the center of the curriculum. Rather than studying separate subjects, the students studied different problems, conducted experiments, and pursued their curiosities, "catching the fundamental three Rs" as they progressed. The classroom served as an embryonic community, active with occupations that reflected the larger society. New subjects would entail manual training, sewing, cooking, and other projects that would help prepare students for living in an industrial economy and yet maintain the family life of the former agrarian society.

In 1919 the Progressive Education Association was founded. Its purpose was to free students from the coercive strictures resulting from the study of academic subjects and to allow students to grow and develop naturally. The PEA's philosophy was couched in the romantic school of thought regarding the nature of children. Jean-Jacques Rousseau, in his book *Emile* (1762), proposed that children are naturally good, and that if reared in a nurturing environment uncontaminated by societal corruptions, children will learn to read, write, and speak correctly if there exists an advantage to learn these skills. Children require environments that allowed them to think freely. Consequently, schools should provide supportive environments so that children can grow and develop to their fullest potential. Other European scholars, Johann Pestalozzi (1746–1827), Frederich Froebel (1782–1852, credited with establishing the kindergarten in the common schools), developed actual lessons, curriculum guides, and materials that appealed to the students' senses and required active physical, emotional, and intellectual participation.

By the middle 1930s the Progressive Education Association had evolved from an organization of private school educators to one consisting of a large number of public school educators. (*Time* magazine, October 31, 1938, put Frederich L. Redefer, executive secretary of the PEA, on the cover and included a feature story on the PEA.) At its zenith, a group of professors at Teacher's College of Columbia University attempted to radicalize the PEA. John Dewey, Harold Rugg, and George Counts were the leaders. Counts published a manifesto, "Dare the Schools Build a New Social Order?"[10] calling for schools to serve as social reconstruction agents. The schools were to reconstruct a just society, one based on communal rather than individualistic values. And, at the PEA's February 1935 annual conference a resolution was passed calling for intercultural education for purposes of educating the children of both "new" and "old" Americans about the cultures of the "new" Americans.[11]

The following month the entire issue of *Progressive Education* was devoted to minority groups. The PEA endorsed cultural pluralism. In 1935, the PEA hired Rachel Davis DuBois, a classroom teacher who developed the idea that harmony was possible through an appreciation of cultural difference, or, intercultural education. DuBois' approach was to develop separate units on the contributions made by different American ethnic groups. Her intent was to build self-esteem in second generation immigrant children who were alienated from their cultural roots because of the strong assimilation activities of the Americanization practices in the common schools. Also, the "old" Americans could learn about the cultures of the "new," thereby lowering prejudices and stereotypes. DuBois' approach, albeit scholarly and thorough, proved to be too liberal for the PEA membership. The concern was that the intercultural education approach encouraged excessive ethnic pride and threatened the "old" immigrants, the group to which the PEA catered. She was fired in 1938. (For more on intercultural education, see Chapter 7.)

Neither the social reconstructionists nor the intercultural educators took hold in the PEA. Rather, the PEA held fast to its promotion of the whole child, eschewing social class and ethnic issues. Yet, at its demise in 1955, the PEA had managed to create an awareness of the importance of child development. It also played an important role in making high school attendance universal. By helping displace the purportedly elitist Renaissance Man subject matter curriculum with life adjustment and vocational education curricula, the PEA made a high school education and diploma seemingly more relevant to the needs of society rather than to the needs of individuals.

The PEA should not take full blame for the condition of schools. The Mr. Fix-It legacy, and all of its willing advocates, share in the blame for attempting to fix social problems through the public schools. The public schools have evolved into variegated systems changing to meet broad-based political agendas. Like Mr. Fix-It, the schools are somewhat good at doing most things. They somewhat prepare workers, citizens, and healthy, well-adjusted individuals, but like Mr. Fix-It, the schools cannot do all things better than average. The schools have been asked to do too much, and as a responsive social agency, the schools have responded in kind, adapting new trends for new interests. The schools have vacillated among the Jeffersonian purpose of schools, politically literate citizens, the common school purpose, the Great Equalizer, the learned person or training of the mind purpose, and the industrial purpose of educating the whole person to be a good worker. This vacillation has its price— mediocrity—as attested by the plethora of educational reports during the 1980s, for example, *A Nation at Risk*. If the schools continue to vacillate between new trends and old purposes, they may become a part of society's problems rather than a part of its solutions. We should retire Mr. Fix-It and replace him with a curriculum that is basically academic with the intent of educating the minds of all students.

EDUCATION OF THE MASSES

That it is possible to educate all of the masses is supported by educators who have assessed the educational systems of societies committed to the education of the entire populace. Hutchins concluded:

> Whatever can be said of the limitations of Soviet Education . . . it has knocked on the head the notion that only a few can understand difficult subjects. The compulsory eight-year school . . . demands that all pupils learn . . . the elements of mathematics, physical and biological science, and at least one foreign language. . . . [A]ccording to western standards the instruction in the subjects has succeeded.[12]

While Professor Hutchins was neither an apologist nor a proponent of Marxist, Soviet education, his assessment of the Soviet education system as well as their subsequent scientific and technological advances validates the notion that a society can educate all of its populace. When the Soviets implemented the policy in the 1920s their people were predominantly poor and illiterate. Within a period of 40 years Soviet society was transformed; by 1960 a sizable proportion were markedly less poor and literate. The motive was to build a strong, vigorous industrial society based on the precepts of Karl Marx.

How much their society is based on the precepts of Marx is an ongoing debate, but that they built a strong, vigorous industrial society, with its predictable problems, is hardly debatable. The Soviet educational policy—a commitment to educate all students—served to elevate the nation from feudal disorganization to scientific, technological and military world prominence, an accomplishment not easily dismissed as communist propaganda.

In our time, the plethora of educational reports have emphasized the necessity to educate all students. Mortimer Adler's *Paideia Proposal*[13] on educational reform takes the position that schools should adopt a basic academic curriculum that is the same for all students. Academic tracks and ability group would be nonexistent; there is only one track. The *Proposal's* aim is to educate the minds of students by teaching them how to think using traditional subjects taught nontraditionally. Upon graduation, under the *Paideia Proposal*, students would be educated enough to learn a job or continue further schooling. Adler's notion is to provide all students with the opportunity to be educated in the conventional sense that the educated person's mind and character are disciplined by the knowledge and use of academic subjects.

Equal educational opportunity is a basic policy of the United States government. The policy means more than just equal access to education. The policy means that all students, regardless of ethnicity, gender, physical condition, race, religion, or social class, have a right to benefit equally from public school programs. In successive landmark Supreme Court decisions and federal legislation, the U.S. government has affirmed a policy of equal educational opportunities for all students. The *Brown* v. *Topeka Board of Education* decision, the U.S. Civil Rights Act, the *Lau* v. *Nichols* decision, Title IX, the Indian Education Act, the Southeast Asian Refugee Children's Act, and the Education for All Handicapped Children Act all prohibit discrimination against special categories of students, establishing a federal policy of educating all students irrespective of race, religion, national origin, gender, language, or handicap. Even though the policy has the force of law and U.S. constitution to enforce its intent, the reality is that some educators are oblivious of the policy, refusing for reasons of ignorance or other spurious arguments, such as local autonomy or states' rights, to translate the policy into educational programs and practices.

My experience shows that the federal policy exists because some state and local educators historically have not provided equal educational opportunities for lower-class, ethnic minority, female, and handicapped students. The need for the policy would be nonexistent were educational opportunities equitably provided to all students. By tradition and law, educational policies have emanated from state and local school officials and these policies have usually reflected the value and belief systems of the state and local communities. Local and regional policies reflected their respective folkways and mores: some policies were proequal opportunity; some simply ignored the issue. In communities hostile or complacent to equal opportunity, the school district officials have been unable or unwilling to rise above the level of their community's norms. Rather than asserting leadership by raising the equal opportunity issue and insisting that all students deserve equal opportunities, some educators have washed their hands of the issue. Indeed, they have ignored the issue, hoping it would go away, a ploy designed to satisfy local power groups without upsetting the status quo. Nonetheless, these educators—quite adept at evading the federal policy—act in violation of the law of the land. An anomaly of American life is that one can be both a respectable citizen and an outlaw.

Some educators view with jaundiced eyes or, even worse, cynically scoff at the idea of making a difference as liberal do-goodism and other idealistic nonsense. Students are the ultimate victims of these views, but teachers are the immediate victims. All too often, teachers become the disenchanted functionaries of an educational system that serves the status quo. In this context, teachers are no more than intermediaries who are forced to have a negative impact on the daily lives of students. Indeed, within this context teacher are replaceable gears in an automated system that destines students to life positions that perpetuate the social caste system of U.S. industrialized society.

All students need to know and learn from committed teachers. Our society demands it. Now more than ever before in our history, students are required to excell as a matter of national survival. The nation can ill afford to miseducate any of its youth, as the youth are one of the few remaining renewable resources.

A SUMMATION

There is absolutely no educational reason why teachers cannot make a difference in the lives of students, especially if they keep a perspective on two societal constants that render effective teachers indispensable: (1) the generic problems of hunger, disease, poverty, and ignorance common to most cultures and nations, and (2) the specific realities of cultural diversity in U.S. society. Teachers, irrespective of whom or where they teach can commit themselves to the eradication of ignorance, disease, or poverty. Teaching a Navajo reservation youngster to read and teaching a White, suburban youngster about Navajos are equally liberating because both teaching acts, by small but potent degrees, can serve to eradicate ignorance and poverty. Students in public school classrooms represent a vast array of groups, which, of course, is reflective of the diversity of U.S. society. To live well in this society, students need both direction and guidance to successfully interact within such a diverse society. To keep a perspective on these societal trends I have proposed that teachers assume a posture of cultural relativism within their teaching-learning universe.

Just as the astronomer Copernicus broadened human understanding of the physical universe, I attempted by analogy to broaden our understanding of the current teaching-learning universe of the U.S. public school classroom, placing middle-class culture within the galaxy of our multiple social and cultural groups rather than at the center. I have argued that teachers should perceive the teaching-learning universe from the vantage point of cultural relativism—the notion that cultures should be perceived from their own perspective rather than compared with middle-class U.S. culture. In the wrong hands, cultural relativism could be a destructive force because it could allow bigoted or sexist teachers to present their cultural positions as valid and thereby justify their acts of discrimination. Since I am aware of this difficulty with cultural relativism, I have argued that narrow-minded teachers have no place in the education profession and that teachers should conduct their classes on the basis of justice, that is, classroom management with human rights.

Cultural relativism operates on several important assumptions. First is the assumption that teachers can understand cultural differences. Just as teachers in the past have been required to learn the "new" math, the "new" English and various other academic innovations, teachers can learn about different cultures within the United States.

The second assumption is that teachers can teach students to understand differences. The instructional models—cultural education and language education, and the instructional strategies—intergroup relations and human rights analyzed in the second half of the text provide teachers with some ways and means by which they can teach students to understand differences. These models and strategies are applicable to any U.S. public school classroom in any social, cultural, or regional setting. They are not intended only for ethnic minority student populations or desegregated schools. Rather, they are intended for all schools and student populations, as well as for urban and rural White and non-White school populations. The bottom line of these models and strategies is that they provide all teachers in all settings with the means to teach understanding of differences.

The third assumption is that students are not mere data bank receptors of knowledge. Rather, cultural relativism operates on the assumption that students can be self-initiating, learning beings if they are directed and allowed to pursue their cultural and personal curiosities. This third assumption is not a call for permissive "do your own thing" ideologies, but rather the assumption challenges teachers to take leadership in their teaching-learning universe by creating for students the culturally correct set of circumstances so that students can use their curiosities to plumb even greater depths of knowledge and understanding. The assumption calls for teachers to empower students to use knowledge not only to pursue their self-interests but also to create a just community wherever they live and work. Teachers therefore should model ethical transcendence in their classrooms so that students can learn to deal with the array of differences existing in their classrooms and in the pluralistic society.

Embracing cultural relativism is not enough. Teachers should understand important sociocultural notions that impinge on teaching and learning. The most fundamental notion is that of "culture." All students have a culture—that is, all students have a culture (even though they may not be conscious of it!) including a system of values, beliefs, and behaviors. There is nothing mysterious about culture. It is not necessarily an exotic rite that occurs in the hinterlands to the beat of frenetic drums, nor is culture classical music resounding in a concert hall. Culture is much more than exotic rites or lofty rhapsodies. Culture is the complex of values, attitudes, behaviors, and materials that provide humans with the sustenance for social existence. While rites and symphonies may be a part of a student's culture, they are not the entire culture.

Students learn their culture and are socialized to live through their families, their peer groups, their communities, and schools. Other socialization agents are the mass media and the church. Students also learn their culture from the communal context into which they are thrust. These communal settings, reflected for example in local and regional cultures such as the Southwest or the Deep South, will influence the attitudes and perceptions of students. Teachers cannot ignore prevalent local or regional cultural attitudes and beliefs. Instead, they need to understand the attitudes and beliefs so as to better reach and thereby teach their students. Teaching and learning in U.S. public schools is ultimately a community affair.

Students also learn their culture through their heritage, be it ethnic, religious, national, or racial. In the United States, it's possible for students to have a nationality, "American" and an ethnic group, "Japanese," affiliation. Some students may identify only with their nationality and consider themselves primarily American. Others may identify with their nationality and ethnic or racial group, thereby considering themselves both ethnic and national, as in African American or Mexican American. The impact of ethnic, racial, or national group heritage upon the student's culture largely depends upon the social status and role ascribed to the student's particular group. Nevertheless, for many students, ethnic, racial, or religious group or social class membership or gender or handicapping conditions are formative aspects of their social identity. And, students learn ethnocentrisms, biases, stereotypes the same way they learn their culture—at home, in schools, among peers, in communities, in the mass media, and even in churches.

Who should be taught to live in a pluralistic society? All female and male students irrespective of cultural backgrounds, handicapping conditions, racial group affiliations, religious denominations, and social classes. Those students not achieving at norm should be provided with an individualized education plan much like the IEPs mandated for handicapped students; social promotion, ability grouping, and academic tracks should be discontinued as educational practices.

Who should teach in the pluralistic society? Anyone who is intellectually competent and committed to the idea that teaching is a liberating force. Teachers should:

1. Stimulate intellectual, cognitive, and social growth;
2. Plan, execute, and evaluate lessons linked to traditional subjects;
3. Infuse experiences and contents into traditional subjects that empower students to pursue their self-interests and create a just community where they live.

What should be taught in a pluralistic society? Educators should take the position that schools cannot continue to vacillate, responding to special interests with every swing of the political pendulum. Rather, teachers should do well what they are best able to do, educate minds. The educated mind operates on three levels of literacy—functional, cultural, and critical. The ultimate aim of every public school system in the United States should be the same—educated humans. Upon high school graduation every student should

- be fully literate in standard American English;
- be fully read in American and global literature;
- speak a modern, foreign language;
- know the rudiments of earth science, biology, chemistry, and physics;
- know the rudiments of mathematics through geometry and trigonometry;
- know American history and the workings of its political institutions;
- know world history and geography;
- operate a computer, play a musical instrument, or develop abilities in other performing arts;
- participate in organized games.

By high school graduation students should be able to learn a job or pursue further training for a job.

Class Dismissed!

NOTES

1. Plato. *Apology.* In B. Jowett, ed. *Five Great Dialogues.* Roslyn, NY: Walter J. Black, 1942, p.49.
2. Ernest Boyer, "Schools of the Future," Hunt Lecture, American Association of Colleges for Teacher Education Annual Conference, February 1987, Washington, D.C.
3. Charlotte P. Taylor. *Transforming Schools.* New York: St. Martin's Press, 1976, p. 96.
4. National Education Association. *Report of the Committee of Ten on Secondary School Studies.* Washington, D.C.: U.S. Government Printing Office, 1893.
5. Michael B. Katz. *The Irony of Early School Reform.* Cambridge: Harvard University Press, 1968.
6. Ellwood P. Cubberley. *Changing Conceptions of Education.* Boston: Houghton Mifflin, 1909, p. 15.
7. Lawrence Cremin. *The Transformation of the Schools.* New York: Knopf, 1961.
8. C. D. Kingsley, ed. *Cardinal Principles of Education.* Washington D.C.: Department of Interior, Bureau of Education *Bulletin,* U. S. Government Printing Office, 1918.
9. For pre-World War I educational experiments, see John Dewey and Evelyn Dewey. *Schools of To-morrow.* New York: Dutton, 1915.
10. George Counts. *Dare the School Build a New Social Order?* New York: John Day, 1932; see also, C. H. Judd. *Education and Social Progress.* New York: Harcourt Brace, 1934.
11. Nicholas V. Montalto. "The Intercultural Education Movement, 1924–1941," in B. Weiss, ed. *American Education and the European Immigrant, 1840–1940.* Champaign: University of Illinois Press, 1982, 142–160.

12. R. M. Hutchins. *The Learning Society*. Baltimore: Penguin Books, 1970, p. 22; see also, V. T. Thayer. *The Role of the School in American Society*. New York: Dodd, Mead, 1960, pp. 334–335; see also, Levitas. *Marxist Perspectives*. London: Routledge and Paul, 1974, pp. 63–71.
13. Mortimer Adler. *The Paideia Proposal*. New York: Macmillan, 1982, pp. 15–37.

Index